MODERN LAW OF
CRIMINAL PROCEDURE
IN KENYA

MODERN LAW OF CRIMINAL PROCEDURE IN KENYA

MUNYAO SILA

PARTRIDGE
A Penguin Random House Company

ISBN:	Hardcover	978-1-4828-0373-0
	Softcover	978-1-4828-0372-3
	eBook	978-1-4828-0374-7

To order additional copies of this book, contact
Toll Free 0800 990 914 (South Africa)
+44 20 3014 3997 (outside South Africa)
orders.africa@partridgepublishing.com

www.partridgepublishing.com/africa

PREFACE

I thought deeply about writing a book on Criminal Procedure Law while I was teaching this subject at the Moi University School of Law. There was a dearth of material on this subject and it was difficult for students to have good reference materials to assist them in their studies. As a legal practitioner, I also found a shortage of materials on this important topic, which I could make reference to when handling criminal cases. This was compounded with the coming into force of the Constitution of Kenya, 2010. The Constitution brought significant changes to the law on Criminal Procedure. New institutions such as the National Police Service, the Office of the Director of Public Prosecutions and the Supreme Court were created. Hitherto unrecognized rights, such as the right to bail irrespective of the offence were also introduced. The law on Criminal Procedure significantly changed.

Upon my appointment as judge in the year 2012, I thought that it would not be possible to write the text. But with encouragement from my wife and my former colleagues at the Moi University School of Law, I found time to write this book while still juggling my busy schedule at the Courts. A lot of research work needed to be done and I had little time for it. Ribin Ondwari, then a student at the Moi University School of Law, dedicated himself to undertake the research work, while at the same time, working on finalizing his LLB studies. I can only describe him as God-sent. It is an understatement to say that his input has been invaluable. For sure this text would not have been completed were it not for his sacrifice. He is a brilliant legal mind who has finalized his LLB studies with distinction and is currently attached as a pupil in a respectable law firm. I have no doubt that his future is bright and that he will do well irrespective of the career path he chooses to take.

This book covers all important aspects of Criminal Procedure Law in Kenya. It is a text that has taken into consideration the changes brought about by the Constitution of 2010, and has utilized a good number of case law decided after 2010. This book is going to prove to be an invaluable companion to any law student, to legal practitioners, judicial officers and the general public.

MUNYAO SILA

ACKNOWLEDGEMENTS

This book would not have been completed without the dedicated input of Ribin Ondwari, then a student at Moi University School of Law, and now training to be an advocate of the High Court of Kenya. He served as my researcher and worked long and hard hours while still needing to catch up with his studies. His brilliance and suggestions made this book what it is. I am unable to thank him enough for his input and sacrifice.

I also wish to thank Justice Fred Ochieng for his advice and suggestions in the Chapters on Sentence and Judgment.

I also thank my former colleagues at the Moi University School of Law, particularly Osogo Ambani, Josphat Ayamunda, Isaiah Orina and Maurice Oduor, who dedicated their time to proof read the manuscript and provide me with advice on the text.

I however take responsibility for any errors in the text.

May I also thank my publishers, Partridge Africa, for agreeing to publish this text.

Last but certainly not least, I sincerely thank my wife, Linda and my two children Sila Jr and Lati, for allowing themselves to suffer a fair amount of loneliness while I worked on this text. Thank you very much.

Munyao Sila

DEDICATION

To my dear wife Linda.

TABLE OF CONTENTS

TABLE OF CASES

The Constitution and List of Statutes

The Constitution of Kenya, 2010

The Criminal Procedure Code, (Chapter 75 of the Laws of Kenya)

The Penal Code (Chapter 63 of the Laws of Kenya)

The Children Act

The Sexual Offences Act

The Anti-Corruption and Economic Crimes Act

The National Police Service Act

The Evidence Act

Commission of Inquiry Act

The Office of The Director of Public Prosecutions Act

Supreme Court Act

Magistrates Court Act

The Witness Protection Act

The International Covenant on Civil and Political Rights

Kenya Defence Forces Act

CHAPTER 1

UNDERSTANDING CRIMINAL PROCEDURE

1.1 Introduction to Criminal Procedure

This text is about criminal procedure and a fundamental question that may arise is, what is criminal procedure? Criminal procedure in its simplest form refers to the process through which a person accused of having committed an offence is taken through, so as to establish his guilt or innocence. If guilty, the accused will be convicted of the offence and he will be punished[1] in accordance with the law; if innocent, the accused will be let free. The entire process from the time the crime is committed, to the investigative stage, to the trial itself and after, and to all antecedents that take place, constitutes criminal procedure.

However, there are some elements of criminal procedure which do not necessarily constitute the taking of a person through a criminal trial, for example, inquests. An inquest is an investigatory process, without there being anyone on trial. There are also persons who may not be offenders, but who may make applications falling within the purview of criminal law. All these, still constitute criminal procedure, for they are tied to some commission or suspicion of commission of an offence.

---

1 Although the term "punishment" may be a misnomer since it is not in all instances that the offender will be "punished" in the actual sense of the word. Sometimes the offender may be discharged, i.e. allowed to go free, in which case he is not really "punished" in the ordinary sense of the word. See *infra* Chapter 12 on Sentence.

Criminal procedure may be distinguished from "civil procedure". Civil procedure involves the process of adjudicating rights and liabilities without anybody being tried for any offence. There may however be an overlap between civil procedure and criminal procedure, the core process being that of contempt of court. Contempt of court implies a disobedience of a court order, which in most instances would befall an order made in a civil process. The civil court has mandate to punish for contempt, and such punishment is no doubt one that is quasi-criminal in nature, for the offender is actually found guilty and punished accordingly, not through a criminal process, but through the process of civil procedure. Overall, however, criminal procedure involves the processes through which an offender is taken through so as to determine his guilt or innocence.

1.2 Systems of Criminal Procedure

There are two core systems of criminal procedure. The first is what is termed as the "Adversarial" system and the second is what is referred to as the "Inquisitorial" system. Generally countries that utilise the English Common Law system lean towards the adversarial system, whereas much of continental Europe utilises the Civil Law system, which leans towards the inquisitorial style of procedure in litigation. Thus, England, Canada and most commonwealth countries that make use of the common law system, have the adversarial procedure in their litigation, whereas countries such as France, Netherlands and the like, that make use of the Civil Law system, have the inquisitorial procedure of litigation.

The intended aim of both systems is to find out the truth, i.e., the guilt or innocence of the accused person, only that they use different routes to reach the result. The adversarial system seeks the truth by pitting the parties against each other in the hope that competition will reveal it, whereas the inquisitorial system, seeks the truth by questioning those most familiar with the events in dispute. Kenya uses the adversarial system in both its criminal and civil procedure.

1.3 The Adversarial System of Criminal Procedure[2]

In this style of litigation, two parties assume opposite positions in determining the guilt or innocence of a person accused of having committed a criminal offence. The judge or magistrate acts like an umpire in the unfolding contest, and after hearing the parties, makes a decision on who has "won" the contest. His role is to ensure fair play. If the prosecution "wins" then the accused is convicted and if the defence "wins" then the accused is acquitted. The Judge or magistrate, just as an umpire, is required to be neutral and must decide the contest between the two parties solely in accordance with the rules of law and procedure and the weight of evidence adduced by the separate parties.

The rationale and basis of the adversarial approach is that by pitting the two sides in a contest, the debate of the two parties will critically analyse the issues and uncover the truth. The role of the prosecutor is to prove that the accused is guilty by adducing evidence to that effect, whereas the role of the defence is to prove that the accused is innocent by attacking the evidence of the prosecution and producing evidence supporting the innocence of the accused. Each party can choose the evidence that it wants to provide or leave out[3], whether or not it will go to assist in uncovering the truth. Generally, there can be no compulsion from one party for the other to produce evidence.[4]

The role of the judge is to decide which of the two parties has outpointed the other, based on the weight and credibility of the evidence tendered. The judge only intervenes to guide procedure and ensure that the rules of evidence are followed; he does not get himself in the arena. The trial is thus decided by a rigorous pro and con argument between the contestants, which in the case of a criminal trial, would be a contest between the prosecution and the accused.

---

2 For an elaborate discussion see James R. Acker, David C. Brody, *Criminal Procedure: A Contemporary Perspective,* Jones & Bartlett Publishers, (2011), John H. Langbein, *The Origins of Adversary Criminal Trial,* Oxford University Press, 2003 and Daniel E. Hall, *Criminal Law and Procedure,* Cengage Learning, (2011).

3 This is the strict position but as we shall see in Chapter 5, the Prosecutor has a duty to produce all the evidence whether or not it goes to incriminate or exonerate the accused.

4 Although many jurisdictions have rules of discovery that may compel the other party, especially the prosecution, to avail certain evidence.

In adversarial systems, the accused generally has a right of silence and is under no obligation to give any evidence that is incriminating to himself. He does not have to answer any questions put to him unless he opts to give evidence on oath, in which case, he may be cross-examined. The adversarial system may have variations with some making use of a jury.[5] Some only have the judge deciding the case, whereas some employ a hybrid, with the judge being aided by assessors.[6]

There are both advantages and disadvantages in the adversarial system. A key advantage is that the neutrality of the judge gives both sides confidence that there will be fairness. An accused also benefits from the presumption of innocence and is under no compulsion to incriminate himself. The disadvantages are however numerous. The truth may be lost in the arguments and contentions of the parties; the prosecutor in striving to obtain a conviction may mask the truth by leaving out evidence which is in favour of the accused; the accused is never interested in the truth but in achieving an acquittal, and may opt to remain silent thus leaving out critical evidence. The system favours the wealthy as they can afford the best lawyers and best experts in their defence. The poor in most cases are unrepresented and have no resources to engage expert witnesses leading to an inequality of arms which may compromise the truth. In adversarial systems, save for where the accused is given legal aid, the accused must use his resources, not only in paying for legal counsel, but also to prepare his defence including gathering forensic and documentary evidence, and paying expert witnesses. Inevitably and in most instances, the prosecution has more resources to spend and there is a possibility of lack of "equality of arms" between the two parties.

Where the prosecution has little evidence, unorthodox means may be used to extract a confession. In a plea bargain.[7]A person may be tempted to plead guilty even when he is innocent, so as to get a lighter sentence and avoid the uncertainties of trial. Indeed in Kenya, most people facing small offences, will tend to plead guilty, even when they are innocent, so as to avoid the rigours of

---

5 As in the American system.

6 Kenya used to have a system of assessors but which was abolished in 2007 by The Statute Law (Miscellaneous Amendments) Act, Act No. 7 of 2007.

7 For plea bargains see Chapter 7.

a trial. On the contrary there are no guilty pleas in inquisitorial systems and the judge must be satisfied that the dossier of information truly points to the guilt of the accused.

Adversarial systems having jury trials are at times criticised for being burdensome to the public, open to bias and external influences, which may dilute the quality of the trial and the result. It is arguable that the rules of procedure in adversarial systems are heavily skewed in favour of the accused. The accused is entitled to be presumed innocent and the prosecution must prove his guilt beyond reasonable doubt. The accused can remain silent and not offer any assistance in the discovery of the truth. He is also entitled to view the evidence against him well before hand and is not obliged to reveal his evidence to the prosecution who stand to be ambushed at the trial. The defence can lay stratagems to lead to the acquittal of the accused and indeed in many cases the accused is set free, not because he is innocent, but because he takes advantage of the rules that are titled in his favour. The adversarial system indeed operates on the principle that it is better to have 10 guilty people set free rather than have one innocent party found guilty.[8]

In adversarial systems, delays are mostly caused by the lengthy trial process as all witnesses must appear and be cross-examined. Not unusually, at times, delays may be a strategy by either prosecution or defence, to procure a conviction or an acquittal, as circumstances touching on the case may change with time, such as the death of a witness.

1.4 The Inquisitorial System of Criminal Procedure[9]

The inquisitorial system is the procedure that is used in most civil law jurisdictions. The judge is an inquisitor thus the name "inquisitorial" system. His

8 This is the so called "Blackstone's formulation" also known as the "Blackstone Ratio" expressed by the English jurist William Blackstone in the work *Commentaries on the Laws of England* published in the 1760s.

9 *Supra* note 2; See also Harry Dammer and Jay Albanese, *Comparative Criminal Justice Systems*, Cengage Learning, 2013 and Morris Ploscowe, *'Development of Inquisitorial and Accusatorial Elements in French Procedure'* Journal of Criminal Law and Criminology, (1932) 233 at pg. 372.

mandate is to inquire as to the truth of the allegations against the suspect. The inquisitorial system requires a judge or a group of judges actively to investigate the case before them. All evidence is supposed to be gathered and presented to the judge who then makes a decision on the guilt or otherwise of the accused. The judge must consider the interests of the prosecution in attempting to push for the guilt of the suspect, but must also consider all evidence that goes to demonstrate the innocence of the suspect. At the end of it, he must make a decision on the guilt or innocence of the suspect, based on the totality of the evidence gathered.

Depending on the system, the judge takes the lead in questioning the suspect and witnesses and although the prosecution and defence may ask questions, these are supplementary to those of the judge who always plays the lead role. The roles of the prosecutor and defence are thus not as central as the role played by the judge in the litigation. The aim is to find the truth, not to pit the prosecution and defence in a contest. Again, depending on the variation of the system, the judge can compel the accused to make a statement and can question him.

In a strict inquisitorial system, there is no presumption of innocence. Neither are there guilty pleas and no plea bargains. Nor is there a point when a prima facie case is proved for the defendant to be called upon to make a defence. A defendant's confession is just one of the wealth of evidence that must be gathered. The matter is decided by the totality of evidence, not the wit of the prosecutor or defendant. The typical inquisitorial system has the police investigating the file and opening an investigation file.[10] However, just as in an adversarial system, the accused has a right to challenge the evidence and call forth his own witnesses to rebut his innocence. It is the process that distinguishes the two. In the adversarial system, the two parties, i.e. the prosecution and the defence, act independently in presenting evidence. The actors are opposing parties. In an inquisitorial system, the onus is on a judicial officer who gathers evidence both for and against the accused. There are generally no exclusionary rules of evidence, all evidence is admissible and deemed important to finding the truth.

---

10 See generally, Franklin D. Strier, *Reconstructing Justice: An Agenda for Trial Reform*, Greenwood Publishing Group, (1994).

Some civil jurisdictions incorporate jury trials for serious offences.[11] Where such is incorporated, the proceedings before the jury proceed in a manner closely similar to adversarial regimes. Some regimes incorporate a two tier system, where there is an investigative pre-trial stage and a trial stage if the magistrate in the pre-trial stage is of the opinion that there is enough evidence against the suspect.[12] The truth in inquisitorial systems is reached by examining those who are familiar with the circumstances. The rights of the accused are therefore not superior to the search for the truth.

There is therefore a clear contrast with an adversarial system, for in the adversarial system, the judge plays the role of an arbiter and he knows nothing of the case, save for what the parties will present. No doubt in the inquisitorial system, the investigator requires great resources to ensure that all aspects of the case are covered. The accused here has a slight benefit as he need not put his resources to the case and can insist on a certain aspect of the investigation being covered. The inquisitorial system obliges the investigator to provide all evidence whether it be in favour or against the accused, so that the trial magistrate can make a determination on the guilt or otherwise of the accused.

Delays are inevitable in criminal trials in the inquisitorial system, as the gathering of evidence may take a considerable time. The pre-trial stage is a formal process which may consume time. Inquisitorial systems are criticised for failing to recognise the accused's right to silence, the presumption of innocence and the reliance on confessions which at times may be procured through unorthodox methods. On the other hand adversarial systems are criticized for being overly protective of the accused and the trial being a contest between the two parties rather than being a search for the truth.

---

11 For example the Assize Courts in France and Italy.

12 For example in France. This is almost similar to the committal system in Kenya that was present in murder trials. The prosecution would gather all evidence and place it in a bundle. This bundle would be tabled before a Magistrate. The Magistrate would peruse the bundle and if satisfied that there appears to be sufficient evidence to warrant the accused to face trial, would then commit him to the High Court, for the High Court to hear the substantive case. The committal proceedings were however abolished in 2003 by the Criminal Law (Amendment) Act, Act No. 5 of 2003.

As a final analysis, both systems have inherent strengths and weakness. There have been attempts to modify the systems in some countries and come up with a hybrid that encompasses attributes of both systems.

International tribunals such as the International Criminal Court, have a sort of a hybrid regime that combines the two systems. There is a pre-trial chamber and a trial chamber.[13] The pre-trial chamber operates in a way that is more aligned to an inquisitorial system. Here the evidence gathered by the prosecutor is tabled and the judge considers whether it is of sufficient weight to warrant committal to trial. A person is then committed to trial by the Trial Chamber. At the trial chamber, the system is more inclined towards the adversarial system.

* * *

---

13 Article 15, 34, 39, and 56 - 60 of the 1998, Rome Statute of the International Criminal Court.

CHAPTER 2

THE COURT SYSTEM IN KENYA AND JURISDICTION TO TRY CRIMINAL CASES

2.1 Introduction

A person suspected to have committed a crime is tried in the courts which have been established by the Constitution or other legislation mandated to do so by the Constitution. A court's jurisdiction flows from the Constitution, since even legislation that establishes courts and gives them jurisdiction, must abide by the dictates of the Constitution.[1] This point that was emphasized by the Supreme Court in the case of *Samuel Kamau Macharia & Another. V. Kenya Commercial Bank & 2 Others,*[2] where the court stated as follows :-

"Where the Constitution exhaustively provides for the jurisdiction of a Court of law, the Court must operate within the constitutional limits. It cannot expand its jurisdiction through judicial craft or innovation. Nor can Parliament confer jurisdiction upon a Court of law beyond the scope defined by the Constitution. Where the Constitution confers power upon Parliament to set the jurisdiction of a Court of law or tribunal, the legislature would be within its authority to prescribe the jurisdiction of such a court or tribunal by statute law."

It follows that the question of jurisdiction is not a mere procedural matter but a substantive issue that goes to the core of the case. One cannot therefore cite

---

1 Article 2, Constitution, which provides that the Constitution is the supreme law.

2 *Samuel Kamau Macharia & Another. V. Kenya Commercial Bank & 2 Others Supreme Court of Kenya Application No. 2 of 2012, (2012) eKLR.*

Article 159 (2) (d) of the Constitution[3] for relief if the court had no jurisdiction. If a court lacks jurisdiction, its judgments and orders, however precisely certain and technically correct, are subject to being declared null and void. Neither can parties agree to confer upon a court jurisdiction, nor can a waiver on the part of parties, confer upon a court jurisdiction.[4]

In criminal matters, the mandate of every trial court is to take an accused person through the criminal trial, and to determine whether or not, the person accused is guilty of the offence charged.[5] It follows that the court which tries the accused person, must have jurisdiction to do so. If there is concurrent jurisdiction, the higher court ought to defer jurisdiction to the lower one.[6]

There is no doubt that if the trial court has no jurisdiction, then the trial is a nullity. It is therefore fundamental to understand the jurisdiction of the various courts and to know which court can try what offence. This inevitably requires an understanding of the judicial structure in Kenya, and the discourse that follows, sets out the structure of the judiciary and the jurisdiction of the various courts in Kenya.

2.2 The Courts and their Jurisdiction.

The Constitution of Kenya, 2010, at Chapter 10, sets out what the Kenya judiciary is comprised of and delineates the jurisdiction of the various courts. In some instances, the Constitution provides, as we shall see shortly, that jurisdiction will be as conferred by Parliament. The only way in which Parliament can

---

3 Which provides that the court ought not to have undue regard to procedural technicalities.

4 *Assanand & Sons (U) Ltd vs East African Records Ltd (1959) E.A. 360.*

5 Although as will be seen later, the court has mandate to convict for an offence which is lesser that one in which the accused was originally charged with. See chapter on Judgment.

6 Put to practice in *Sum Model Industries Ltd vs Industrial and Commercial Development Corporation*, Supreme Court, Civil Application No. 1 of 2011, where in a matter where both Court of Appeal and Supreme Court had jurisdiction on the question of leave to appeal to the Supreme Court, the Supreme Court deferred the matter to the Court of Appeal, as the Court of Appeal was the less superior of the two.

confer jurisdiction upon a court is through legislation. Jurisdiction of the courts is therefore elaborated in both the Constitution and in legislation. However, if there is a conflict between the two, inevitably the provisions of the Constitution will prevail owing to the provisions of Article 2 of the Constitution which provide that the Constitution is the supreme law.

The Constitution categorises the courts into Superior Courts and Subordinate Courts. The Superior Courts are the Supreme Court, the Court of Appeal, the High Court, the Industrial Court, and the Environment and Land Court. The first three are established by Article 162 (1) of the Constitution, whereas the Constitution under Article 162 (2) commanded Parliament to establish the latter two. They were eventually established by the Industrial Court Act[7] and the Environment and Land Court Act.[8]

Article 162(4) of the Constitution provides that the subordinate courts are the courts established under Article 169 of the Constitution, or by Parliament, in accordance with that Article. Article 169 of the Constitution establishes the following courts as the subordinate courts.

(a) The Magistrates Courts,
(b) The Kadhis' Courts,
(c) The Court Martial and
(d) Any other court or local tribunal as may be established.

Parliament is mandated to enact legislation conferring jurisdiction, functions and powers on these subordinate courts.

2.3 The Superior Courts

As we have seen above, the Constitution has established the Supreme Court, the Court of Appeal, the High Court, the Industrial Court and the Environment and Land Court as the superior courts.

---

7 Industrial Court Act, Act No.20 of 2011, CAP 234, Laws of Kenya.

8 Environment and Land Court Act, Act No. 19 of 2011, CAP 12A Laws of Kenya.

2.3.1. The Supreme Court

This is the highest court in the land and is established by Article 163 of the Constitution. It comprises of the Chief Justice, who is the President of the Court, the Deputy Chief Justice who deputizes for the Chief Justice and is the Vice-President of the Court, and five other Judges. The jurisdiction of the Supreme Court is provided exhaustively under the Constitution and is further elaborated in the Supreme Court Act.[9] The Supreme Court has original, appellate, and advisory jurisdiction. Apart from these three matters, the Supreme Court has no other jurisdiction. When the Supreme Court Act was enacted, Section 14 thereof purported to give "special jurisdiction" to the Supreme Court. The said provision is drawn as follows:-

(1) *To ensure that the ends of justice are met, the Supreme Court shall, within twelve months of the commencement of this Act, either on its own motion or on the application of any person, review the judgments and decisions of any judge—*

  (a) *removed from office on account of a recommendation by a tribunal appointed by the President, whether before or after the commencement of this Act; or*
  (b) *removed from office pursuant to the Vetting of Judges and Magistrates Act (Cap. 8B); or*
  (c) *who resigns or opts to retire, whether before or after the commencement of this Act, in consequence of a complaint of misconduct or misbehaviour.*

(2) *To qualify for review under subsection (1), the judgment or decision shall have been the basis of the removal, resignation or retirement of, or complaint against, the judge.*
(3) *The Court shall, in exercise of its powers under this section—*

  (a) *conduct a preliminary enquiry to determine the admissibility of the matter; and*
  (b) *have all the necessary powers to determine the review under this section, including calling for evidence.*

---

9 Supreme Court Act, CAP 9A, Laws of Kenya.

(4) *An application for review in respect of a judgment or decision made before the commencement of this Act shall not be entertained two years after the commencement of this Act.*

(5) *Nothing in this section shall be construed as limiting or otherwise affecting the inherent power of the Court, either on its own motion or on the application of a party, to make such orders as may be necessary for the ends of justice to be met or to prevent abuse of the due process of the Court.* The Supreme Court in the case of *S.K. Macharia vs KCB*[10] held that the said provision of the law was unconstitutional. The court stated as follows:-

> *"Section 14 of the Supreme Court Act is unconstitutional insofar as it purports to confer "special jurisdiction" upon the Supreme Court, contrary to the express terms of the Constitution. Although we have a perception of the good intentions that could have moved Parliament as it provided for the "extra" jurisdiction for the Supreme Court, we believe this, as embodied in Section 14 of the Supreme Court Act, ought to have been anchored under Article 163 of the Constitution, or under Section 23 of the Sixth Schedule on "Transitional Provisions."*

2.3.1.1 Original Jurisdiction of the Supreme Court

The only original jurisdiction, that is, jurisdiction to commence a case and pass judgment on it, vested upon the Supreme Court, is jurisdiction to hear matters relating to presidential elections.[11] Indeed the Supreme Court did have occasion to hear and determine the case relating to the presidential elections of 2013.[12]

---

10 *Supra*, note 2.

11 Constitution, Article 163 (3) (a).

12 *Raila Odinga & 5 Others vs Independent Electoral and Boundaries Commission & 3 Others, Supreme Court Petitions 3,4 & 5 of 2013, (2013) eKLR.*

2.3.1.2 Advisory Jurisdiction of the Supreme Court

The Supreme Court is empowered to render advisory opinions with respect to matters concerning the County Government. The only entities permitted to request the Supreme Court for an advisory opinion are the National Government, any State Organ, or any County Government.[13]

It will be seen that the jurisdiction to provide advisory opinions is very narrow. The only matter that may be subject to an advisory opinion is an issue concerning County Governments and the bodies that can approach the court are limited. It is apparent that private individuals cannot ask the court to render an advisory opinion.

In as much as the advisory jurisdiction is limited, it is the first time in Kenyan jurisprudence that a court has been given power to render advisory opinions. The Constitution of 2010, introduced County Governments into our political system, a system that has never before been present in Kenya. It is probable that the Constitution thought it wise to provide for the advisory jurisdiction, so as to provide a forum for guidance and interpretation of the law relating to County Governments, given that Kenya has had no experience with such system before.

In the matter of the Interim Independent Electoral Commission[14] the Supreme Court elaborated that an advisory opinion is in the nature of legal advice and does not fall in the category of judgment, ruling, order, or decree.[15] However, the same must be treated as an authoritative statement of the law, and the organs that sought it and all government or public action, must be guided by it. The same therefore has the same binding effect as any other decision of the court.[16]

This matter was filed by the Interim Independent Electoral Commission, and the court held that the Commission fell within the definition of "State Organ" and was therefore permitted to seek an advisory opinion from the Supreme

---

[13] Constitution, Article 163 (6).

[14] *In the matter of the Interim Independent Electoral Commission* Supreme Court Application No. 2 of 2011, (2011) eKLR.

[15] *Ibid*, Paragraph 33.

[16] *Ibid*, paragraph 93 and 94.

Court.[17] As to the subject matter *"any matter touching on county government"* the Supreme Court was of the opinion that it should be so interpreted as to incorporate any national-level process bearing a significant impact on the conduct of county government. The matter before court touched on when the first elections after the promulgation of the Constitution of 2010 should be held, and the court was of the view that the issue, is a question central to county government as to lie within the advisory jurisdiction of the Supreme Court. The court however declined to render an advisory opinion as it was of the view that the question before it could be determined by the High Court as the parties were not asking for a plain opinion statement of the date of the election, but rather, an interpretation of the Constitution, which could be done by the High Court.[18]

This being the first case in which the Supreme Court was faced with an application for an advisory opinion, the Supreme Court seized the opportunity to set down guidelines for the invocation of its advisory jurisdiction. It stated as follows:-

(i) For a reference to qualify for the Supreme Court's Advisory-Opinion discretion, it must fall within the four corners of Article 163(6): it must be 'a matter concerning county government.' The question as to whether a matter is one 'concerning county government' will be determined by the Court on a case-by case basis.

(ii) The only parties that can make a request for an Advisory Opinion are the national government, a State organ, or a county government. Any other person or institution may only be enjoined in the proceedings with leave of the Court, either as an intervener (interested party) or as amicus curiae.

(iii) The Court will be hesitant to exercise its discretion to render an Advisory Opinion where the matter in respect of which the reference has been made is a subject of proceedings in a lower Court....

(iv) Where a reference has been made to the Court the subject-matter of which is also pending in a lower Court, the Court may nonetheless render an Advisory Opinion if the applicant can demonstrate that the issue is of great public importance and requiring urgent resolution through an Advisory Opinion.

17 *Ibid*, paragraph 36.

18 *Ibid*, paragraph 46 and 96.

> *In addition, the applicant maybe required to demonstrate that the matter in question would not be amenable to expeditious resolution through adversarial Court process.*[19]

In *Re Speaker of the Senate & Another vs The Honorable Attorney General & Another & 3 Others*[20] the Supreme Court held that the Speaker of the Senate qualifies to be included in the definition of a "State Organ" and could thus file a matter in the Supreme Court seeking an advisory opinion. The matter concerned debate over the Division of Revenue Bill which the Speaker of the National Assembly had declared that it could be debated solely by the National Assembly without input from the Senate. The Supreme Court accepted jurisdiction and held that the matter concerned the County Government. It also held that the matter was a proper case for the court to invoke its advisory jurisdiction given that the issues raised were of great public interest and the parties needed constitutional guidance.

2.3.1.3 Appellate Jurisdiction of the Supreme Court

In so far as the appellate jurisdiction of the Supreme Court is concerned, the Supreme Court has jurisdiction to hear appeals from the Court of Appeal and from any other court or tribunal as prescribed by national legislation.[21] Only two types of appeal lie from the Court of Appeal to the Supreme Court[22]. The first is an appeal as of right, if the matter involves the interpretation of the Constitution.[23] In these types of cases, leave is not required before appealing to the Supreme Court.

The second type of an appeal is one which does not involve the interpretation of the Constitution. For such appeal to be entertained by the Supreme Court, it must be one which has been certified as involving a matter of general public

---

19 *Ibid*, paragraph 83.

20 *Re Speaker of the Senate & Another vs The Honorable Attorney General & Another & 3 Others* Supreme Court, Advisory Opinion No. 2 of 2013, (2013) eKLR.

21 Constitution, Article 163 (3) (b) (ii).

22 *Ibid*, Article 163 (4).

23 *Ibid*, Article 163 (4) (a).

importance.[24] The Constitution provides that the certification can either be by the Court of Appeal or by the Supreme Court. If the certification is by the Court of Appeal, the Supreme Court has power to review it, and can either affirm it, vary it, or overturn it.[25]

In the case of *Lawrence Nduttu & 6000 Others v. Kenya Breweries Limited & Another*,[26] it was affirmed that it is only the two types of appeals that are envisaged. The Supreme Court stated as follows:-

"At the outset, we consider it crucial to lay down once again the principle that only two types of appeal lie to the Supreme Court from the Court of Appeal. The first type of appeal lies as of right if it is from a case involving the interpretation or application of the Constitution. In such a case, no prior leave is required from this Court or Court of Appeal. The second type of appeal lies to the Supreme Court not as of right but only if it has been certified as involving a matter of general public importance. It is the certification by either Court which constitutes leave. This means that where a party wishes to invoke the appellate jurisdiction of this Court on grounds other than that the case is one which involves the interpretation or application of the Constitution, then such intending appellant must convince the Court that the case is one involving a matter of general public importance. If the Court of Appeal is convinced that such is the case and the certification is affirmed by the Supreme Court, then the intending appellant may proceed and file the substantive appeal..."[27]

These two types of appeals are the only ones envisaged by the Constitution.

(a) *Appeal as of right*

If a matter involves the interpretation of the constitution, then one has a right to appeal to the Supreme Court. Leave is not necessary. However, the simple citation of the Constitution in an appeal to the Supreme Court, does not

---

24 *Ibid*, Article 163 (4) (b).

25 *Ibid*, Article 163 (5).

26 *Lawrence Nduttu & 6000 Others v. Kenya Breweries Limited & Another* Supreme Court Appeal No. 3 of 2012, (2012) eKLR.

27 *Ibid*, paragraphs 20 and 21.

convert the matter into one requiring the interpretation of the Constitution. The matter of interpretation of the Constitution must have been in contest in the previous courts. This is to avoid a transmutation of a matter, in order to escape the requirement for certification.[28] Where the case to be appealed from had nothing or little to do with the interpretation or application of the Constitution, it cannot support a further appeal to the Supreme Court under the provisions of Article 163 (4) (a) of the Constitution.[29]

(b) Appeal with leave

The threshold must be met, that the case be one in which a "matter of general public importance is involved", and before such appeal is allowed to be filed, there must be certification that the matter involves a question of public importance. The Constitution uses the words "certification", but the Supreme Court Act uses the word "leave"[30]. In the case of *Lawrence Nduttu*[31], the Supreme Court held that the two words mean the same thing.[32] The Constitution and the Supreme Court Act, provide that one may have the certification either from the Court of Appeal or the Supreme Court itself. In the case of *Sum Model Industries vs Industrial and Commercial Development Corporation*[33] the Supreme Court was of the opinion, that although the Constitution permits the Supreme Court to issue a certification, it would be good practice for such applications to be originated in the Court of Appeal. If any party is aggrieved, the party may ask the Supreme Court to overrule such certification.

Before leave is granted, the court must be satisfied that the issue raised is one of general public importance. The question that arises, is, what then is a matter of general public importance? Way before the Constitution of 2010 was envisaged, Madam JA sitting in the case of *Murai v Wainaina,*[34], opined obiter, that a question of general public importance *"is a question which takes into account the*

---

28 *Peter Oduor Ngoge vs Honorable Ole Kaparo & Others* (Supreme Court Petition No. 2 of 2012) (2012) eKLR.

29 *Lawrence Nduttu* case, *supra* note 26.

30 Supreme Court Act, *Supra* note 9, Section 15.

31 *Supra* note 26.

32 *Supra* note 22, paragraph 18.

33 *Supra*, note 6.

34 *Murai v Wainaina* (1982) KLR 38.

well-being of the society in just proportions". The judge was further of the view that a matter touching on personal freedoms and a question touching on ownership of land were questions of general public importance.

The first case in which the Supreme Court had occasion to give pronouncement on what a question of "general public importance" constitutes, was the case of *Hermanus Phillipus Steyn v. Giovanni Gnecchi-Ruscone*[35]. The court was of the view that a matter of "general public importance" goes beyond a question of law. It could be related to a question of general public interest, or it may involve a substantial point of law, the determination of which has a bearing on public interest. The court then proceeded to provide guidelines on how to determine a question of general public importance. It pronounced itself as follows:-

In summary, we would state the governing principles as follows:

(i) for a case to be certified as one involving a matter of general public importance, the intending appellant must satisfy the Court that the issue to be canvassed on appeal is one the determination of which transcends the circumstances of the particular case, and has a significant bearing on the public interest;

(ii) where the matter in respect of which certification is sought raises a point of law, the intending appellant must demonstrate that such a point is a substantial one, the determination of which will have a significant bearing on the public interest;

(iii) such question or questions of law must have arisen in the Court or Courts below, and must have been the subject of judicial determination;

(iv) where the application for certification has been occasioned by a state of uncertainty in the law, arising from contradictory precedents, the Supreme Court may either resolve the uncertainty, as it may determine, or refer the matter to the Court of Appeal for its determination;

(v) mere apprehension of miscarriage of justice, a matter most apt for resolution in the lower superior courts, is not a proper basis for granting certification for an appeal to the Supreme Court; the matter to be certified for a final appeal in the Supreme Court, must still fall within the terms of Article 163 (4)(b) of the Constitution;

---

35 *Hermanus Phillipus Steyn v. Giovanni Gnecchi-Ruscone,* Supreme Court Application No. 4 of 2012, (2013) eKLR.

(vi) *the intending applicant has an obligation to identify and concisely set out the specific elements of "general public importance" which he or she attributes to the matter for which certification is sought;*

(vii) *determinations of fact in contests between parties are not, by themselves, a basis for granting certification for an appeal before the Supreme Court.*

In the event, the Supreme Court declined to certify the matter as involving a question of general public importance, the issue in the case being whether the applicant was entitled to be paid some commission as brokerage fees.

We have already seen that the certification by the Court of Appeal is subject to review by the Supreme Court. This was precisely what transpired in the case of *Malcolm Bell vs Hon. Daniel Toroitich arap Moi & Another.* [36] In the case, the Court of Appeal in granting a certification, had held that the matter was of *general public importance;* and that *substantial miscarriage of justice may occur* unless the appeal is heard. This was reversed by the Supreme Court. In the view of the Supreme Court, the issues in the case revolved around questions of adverse possession which involve legal principles that have been settled and which the Court of Appeal itself had settled in the matter. The court also held that Section 16 (1) and (2) (b) of the Supreme Court Act, upon which the Court of Appeal had relied on, was unconstitutional. The same provides as follows:-

S.16

*(1) The Supreme Court shall not grant leave to appeal to the Court unless it is satisfied -that it is in the interests of justice for the Court to hear and determine the proposed appea*l.

(2) It shall be in the interests of justice for the Supreme Court to hear and determine a proposed appeal if—

(a) the appeal involves a matter of general public importance; or

*(b) a substantial miscarriage of justice may have occurred or may occur unless the appeal is hear*d.

[36] *Malcolm Bell vs Hon. Daniel Toroitich arap Moi & Another,* Supreme Court, Civil Application No. 1 of 2013, (2013) eKLR.

The Supreme Court held that this donation by statute was contrary to the provisions of Article 163 of the Constitution, as the Constitution only limits appeals to the Supreme Court, where the matter solely involves a question of general public importance. It was therefore wrong for the Court of Appeal to provide a certification on the reasons that a substantial miscarriage of justice could occur. The certification by the Court of Appeal was therefore reversed.

There can be no certification where the matter was one concluded before the promulgation of the Constitution of Kenya, 2010 since the said provisions do not act retrospectively.[37] The decisions of the Supreme Court bind all other courts.[38] This entrenches in the Constitution the doctrine of *stare decisis*. This is significant since trial courts will have to follow the determinations of the Supreme Court on critical matters touching on criminal procedure.

From the above discourse, it will be seen that the Supreme Court may only be seized of a criminal matter, in an appeal, where such appeal involves a question relating to the interpretation of the Constitution for which a party may appeal as of right, or, where the matter involves a question of general public importance, for which certification must first be sought. It is unlikely, that the advisory jurisdiction may be invoked in a criminal matter, since as we have seen, the advisory jurisdiction is only limited to matters concerning the County Government.

2.3.2 The Court of Appeal

The Court of Appeal is established by Article 164 of the Constitution. The Constitution provides that it shall have no fewer than 12 judges.[39] The jurisdiction of the Court of Appeal is to hear appeals from the High Court and any other court or tribunal as prescribed by an Act of Parliament.[40] The Court

---

37 *Greenfield Investments Limited vs Barber Alibhai Mawji*, Court of Appeal at Nairobi, Civil Application No. 5 of 2012 (2013) eKLR.

38 Constitution, Article 163 (7).

39 *Ibid*, Article 164 (1) (a).

40 *Ibid*, Article 164 (3).

of Appeal does not have original jurisdiction to hear and determine a matter.[41] It only hears appeals. Thus where one is dissatisfied with a matter arising out of a criminal trial from the High Court, or from a decision of the High Court while in exercise of its appellate jurisdiction, he has recourse to appeal to the Court of Appeal. The Court of Appeal does not however hear appeals where the appeal solely touches on the severity of the sentence.[42]

The threshold of "a question of general public importance" which is required for an appeal to be referred to the Supreme Court is not a requirement for one to appeal to the Court of Appeal. Therefore, unless expressly excluded by statute, one will have a right to appeal to the Court of Appeal if aggrieved by a decision of the High Court in either its original or appellate jurisdiction.

2.3.3. The High Court

Article 165 of the Constitution establishes the High Court. The High Court has the following jurisdiction as set out in Article 165 (3):-

a) *unlimited original jurisdiction in criminal and civil matters;*
b) jurisdiction to determine the question whether a right or fundamental freedom in the Bill Rights has been denied, violated, infringed or threatened;
c) jurisdiction to hear an appeal from a decision of a tribunal appointed under the Constitution to consider the removal of a person from office, other than a tribunal appointed under Article 144;
d) jurisdiction to hear any question respecting the interpretation of the Constitution including the determination of:-

> *The question whether any law is inconsistent with or in contravention of the Constitution;*
> *The question whether anything said to be done under the authority of the Constitution or of any law is inconsistent with, or in contravention of, the Constitution;*

---

41 Save for the jurisdiction to punish for contempt. See *R v Tony Gachoka & Another,* Court of Appeal, Criminal Application No.4 of 1999, (1999) eKLR.

42 See Chapter 13 on Appeals.

Any matter relating to constitutional powers of State organs in respect of county governments and any matter relating to the constitutional relationship between the levels of government; and
iv. A question relating to conflict of laws under Article 191; and

e) Any other jurisdiction, original or appellate, conferred on it by legislation.

In so far as criminal matters are concerned, the High Court always has original unlimited jurisdiction. It means that it can try any offence. This position is buttressed by the provisions of sections 4 and 5 of the Criminal Procedure Code (CPC).[43] Section 4 makes provision for the trial of the offences set out in the Penal Code.[44] It provides that subject to the CPC, an offence under the Penal Code may be tried by the High Court, or by a subordinate court by which the offence is shown in the fifth column of the First Schedule to the CPC to be triable.[45] Section 5 of the CPC, makes provision for the trial of offences that are set out in other law separate from the Penal Code. It provides that if a court is mentioned, the offence shall be tried in the court mentioned[46], and if not court is mentioned, then subject to the CPC, the offence may be tried by the High Court, or a subordinate court as noted in the Fifth Column of the CPC[47].

Thus, both legally and theoretically, the High Court can hear and determine any criminal case.[48] However, in practice, the lowest court having jurisdiction to hear the case is the court that will try the matter thus giving avenue to an aggrieved party to proceed to the High Court on appeal. If the High Court proceeded to determine such cases, pursuant to its original jurisdiction, then the accused will lose one rung in pursuing his right of appeal. It is therefore prudent, in order to preserve the entitlement of an accused to fully enjoy his

---

43 Chapter 75, Laws of Kenya.

44 Chapter 63, Laws of Kenya.

45 The Fifth Column of the CPC provides for the various offences set out in the Penal Code (CAP 63) Laws of Kenya, and the particular court with jurisdiction to try the offence. See also below, jurisdiction of subordinate courts.

46 CPC, Section 5 (1).

47 *Ibid*, Section 5 (2).

48 But see *John Swaka v DPP & 2 Others*, High Court at Nairobi, Constitutional Petition No.318 of 2011, (2013) eKLR where the judges seemed to suggest that the High Court cannot hear a criminal matter which is triable by a subordinate court.

right of appeal, for the case to be tried by the lowest court with jurisdiction to hear the case. However, there are some offences which are solely triable by the High Court.[49] The High Court is further empowered under Section 6 of the CPC to pass any sentence authorized by law. This is unlike subordinate courts which have limitations of sentence.[50] This in essence confirms the unlimited powers conferred upon the High Court by the Constitution.

As to hearing appeals, it will be observed under Article 165 (3) (e) of the Constitution, that the High Court has appellate jurisdiction, as may be conferred by legislation. The CPC prescribes that the High Court can hear appeals from trials conducted in Magistrates courts,[51] and therein lies its jurisdiction to hear appeals from trials conducted by subordinate courts.

In addition, under the provisions of Article 165 (6) of the Constitution, the High Court has supervisory jurisdiction over the subordinate courts and over any person, body or authority exercising a judicial or quasi-judicial function but not over a superior court. Article 165 (7) prescribes that the High Court in exercising this jurisdiction, is empowered to call for the record of any proceedings before any subordinate court or person, body or authority and may make any order or give any direction it considers appropriate to ensure the fair administration of justice. This supervisory jurisdiction in criminal matters is usually manifested by the power of Revision.[52] But it will be a fallacy to say that the supervisory jurisdiction is only exercisable through revision.

The supervisory powers in Article 165 are wide ranging powers provided to give the High Court a supervisory role to all judicial and quasi-judicial bodies. In the exercise of this supervisory jurisdiction, the High Court can call for the record of any proceedings be it a criminal or civil proceeding. As may be discerned this supervisory power extends beyond supervising the standard courts but also to supervising anybody or authority exercising a judicial or quasi-judicial function. The High Court in exercising this supervisory jurisdiction can make any order

---

49 Such as the offences of murder and treason. See CPC, Column 5.

50 Below, on jurisdiction of subordinate courts.

51 CPC, Section 347.

52 See Chapter 13 and 14 on Appeals and Revision respectively.

or give any direction it considers appropriate to ensure the fair administration of justice.

It can therefore safely be concluded that the High Court has original, appellate and supervisory jurisdiction. The jurisdiction of the High Court is however limited by Article 165 (5) which specifically provides that the High Court shall not have jurisdiction in respect of matters reserved for the exclusive jurisdiction of the Supreme Court under the Constitution; or falling within the jurisdiction of the courts contemplated in Article 162 (2) which are the Industrial Court and the Environment and Land Court.[53] These courts determine disputes touching on employment and labour relations[54], and the environment and the use of and occupation and title to land[55] which are ordinarily disputes of a civil nature. The jurisdiction of the High Court, to hear criminal matters is therefore unaffected by the presence of these two superior courts.

Note also that vide the powers conferred by Article 163 (3) (d) of the Constitution the High Court can sit as a Constitutional Court and can hear and determine constitutional issues that arise in the course of a criminal trial in the subordinate courts. The High Court is also vested with prerogative powers of *mandamus, certiorari,* and *prohibition* exercised through the avenue of Judicial Review[56] and which can be used to control criminal trials. Through these tools, the High Court can prohibit the trial of an individual or quash the decision or proceedings of a subordinate court.

2.4 The Subordinate Courts

The Constitution under Article 169 (1) provides for the subordinate courts. The Article states that the subordinate courts are;-

the Magistrates courts;

---

53 *Supra*, notes 7 and 8.

54 For the Industrial Court.

55 For the Environment and Land Court.

56 The procedure for the invocation of prerogative orders is provided for under Order 53 of the Civil Procedure Rules, 2010 made under the Civil Procedure Act, Chapter 21, Laws of Kenya.

the Kadhis' courts;

the Courts Martial; and

any other court or local tribunal as may be established by an Act of Parliament, other than the courts established as required by Article 162 (2).[57]

2.4.1 Magistrates Courts

The various Magistrates courts and their jurisdiction are elaborated by the Magistrates' Courts Act.[58] There are various categories of magistrates. In the order of seniority, these are Chief Magistrate, Senior Principal Magistrate, Principal Magistrate, Senior Resident Magistrate, Resident Magistrate and District Magistrate.[59] Excluding the District Magistrate, the other magistrates comprise of the "Resident Magistrate's Court".[60] The District Magistrate, sits as a "District Magistrate's Court".[61] Magistrate courts can be of the first class or third class. It is a Magistrates Court of the first class if it is a "Resident Magistrates' Court"[62] or a District Magistrate's Court held by a district magistrate of the first class. Magistrate's court of the third class means a district magistrate's court held by a district magistrate having power to hold a magistrate's court of the third class.[63]

2.4.1.1 Original Criminal Jurisdiction of Magistrates Courts

The magistrates courts, unlike the High Court do not have unlimited jurisdiction and therefore cannot hear any case. They have limits as to the nature of cases that they can hear and the level of sentence that they can mete out depending

---

57 The Industrial Court and the Environment and Land Court.

58 Chapter 10, Laws of Kenya.

59 *Ibid*, Section 2.

60 *Ibid*, Section 3.

61 *Ibid*, Section 6.

62 Meaning either Chief Magistrate's, Senior Principal Magistrate's, Principal Magistrate's, Senior Resident Magistrate's, or Resident Magistrate's courts.

63 Magistrate's Courts Act, Section 2, *supra* note 58.

on their rank. To determine which court can try what offence prescribed in the Penal Code, one must refer to the Fifth Column of the CPC.[64] For offences under other law (not those in the Penal Code), one must refer to the statute prescribing the offence and the maximum sentence provided, so as to determine which Magistrates' Court has jurisdiction to try the offence.

Section 7 of the CPC provides for the sentences that the respective courts can pass. Save for the Resident Magistrates' Courts, the Magistrates' Courts of the First Class, can pass any sentence authorised by law for an offence that is triable by that court. The Resident Magistrate's Court cannot pass sentence exceeding 7 years or a fine exceeding Kshs.20, 000/=. It follows therefore that such court cannot try an offence where the maximum penalty exceeds 7 years or a fine beyond Kshs. 20,000/=.[65] The exceptions are offences set out in Section 278, 308(1) and 322 of the Penal Code[66] or those under the Sexual Offences Act.[67]

District Magistrates of the First Class can only try offences where the maximum penalty is 7 years and the maximum fine is Kshs.20,000/=[68] while District Magistrates of the Second Class, can only try offences where the maximum penalty is 2 years and the fine does not exceed Kshs. 10,000/=.[69] In so far as territorial jurisdiction is concerned, Resident Magistrates' courts have jurisdiction throughout Kenya, whereas, District Magistrates' Courts only have jurisdiction within the District.[70]

---

64 The Fifth Column of the CPC sets out the jurisdiction of the various courts to try the offences noted in the Penal Code.

65 CPC, Section 7 (1) (b) as read with Section 7 (2).

66 Respectively being the offences of Stealing Stock which carries a maximum sentence of 14 years; being armed with a dangerous weapon which carries a maximum sentence of 15 years; and handling stolen goods which carries a maximum sentence of 14 years.

67 Sexual Offences Act, Chapter 62A, Laws of Kenya. The Act covers offences such as rape, defilement, and Indecent Assault. The sentences under the Sexual Offences Act, for some of the offences, go up to life imprisonment.

68 CPC, Section 7(2).

69 CPC, Section 7(3).

70 Magistrates Court Act, *supra* note 58, Sections 3(2) and 7(3).

2.4.1.2 Appellate Criminal Jurisdiction of Magistrates Courts

Resident Magistrate's Courts do have appellate jurisdiction in criminal matters from the judgments of Magistrate's Court of the third class.[71] Thus a person who is convicted of an offence on a trial held by a magistrate's court of the third class, or the Attorney-General where such person has been acquitted, has avenue to make an appeal to the Resident Magistrate's Court. However, in practice, Magistrates Courts of the 3rd Class are virtually non-existent, and therefore it is rare to find the Resident Magistrates' Courts exercising their appellate jurisdiction.

2.4.1.3 Inquisitorial Criminal Jurisdiction of Magistrates' Courts

Magistrates Courts are also authorized to hold inquests.[72] Inquests can be held by magistrates of the first or second class, or one specially empowered by the Chief Justice. The power to hold inquests is only vested in the Magistrates' court and the High Court, (since it presided by a judge, and not magistrate), has no power to hold an inquest.

In *Re Muge,*[73] the then Attorney General of the Republic of Kenya, purported to order the Chief Justice to appoint a Judge to conduct an inquest into the death of Bishop Alexander Muge who was killed in a road traffic accident. At the same time, one Mr. Onkoba was charged with the offence of Causing Death by Dangerous Driving arising out of the same accident that killed Bishop Muge. The widow of the deceased applied for an order of prohibition to stop the Magistrate from proceeding with the traffic case as there had been intimation that an inquest would be held. It was the position of the applicant that it would be futile to hold an inquest if the traffic case proceeded to conclusion, as the whole purpose of the intended inquest, would be defeated by the trial. In the first instance, the High Court dismissed the application, on the technicality of the supporting affidavit, which it considered to be defective. The applicant appealed and in the Court of Appeal, the decision turned on whether or not

---

71 *Ibid*, Section 10.

72 CPC, Section 385.

73 *Re Muge* (1991) KLR 51.

the purported directive to the Chief Justice had any basis in law. If not, then the purported inquest could not be held, and thus the applicant could not be said to have suffered any injury. The Court of Appeal held that the direction by the Attorney General had no basis in law as it was not sanctioned by any constitutional or statutory provision. In other words, the Attorney General could not direct that a Judge of the High Court be appointed to hold an inquest.

2.4.2 Special Magistrates Courts

2.4.2.1 Children's Courts

The Children's Courts are established by the Children Act.[74] The Children's Courts are staffed by Magistrates who are specifically appointed by the Chief Justice to preside over cases involving children in any part of the country. Such Magistrates constitute the Children's Court when so sitting to hear cases involving children. The jurisdiction of the Children's Court *inter alia* includes hearing of any charge against a child, other than a charge of murder or a charge in which the child is charged together with a person or persons above the age of eighteen years. [75]

The Children's Court also presides over charges against any person accused of an offence under the Children Act.[76]

Any sentence prescribed for the particular offence can be passed by the Magistrate mandated to hear matters covered by the Children's Court, irrespective of any limitations that may be prescribed by the *CPC* as to the particular sentence that the particular rank of magistrate may pass. Thus all magistrates gazetted to sit in Children's Courts have the same powers irrespective of their ranks in the magistracy.

---

74 The Children Act, Chapter 141 Laws of Kenya was assented on the 31st day of December 2001.

75 *Ibid*, Sections 73 and 184.

76 *Ibid.*

2.4.2.2 The Anti-Corruption Courts

The Anti-Corruption Courts are established pursuant to the provisions of the Anti –Corruption and Economic Crimes Act.[77] This Act provides for the prevention, investigation and punishment of corruption, economic crimes and related offences and for matters incidental and connected therewith.[78] The statute empowers the Chief Justice to appoint Special Magistrates, to hear offences under the statute, which are offences related to corruption and economic crimes.[79]Only the Special Magistrates so appointed have jurisdiction to hear such matters. Unless, so appointed, a magistrate would not have jurisdiction to hear the offences of corruption and economic crimes set out in the Act.[80] As a special magistrate, a magistrate sitting in the Anti-Corruption Court can pass any sentence authorised by the statute. All magistrates in the Anti- Corruption Court exercise the same jurisdiction irrespective of rank.

2.5 Kadhis' Courts

Under Article 162(5) of the Constitution, the jurisdiction of a Kadhis' Court is limited to the determination of questions of Muslim law relating to personal status, marriage, divorce or inheritance in proceedings in which all the parties profess the Muslim religion and submit to the jurisdiction of the Kadhis' Courts. The Kadhis' Court therefore does not have jurisdiction to try criminal matters and cannot prosecute suspected offenders.

2.6 Courts Martial

The Courts Martial is provided for in the Constitution and established by the Kenya Defence Forces Act (KDF Act).[81] Its purpose is to try offences under the same statute which are basically offences committed by members of the armed

---

77 The Anti-Corruption and Economic Crimes Act, Cap 65 Laws of Kenya.

78 *Ibid*, The Preamble.

79 *Ibid*, Section 3.

80 *Ibid*, Section 4.

81 Kenya Defence Forces Act Chapter 199, Laws of Kenya.

forces. Section 160 of the Kenya Defence Forces Act provides that the Courts Martial shall consist of

(a) a Judge Advocate, who shall be the presiding officer;
(b) at least five other members appointed by the Defence Court-Martial Administrator if an officer is being tried; and
(c) not less than three other members in any other case.

At least one of the members shall be of equivalent rank as the accused person where the accused person is an officer and the lowest ranking officer in the Defence Forces where the accused person is a service member. The judge advocate is either a magistrate or an advocate of the High Court of Kenya of not less than 10 years standing appointed by the Chief Justice.

Under Section 186 of the KDF Act, appeals from the court martial are heard by the High Court and there is a further right of appeal to other superior courts.[82]

The court martial being a subordinate court, is also subject to the supervisory powers of the High Court.

2.7 Effect of Limitation of Jurisdiction of Subordinate Courts

A subordinate court cannot preside over a matter beyond the empowering constitutional or statutory provision. This is unlike the High Court which has unlimited jurisdiction in trials.

Lack of jurisdiction by a subordinate court can be raised as a ground of appeal to nullify the proceedings and judgment. In the Ugandan case of *Martino Judayi & Others v. West Nile District Administration,*[83] the appellants were charged in the District African Court of West Nile with an offence under Section 228 of the Penal Code of Uganda. The appellants were convicted but

---

82 This is unlike the previous position in the former Armed Forces Act (repealed by the KDF Act) where one had a right of appeal to the High Court and no further right of appeal. See *Ondari & 17 Others v Republic* (1986) KLR at 776.

83 *Martino Judayi & Others v. West Nile District Administration* (1963) E.A. 406.

the conviction was quashed as the court had no jurisdiction to try the offence. The trial was declared a nullity.

In the case of *R. V. Ambari s/o Juma*[84] at the High Court of Tanganyika, an accused was charged with defilement of a girl under the age of twelve, contrary to section 136 of the Tanzanian Penal Code. He was taken before a third-class magistrate who had no jurisdiction to try the case. This magistrate read and explained the charge to the accused, who pleaded not guilty. Subsequently the accused was tried by a first-class magistrate, who convicted him of indecent assault. There was no record that the accused was again asked to plead to the charge at its trial, nor was there any record that he was then reminded of his earlier plea. In the exercise of its jurisdiction in revision, the High Court considered the validity of the proceedings. The Court considered that in view of the terms of Section 203 of the Tanzanian CPC, the plea of the accused could not be lawfully taken by a court which has no jurisdiction to try the offence. The conviction and the sentence were hence set aside for a new trial. *Mahon, Ag. C. J.* In his ruling stated;

"An accused cannot be lawfully arraigned in this territory before a court which has no jurisdiction to try him, although such a court may, of course, remand him or admit him to bail. It follows, therefore, that the proceedings before the third-class magistrate were a nullity in so far as the taking of a plea was concerned, and as the accused was not thereafter called upon to plead and did not in fact plead, the trial was a nullity, the irregularity not being one which can be cleared by s. 346 of the CPC."

A court which has no power to impose a minimum sentence required by the penal provisions cannot have jurisdiction to try and determine the offence under such penal provisions. Such a trial is a nullity.

* * *

---

[84] *R. V. Ambari s/o Juma* (1959) E. A. 85

CHAPTER 3
INVESTIGATING CRIME

3.1. Introduction

Investigation in relation to a crime is the process of gathering information, analyzing it, identifying the relevant parties, and organizing this information in a form that makes sense. The purpose of any investigation is to determine whether an offence has been committed, and if so, who has committed the said offence. It also serves the purpose of gathering evidence that may be presented during trial.

In an investigation, a wide range of information is gathered. These include the statements of witnesses; forensic tests; photographs; samples from the crime scene, victim or suspect; medical reports and other important material that may give information on the crime being investigated. It is the totality of the evidence gathered during investigation that guides the State in deciding whether there is enough evidence to put a person on trial. The process of investigation is critical since the burden of proving a criminal case is placed upon the prosecution and therefore there must be adequate evidence gathered to sustain a conviction.

3.2 Role of the Police in Investigations

The onus of investigating crimes is not just on the police department. Indeed there is no monopoly granted to any institution or individual when it comes to investigating crimes. Any person or entity is free to investigate a crime. However, the Police Department is a unit that is specifically equipped for purposes of investigating, arresting and preferring charges against individuals suspected to having committed an offence. Article 243 of the Constitution[1] establishes the National Police Service (NPS). These constitutional provisions were put to effect by the enactment of the National Police Service Act (NPSA).[2]

The NPS consists of the Kenya Police Service[3] and the Administration Police Service.[4] The Constitution also establishes the office of the Inspector-General (IG) of the NPS who shall have independent command over the NPS.[5] The Cabinet Secretary responsible for the police is at liberty to give direction to the IG with respect to any matter of policy[6], but no person may give a direction to the IG with respect to, *inter alia*, the investigation of any particular offence or crime.[7] Article 157(4) of the Constitution, however gives the Director of Public Prosecutions (DPP) the mandate to direct the IG to investigate any information or allegation of criminal conduct[8] which opens the debate whether the provisions of Article 245 (5) and Article 157 (4) of the Constitution are contradictory.

The constitutional provisions relating to the police service, were elaborated when parliament enacted the National Police Service Act (NPSA)[9], whose object is to give effect to the provisions of Articles 238, 239, 243, 244 and 247 of the Constitution.[10] Section 24 of the NPSA sets out the functions of the police which functions include, the investigation of crimes, collection of criminal intelligence, prevention and detection of crime, and apprehension of

---

1 Constitution of Kenya, 2010.

2 Act No. 11A of 2011, now Chapter 284 of the Laws of Kenya, assented to on 27th August 2011 and commenced on 30th August 2011.

3 Constitution, Article 243(2).

4 *Ibid*, and the NPSA, Section 25.

5 Constitution, Article 245 (1) and (2); this position is also reflected in section 8 (1) of the NPSA.

6 Which directions should be in writing pursuant to Article 245 (5) of the Constitution.

7 *Ibid*, Article 245 (4) (b).

8 Article 157 (4) of the Constitution provides, *"The Director of Public Prosecutions shall have power to direct the Inspector-General of the National Police Service to investigate any information or allegation of criminal conduct and the Inspector-General shall comply with any such direction."*

9 Act No. 11A of 2011, Laws of Kenya, assented to on 27th August 2011 and commenced on 30th August 2011.

10 *Ibid*, Section 3.

offenders.[11] Further, pursuant to the provisions of Section 22 and S.118 of the Criminal Procedure Code[12] (CPC) the police can carry out searches of premises and vessels. The right to search is also accorded to the police by Section 60 of the NPSA.

Section 28 of the NPSA provides for the establishment of the directorate of Criminal Investigations Department.[13]The functions of the directorate include the investigations of serious crimes including homicide, narcotic crimes, human trafficking, money laundering, terrorism, economic crimes, piracy, organized crime, and cyber-crime among others; the conduction of forensic analysis and investigation of any matter that may be referred to it by the Independent police Oversight Authority.[14]

There is no doubt that the investigation of a crime may be a complicated process and may involve multiple procedures. It is beyond the scope of this book to enumerate all of them. However, three of the investigative processes are important and have a huge bearing on the criminal trial, and therefore deserve a special mention. First, is the recording of statements; second, is the process of an identification parade and third, is search and seizure. Let us have a closer look at these three critical aspects of investigation.

3.3 Statements

3.3.1 Recording of Statements

Statements are critical as they form the foundation upon which oral evidence is presented before court in a criminal trial. Much of the law on this point is covered in the new NPSA, which repealed the former Police Act,[15] and in judicial decisions. Prior to the coming in force of the NPSA[16] the operative provisions touching on the taking of statements were covered in the Police

11 *Ibid*, Section 24 (e)-(h).

12 Chapter 75, Laws of Kenya.

13 NPSA, Section 28.

14 *Ibid*, Section 35.

15 The Police Act is the former Chapter 84, Laws of Kenya, which was repealed by Section 130 of the NPSA, the current Chapter 84, Laws of Kenya.

16 *Supra* note 9.

Act (now repealed).[17] The NPSA is therefore the current statute laying out procedures for the taking of statements.

Section 52 of the NPSA authorizes the police to record statements not just from suspects but also from any person they feel has information that can help in their investigations. It provides as follows :-

(1) A police officer may, in writing, require any person whom the police officer has reason to believe has information which may assist in the investigation of an alleged offence to attend before him at a police station or police office in the county in which that person resides or for the time being is.

(2) A person who without reasonable excuse fails to comply with a requisition under subsection (1), or who, having complied, refuses or fails to give his correct name and address and to answer truthfully all questions that may be lawfully put to him commits an offence. (3) A person shall not be required to answer any question under this section if the question tends to expose the person to a criminal charge, penalty or forfeiture.

(4) A police officer shall record any statement made to him by any such person, whether the person is suspected of having committed an offence or not, but, before recording any statement from a person to whom a charge is to be preferred or who has been charged with committing an offence, the police officer shall warn the person that any statement which may be recorded may be used in evidence.

(5) A statement taken in accordance with this section shall be recorded and signed by the person making it after it has been read out to him in a language which the person understands and the person has been invited to make any correction he may wish.

(6) Notwithstanding the other provisions of this section, the powers conferred by this section shall be exercised in accordance with the Criminal Procedure Code (Cap. 75), the Witness Protection Act (Cap. 79) or any other written law.

(7) The failure by a police officer to comply with a requirement of this section in relation to the making of a statement shall render the statement inadmissible in any proceedings in which it is sought to have the statement admitted in evidence.

---

17 The NPSA repealed both the Police Act (former CAP 84) and the Administration Police Act (CAP 85).

From these above provisions, it will be discerned first, that every individual has a duty to assist the police in investigation and has a duty to attend at a police station upon being summoned, and also to answer questions truthfully. However, one cannot be compelled to answer questions which tend to incriminate him, a manifestation of the right to remain silent, and the right not to make any confession or admission, which rights are enshrined in Article 49 (b) and (d) of the Constitution.

Broadly speaking, there are two categories of statements. The first is what in common parlance is termed as a "Statement under Inquiry." The second is in common parlance termed as a "Statement under Caution".[18]

3.3.1.1 Statement under Inquiry

The police have power to summon any person whom they feel has information that can assist in investigation and a police officer may record a statement from such person, whether the person is a suspect or not. This is the form of statement which in practice is called a "Statement under inquiry." It is termed so, because at this point in time, the police are still at the stage of making inquiries with the aim of uncovering the truth underlying the suspected offence. Such statements were previously canvassed under section 22 (1) of the Police Act (repealed).[19]

3.3.1.2 Statement under Caution or Warning

Second, is the statement "under caution" or statement "under warning". [20] The Police, after making inquiries and investigating the circumstances of the

---

18 In common parlance, since these words do not appear in the NPSA.

19 Section 22 (1) of the Police Act (repealed) provided that, *"A police officer may by writing under his hand require any person who he has reason to believe has information which will assist him in investigating an alleged offence to attend before him at a police station or police office in the district in which such person resides or for the time being is."*

20 Section 52 (4) of the NPSA provides, *"A police officer shall record any statement made to him by any such person, whether the person is suspected of having committed an offence or not, but, before recording any statement from a person to whom a charge is to be preferred or who has been charged with committing an offence, the police officer shall warn the person that any statement which may be recorded may be used in evidence."*

subject crime, may be of the view that they have identified the person that they suspect to have committed the offence. The police are empowered to take a statement from the person so suspected. But before taking down the statement from such person, the Police officer must first warn or caution such person that any statement he makes may be used in evidence. Before a statement under warning is made, the suspect must be provided with the details of the charge that he is suspecting to have committed, and warned before being invited to make any statement.

Such person still retains the right to remain silent or not to make a statement that incriminates him. Indeed it is arguable that one has a right not to make any statement upon warning. This type of statement was previously canvassed in section 22 (3) of the Police Act (repealed).[21]

The distinction between these two statements is that in the latter statement (the statement under warning), the police officer has narrowed down on the person whom he suspects to have committed the offence. In the former, the police officer is merely taking down statements that will assist him in investigation. If a person who has made a statement under inquiry ends up being a suspect, then he may be called upon to make a second statement, but this statement must be under warning, and the suspect still retains his right to remain silent or his right not to make any statement that incriminates him.

The statements must be taken as provided by law otherwise such statement may be rendered inadmissible.[22]

It is critical to underline that any person who has been arrested, has a constitutional right of silence i.e. he need not make any statement and can opt to remain silent. This right of silence is enshrined in Article 49 (1) of the 2010

---

21 Section 22 (3) of the Police Act (repealed) provided that, *"Any police officer may record any statement made to him by any such person, whether such person is suspected of having committed an offence or not, but, before recording any statement from a person whom such police officer has decided to charge or who has been charged with committing an offence, the police officer shall warn such person that any statement which may be recorded may be used in evidence."*

22 Section 57 (7), NPSA.

Constitution,[23] and Section 52(3) of the NPSA.[24] Further, as noted by Section 52(4) of the NPSA, the person must first be warned that such statement may be used in evidence against him.[25] After the statement has been put down in writing, it must be read to him in a language that he understands and he must be invited to make any amendments to the statement.

Usually the police will make a certificate to state that the statement has been given voluntarily and that the suspect has been warned; the suspect will also sign the certificate. Both the statement under inquiry and the statement under warning can be used in evidence against the maker by the Prosecution. Where the statement is inculpatory, it may amount to a confession, which may be valuable evidence for the prosecution in the trial of the suspect.

3.3.2 Who May Take Down a Statement

3.3.2.1 Rank of Police Officer

The NPSA does not restrict any police officer from taking down statements. However, The Evidence Act provides under Section 29 that *"no confession made to a police officer shall be proved against a person accused of any offence unless such police officer is of or above the rank of or equivalent to inspector or an administrative office holding first or second class magisterial powers and acting in the capacity of a police officer."*[26]

Thus, in as much as there are no restrictions on the rank of the officer who may take the statements, such statement will be inadmissible as a confession, if not taken by a police officer of the rank of Inspector and above or its equivalent. The practice therefore is for the police officer, if below the rank of Inspector,

---

23 Constitution, Article 49 (1), provides, *"An arrested person has the right (a) to be informed promptly, in language that the person understands, of--(ii) the right to remain silent; and (iii) the consequences of not remaining silent; (b) to remain silent."*

24 NPSA, Section 52(3) provides, *"A person shall not be required to answer any question under this section if the question tends to expose the person to a criminal charge, penalty or forfeiture."*

25 *Supra* note 20.

26 Chapter 80, Laws of Kenya.

to have the suspect record any statement made under warning before an officer of the superior rank.

3.3.2.2 Position of Investigating Officer

Ordinarily, it would be the investigating officer who takes down statements under inquiry, since he is the officer investigating the offence. The question that arises is whether the same officer is also entitled to take down the statement under warning. The NPSA does not bar an investigating officer from taking down a statement under warning and the case law does not outlaw it. In *Mwaiseje and Another v R*[27] it was stated that *"If after being duly cautioned the accused person then voluntarily makes a statement we see no reason for excluding such evidence merely because the investigating officer of the case already knew something about it from other suspects. The trial judge, however, must fully satisfy himself that the statement in issue was in fact made by the accused person and that it had not come from the investigating officer's prior knowledge of the circumstances of the offence."*[28]

It is therefore, always prudent, and it is good practice, that the statement under warning be taken down before another officer, and not by the investigating officer. This puts aside the suspicion that the second statement may have been influenced by the knowledge of the investigating officer, and though not specifically outlawed, courts generally frown upon the practice of an investigating officer taking down the statement under warning.[29] In the case of *Njuguna Kimani v R*[30]the court stated obiter that *"it is inadvisable, if not improper, for the police officer who is conducting the investigation of a case to charge and record the caution statement of a suspect."*

However, the arguments of whether or not an investigating officer should take down the statements has now been obviated by the provisions of Section 25A

---

27 Court of Appeal, Nairobi Criminal Appeal No. 17 of 1991, (1992) eKLR.

28 See also *Bassan & Another v R* (1961) EA 521; *Njuguna v Republic* (1965) E.A. 583 and *Israel Kamukolse v R* (1956) EACA 521.

29 *Njiru & Others v R* (2002) 1 EA 218.

30 21 EACA 316.

of the Evidence Act, at least in so far as confessionary statements are concerned, as the law provides that a confession taken before the investigation officer is not admissible. But what about the same officer taking down the several statements from the several suspects? It is arguable that the officer after taking down one statement will have some knowledge of the circumstances surrounding the offence which may influence how the later statements are recorded. In *Ngoya v R*[31] the court stated as follows :-

"as regards the taking of charge and caution from more than one accused person by the same police officer, we know of no authority for the proposition that this is irregular. It is no doubt preferable that each statement should be taken by different officers, but some regard must be had to practical considerations. If there are, for instance, 10 co-accused persons; it would hardly be a practical proposition to assemble 10 officers of the requisite rank to record the 10 statements, without undue wastage of time, effort and expense."[32]

Thus although not outlawed, it is prudent, if practicable, to have different officers take down the statements of each suspect. This gives the statements higher credence and removes the suspicion that the later statements could have been influenced by the earlier ones.

3.3.2.3 The Judges' Rules

Owing to the danger that is inherent in tailoring the statement to suit what would favour the investigators, the judges in England developed what are termed as the Judges' Rules in 1912. These are administrative directions aimed at safeguarding the rights of a suspect, but are not part of statutory law, and in case of any conflict with statutory provisions, must give way to the statutory provisions.[33] In *Balbir Sain Joshi v R,*[34] it was held that where questions relating to the admissibility of statements made to the police by accused persons were not governed by statutory provisions in force in Kenya, the court must be

31 (1985) KLR 309.

32 *Ibid.*

33 *R v Voisin* (1918) 1 KB 531.

34 (1951) 18 EACA 228.

guided by the Judges Rules. The judge or magistrate therefore has discretion to follow the Judges Rules for matters not covered by statute and can reject a statement which was taken down in contravention of the Judges Rules.[35]

It is therefore important that the Judge's Rules are followed when making a statement under inquiry and a statement under warning. Failure to follow the Judge's Rules may make the statements inadmissible. According the question that begs an answer is what then are the Judges' Rules?

The Judge' Rules as acknowledged in Kenya, are nine in number.[36]

1. When a police officer is endeavouring to discover the author of a crime, there is no objection to his putting questions in respect thereof to any person or persons, whether suspected or not, from whom he thinks that useful information can be obtained.
2. Whenever a police officer has made up his mind to charge a person with a crime, he should first caution such person before asking him any questions, or any further further questions, as the case may be.
3. Persons in custody should not be questioned without the usual caution being first administered.
4. If the prisoner wishes to volunteer any statement, the usual caution should be administered. It is desirable that the last two words of such caution be omitted and that the caution should end with the words "be given in evidence."
5. The caution to be administered to a prisoner, when he is formally charged, should therefore be in the following words: *"Do you wish to say anything in answer to the charge? You are not obliged to say anything unless you wish to do so, but whatever you say will be taken down in writing and may be given in evidence."*
6. A statement made by a prisoner before there is time to caution him is not rendered inadmissible in evidence merely by reason of no caution having been given, but in such case he should be cautioned as soon as possible.

---

35 *Gathuri Njuguna v Republic* (1965) EA 538; see also *R v Bass (1953)* 1 All ER 1064; *Anyangu v Republic* (1968) E.A. 239 and *R. v Voisin* (1918) *supra* note 33.

36 As noted in Chapter 46 of the Police Force Standing Orders. Force Standing Orders have their authority in Section 10 (1) (r) of the NSPA. As noted in Section 10 (2) Force Standing Orders are administrative in nature.

7. A prisoner making a voluntary statement must not be cross-examined, and no questions should be put to him about it except for the purpose of removing ambiguity in what he has actually said. For instance, if he has mentioned an hour without saying whether it was morning or evening, or has given a day of the week and day of the month which do not agree, or has not made it clear to what individual or what place he intended to refer in some part of his statement, he may be questioned sufficiently to clear up the point.
8. When two or more persons are charged with the same offence and statements are taken separately from the persons charged, the police should not read these statements to the other persons charged, but each of such persons should be furnished by the police with a copy of such statements and nothing should be said or done by the police to invite a reply. If the person charged desires to make a statement in reply, the usual caution should be administered.
9. Any statement made in accordance with the above Rules should, whenever possible, be taken down in writing and signed by the person making it after it has been read to him and he has been invited to make any corrections he may wish.

It should be noted that the Judges' Rules do not usurp the provisions of statute but are only meant to provide administrative guidelines. However, where statute is silent on an issue, the Judges' Rules may be utilized to fill in the void.

3.3.3 Confessionary Statements

A confession is defined in Section 25 of the Evidence Act to mean words or conduct, or a combination of words and conduct, from which, whether taken alone or in conjunction with other facts proved, an inference may reasonably be drawn that the person making it has committed an offence. In 2003, the Criminal Law Amendment Act 2003, took away from the police the power to record confessions from persons suspected of crimes.[37] The amendment introduced a Section 25A into the Evidence Act, which provided that, *"A*

37 The Criminal Law, Amendment Act, 2003, Act No.5 of 2003, which commenced on 25 July 2003.

confession or any admission of a fact tending to the proof of guilt made by an accused person is not admissible and not be proved against such a person unless it is made in court."

In the case of *R v Maalim Komora Godana*[38] decided in 2006, the judge had this to say about the power given by statute empowering magistrates to take down confessionary statements :-

"To ask magistrates to record confessions of suspects in matters yet to be taken to Court is to ask them to be part of the police investigation team. The inevitable consequence would not only create a clear conflict of roles but also be against public policy."

It was the court's view that that provision needed to be interpreted to refer only to confessions made during the trial, and not to cover a procedure where the suspect was presented before the magistrate, at the investigatory stage of the proceedings, so as to record a confession.

That decision obviously rendered the amendment worthless and it is probably because of this that Section 25A was again amended in 2007[39] to add to the then existing Section 25A and to add a subsection 2. The section as amended and which comprises the current law, reads as follows:-

(1) A confession or any admission of a fact tending to the proof of guilt made by an accused person is not admissible and shall not be proved as against such person unless it is made in court before a judge, a magistrate or before a police officer (other than the investigating officer), being an officer not below the rank of Chief Inspector of Police, and a third party of the person's choice.

(2) The Attorney-General shall in consultation with the Law Society of Kenya, Kenya National Commission on Human Rights and other suitable bodies make rules governing the making of a confession in all instances where the confession is not made in court.

---

38 Malindi High Court Criminal Case No. 4 of 2006, (2006) eKLR.

39 Amended by the The Statute Law (Miscellaneous Amendments) Act, Act No. 7 of 2007 which came into effect on 15 October 2007.

It will be seen from the above, that a confessionary statement can only be admissible if made before :-

(a) A judge or magistrate; or
(b) A police officer, not being the investigating officer, who must not be below the rank of Chief Inspector of Police.

There is also the requirement that there be a third party of the person's choice.

The reasoning advanced in the *Komora* case arguably still applies to the provision of law permitting the courts to take down confessions. It is therefore more advisable to have confessions taken down by the authorized police officers rather than by courts, since a suspect always has an option to plead guilty to an offence, or give evidence admitting the offence, in the course of trial, which has a greater validity and weight than a confession.

Although subsection 2 of Section 25A of the Evidence Act, has made provision for the Attorney General to make rules as to how confessions are to be taken down by police officers, so far, no such rules have been made. It is probable that the statute had in contemplation rules such as the Judges' Rules, to be made to apply to the circumstances of Kenya.

3.3.4 Admission of Confessionary Statements in a Trial

Where a confession is not retracted it is sufficient to sustain a conviction.[40] However, if the statement is challenged in court either by way of a retraction or repudiation, a "trial within a trial" must be held to determine whether the said statement will be admissible in court. An accused person may retract or repudiate the statement. The difference between the two was considered in the case of *Tuwamoi v Uganda*[41] where the court made the distinction by stating that a "retracted statement" occurs when the accused person admits that he made the statement recorded but now seeks to recant, to take back what he

---

40 *John Kinywa Miriti v Republic,* Court of Appeal at Nairobi, Criminal Appeal No.325 of 2007, (2011) eKLR.

41 (1967) EA 90.

said, generally on the ground that he had been forced or induced to make the statement; in other words that the statement was not a voluntary one. On the other hand, a "repudiated statement" is one which the accused person avers he never made. However, the court went on to state further, that in its view, there was no real distinction in principle between a repudiated and a retracted confession.

A trial court should accept any confession which has been retracted or repudiated, or both retracted and repudiated with caution, and must before founding a conviction on such a confession, be fully satisfied in all the circumstances of the case, that the confession is true. The same standard of proof is required in all cases, and usually, a court will only act on the confession, if corroborated in some material particular by independent evidence accepted by the court. But corroboration is not necessary in law and the court may act on a confession alone, if it is fully satisfied after considering all the material points and surrounding circumstances that the confession cannot but be true.[42]

The earlier position had been that a retracted confession required to be corroborated by other evidence to sustain a conviction but a repudiated confession did not require such corroboration and the court could convict solely on the repudiated confession if satisfied that it was made and it is true.[43]

In *Anasuerus Najared Likhanga v Republic*[44] the court held that the onus is on the prosecution to prove that the statement was made voluntarily without any threat or inducement of any kind. In *Daniel Kamau Njoroge v Republic*[45] the court held a confession to be inadmissible because the circumstances revealed evidence of threats and actual bodily harm prior to the giving of the

---

42 *Ibid*; See also *Grace Wambui Njoroge & 4 others v Republic* (2006) eKLR; *James Muturi Kuria & 5 Others v Republic* (2006)eKLR; *John Wachira Wandia and Another v republic* (2006) eKLR

43 See *R. v Labasha* 3 EACA 48; *R v Mutwiwa* (1935) 2 EAC 66; *James Muturi Kuria & 5 Others v Republic* High Court at Nyeri, Criminal Appeal No. 124-129, (2006) eKLR; and *John Wachira Wandia and Another v Republic*, Court of Appeal at Nyeri, Criminal Appeal No. 57 & 58 of 2004, (2006) eKLR.

44 Court of Appeal at Kisumu, Criminal Appeal No. 93 of 2005, (2006) eKLR.

45 Court of Appeal at Nakuru, Criminal Appeal No. 13 of 1994, (1994) eKLR.

confession.[46] There was evidence that the appellant "was worried and not at ease" when he was taken before the officer to record his statement. At the prison dispensary he was noted to be coughing blood and complained of chest pains and of having been assaulted. The Court of Appeal held that the trial court was wrong in accepting the confessionary statement of the appellant given these circumstances. The court observed that the only reasonable conclusion is that the appellant received the injuries he complained of while he was in custody and before he recorded the confessionary statement. The statement was therefore not voluntarily given thus inadmissible.

Where a court is called upon to consider the voluntary character of statements made by suspected persons in police custody, it must take into consideration the length of time the accused has been kept in police custody and to what extent he has been subjected to questioning.[47]

The charge should also be read out before the accused person is invited to make the statement under caution as was held in *Bassan & Another v Republic*.[48] The court was of the view that writing of the statement before the charge is read out it was a grave omission. The court further averred that the onus is on the prosecution to prove that such a statement made in response to the charge which the accused was expected to face. After the statement is admitted, it must be read out in court and any other accused person affected by its admission given opportunity to cross-examine on it.[49]

If a statement is retracted or repudiated, a "trial within a trial" must be held to determine whether the statement is admissible in evidence. A trial within a trial is a mini-trial conducted within the trial of the main suit, held with the sole purpose of determining the issue of admissibility of the statement. Such

---

46 Ibid; See also *James Nduku Gitau v Republic* (2006) eKLR

47 See *James Nduku Gitau v R*, High Court at Nairobi, Criminal Appeal No. 1235 of 2002, (2006) eKLR where the appellant had been shot and questioned 13 days after being kept in custody. See also *Mwangi s/o Njoroge v Republic* (1954) EACA 377; and *Francis Kamunya Ruchunu & Another v Republic*, Nairobi High Court, Criminal Appeal Case No. 827 of 2003, (2006) eKLR.

48 (1961) EA 521.

49 *Francis Kamunya Ruchunu & Another v Republic* supra note 47.

trial is no different from the manner in which the trial of the main suit is held, probably the reason why it is described to be a "trial within a trial".

Once an objection to the admissibility of the statement is made, the prosecution must begin by providing evidence going to show why such statement should be admitted in evidence. This is done by providing witnesses who will affirm that such statement was made voluntarily, without coercion or inducement. Such witnesses are liable to be cross-examined by the defence. The prosecution will then rest its case and the accused will have his chance to call forth evidence to show that it was either not made by him or was not made voluntarily. His avenues of providing evidence are similar to the situation where the accused has been put on defence. He can opt to make an unsworn statement with or without witnesses or can make a sworn statement with or without calling witnesses. He can also opt to keep quiet. If witnesses are called, they may be cross-examined by the prosecution. After taking evidence from both prosecution and the accused, the court will make a determination on whether or not the statement is admissible.

It is incumbent upon the judge to examine carefully every circumstance relevant to the making of the statement before coming to a decision. Such circumstances as we have seen above may be the length of duration in custody, allegations of beatings or other forms of ill treatment or threats thereof, allegations of inducement to make the statement, fear and apprehension, extent of questioning by the police, and any other relevant circumstance. In *Gathuri Njuguna v R,*[50] the court was of the view that these two factors: how long the person making the statement had been in custody and to what extent he was subjected to questioning were relevant. In *Edong s/o Etat v R,*[51] the Court of Appeal did not take it well that the trial court had failed to consider whether there had been any questioning or cross-examination of the appellant while in custody and it thought this to have been a serious non-direction. During the course of the trial the trial Judge ruled that the statement was voluntarily made and admissible and the appellant was convicted. He appealed against the conviction. The Court of Appeal made a careful examination of the circumstances in which the statements were made and were of the view that the statements could not

50 (1965) EA 538.

51 (1954) 21 EACA 338.

be considered to have been taken voluntarily and declared them inadmissible in which event the appeal succeeded.

If a person makes more than one statement which are in conflict, all statements must be tendered in evidence.[52] Where there are more than one accused persons, it would be appropriate to have separate trials within a trial. This was impressed in the case of *Imbindi v R.*[53] In this case a joint trial within trial was held for all co-accused as the statement were recorded by the same officer. The Court held that this was wrong, and separate trials within a trial, should have been held for each impugned statement, as each challenge is entitled to its individual consideration.

3.3.5 Confession Implicating a Co-accused

Such statements are admissible. This is provided for under *section 32(1)* of the *Evidence Act* to the effect that, 'When more persons than one are being tried jointly for the same offence, and a confession made by one of such persons affecting himself and some other of such persons is proved, the court may take the confession into consideration as against such other person as well as against the person who made the confession.' This evidence is however said to be the weakest kind of evidence that can be taken into account; nevertheless, it is accepted that such evidence lends assurance to an otherwise strong case against the accused.[54]

This evidence must satisfy the legal requirements of circumstantial evidence to warrant or justify conviction. It must irresistibly point to the co-accused to the exclusion of all others within the meaning of *R v Kipkering Arap Koske & Another*[55] where it was, *inter alia*, held that;

---

52 *Tuwamoi v Uganda*, Supra note 41.

53 *Imbindi v R* (1983) KLR 344.

54 See *Raphael Oduor Ngoya & 5 others v. Republic* Cr. Appeal No. 136 of 1981(Unreported), and *Stephen M'riungi and 3 Others v Republic* Cr Appeals Nos 134, 135, 136 and 137 of 1982 (unreported).

55 (1949) 16 EACA, 135.

> *"In order to justify the inference of guilt, the inculpatory facts must be incompatible with the innocence off the accused, and incapable of any explanation upon any other reasonable hypothesis than that of his guilt. The burden of proving facts which justify the drawing of this inference from the facts to the exclusion of any reasonable hypothesis of innocence is always on the prosecution and never shifts to the accused."*[56]

It is also necessary that before drawing this inference the court must be sure that there are no co-existing circumstances which would weaken or destroy the inference.[57]

3.4 Identification Parades

Identification parades are utilized to enable eyewitnesses point out the person whom they allege to have seen participating in a crime. Therefore an identification parade can be said to be the process through which the veracity of a witness's assertion is tested to prove that the accused was at the scene of the crime by putting the accused in a row together with other people and see if the witness can single him out. It is important to note that, identification parades are held where the suspect was not known to the witness before the incident, as there would be no purpose of holding one, where the suspect is well known to the witness.

The Police Force Standing Orders provide for how identification parades should be conducted.[58] The core provision is Standing Order No. 6 which provides as follows:-

6 (i) The necessity and value of holding identification parades in appropriate cases cannot be overstressed. The police should not take a witness direct to an accused/suspected person for the purpose of identification except when they are sure that the accused/suspect is well known to him/her. When the whereabouts of the accused/suspected person is known to the police, but there is some doubt as to whether he/she is the correct person, the only way

---

56 *Ibid.*

57 *Teper v The Queen* (1952) AC 480.

58 Police Force Standing Orders, Chapter 46.

to ensure a fair and correct identification is by means of an identification parade.

(ii) Any person may refuse to appear in an identification parade, and if the accused/suspected person takes this attitude, he/she cannot be compelled to take part in the parade. In such instances if the accused/suspected person is subsequently charged, evidence will be given of his/her refusal to take part in an identification parade.

(iii) Whenever an identification parade is held, the conducting officer will make use of and complete all relevant portions of Form P.156 "Report of an identification Parade." This form will completed at the time of holding the parade and if necessary will be used by the conducting officer as a means of refreshing his/her memory in any subsequent court proceedings as authorized by Section 167(i) of the Evidence Act.

(iv) Whenever it is necessary that a witness be asked to identify an accused/suspected person, the following procedure must be followed in detail:-

(a) The accused/suspected person will always be informed of the reasons for the parade and that he/she may have a counsel or a friend present when the parade takes place;

(b) The police Officer-in-Charge of the case, although he/she may be present, will not conduct the parade.

(c) The witness or witnesses will not see the accused before the parade.

(d) The accused/suspected person will be placed among at least eight persons, as far as possible of similar age, height, general appearance and class of life as him/her. Should the accused/suspect be suffering from a disfigurement, steps should be taken to ensure that it is not especially apparent. Not more than one accused/suspected person should appear on identification parade.

(e) The accused/suspected person will be allowed to take any position he/she chooses and will be allowed to change his/her position after each identifying witness has left if he/she so desires.

(f) Care will be exercised that witnesses do not communicate with each other.

(g) If the witness desires to see the accused/suspected person walk, hear him/her speak see him/her with hat on or off, this should be done, but in this event the whole parade should be asked to do likewise.

(h) The conducting officer will ensure that the witness indicates the person identified, without the possibility of error e.g. by touching.
(i) At the termination of the parade, or during the parade, the officer conducting it should ask the accused/suspected person if he/she is satisfied that the parade is being/has been conducted in a fair manner and make a note in writing of his/her reply thereto.
(j) When explaining the procedure to a witness the officer conducting the parade will tell him/her that he/she will see a group of people which may not include the person responsible. The witness should not be told, "to pick out somebody" or be influenced in any way whatsoever.
(k) A careful note must be made after each witness leaves the parade, to record whether he/she identified the accused/suspected person and in what manner.
(l) A record should be made by the officer conducting the parade of any comment made by the accused/suspected person during the parade, particularly comments made when the accused/suspected person is identified.
(m) The parade must be conducted with scrupulous fairness, otherwise the value of the identification(s) as evidence will be lessened or nullified.
(n) Unless a police officer is accused/suspected police officers will not be used to make up the parade.

(v) Parades should be conducted with as much privacy as possible. They should not, unless unavoidable, be held in view of the public but in an enclosed compound or yard from which all spectators and unauthorized persons are excluded.
(vi) If a witness desires to keep his/her identity secret, and the circumstances are such that the Officer-in-Charge of the case deems such a course advisable for reasons of security, victimization etc., arrangements will be made for the witness to view the parade from a concealed vantage point (e.g through a window, from a room or from behind a screen). If the witness identifies one or more of the persons on the parade, the person(s) so identified will be removed and confronted with the witness, who will be asked to confirm the identification in the normal way, i.e. by clearly indicating that he/she is the person concerned.

(vii) If it is necessary to endeavour to establish the identity by means of photographs the witness will be shown at least eight photographs of different persons of the same race as the accused/suspected person. Care should be taken to ensure that the photographs are of the same size and type, thereby excluding any possibility of the accused/suspected person's photograph being of a distinct type.

(viii) When the procedure outlined in subparagraph (vii) above has been adopted, it must be remembered that it is still necessary for a physical identification parade as described in paragraph 6(iii) and 6(iv) to be held to corroborate any photographic identification.

(ix) When a number of witnesses are invited to view photographs immediately one identification has been made, this method of identification will cease. Those witnesses who have not yet had an opportunity of seeing the photographs must be precluded from doing so. The accused/suspected person should then be put on an identification parade in the usual way for the purpose of identification by all the witnesses.

(x) When a photograph used for identification purposes is obtained from the identification bureau, the prosecution will inform the defence of this fact beforehand and evidence of this point will not be led in the examination-in-chief lest the court should draw any inference regarding the accused having a criminal record. If the defence wishes to refer to the question of photograph in cross-examination, it is their responsibility. When a photograph used for identification purposes is obtained from any other source, such as newspaper, Government office, or accused's own home evidence can be given freely and without prejudice to the accused.

The above provisions speak for themselves. Failure to abide by the above rules may invalidate the identification parade and render evidence on the identification parade worthless.[59] However, a failure to observe some of them will not necessarily render the parade a complete nullity and it behoves upon the court to determine for itself whether the violation went to the root of the identification parade as to render it unreliable.[60]

---

59 *James Muturi Kuria & 5 Others v Republic*, High Court at Nyeri, Criminal Appeal No. 127-129 of 2001, (2006) eKLR.

60 *Sentale v R* (1968) EA 365.

In *David Mwita Wanja & 2 others v R* [61] the court held that the value of an identification parade as evidence would depreciate considerably unless it was held with scrupulous fairness and in accordance with the instructions contained in the Police Force Standing Orders.[62] In *Njihia v Republic*[63] the court stated as follows :-

"It is not difficult to arrange well-conducted parades. The orders are clear. If properly conducted, especially with an independent person present looking after the interests of a suspect, the resulting evidence is of great value. But if the parade is badly conducted and the complainant identifies a suspect the complainant will hardly be able to give reliable evidence of identification in court. Whether that is possible, depends upon clear evidence of identification apart from the parade."

In *Kella v Republic*[64] an identification parade held after lapse of 2 ½ years was held to be unsatisfactory.[65] In *Njiru & Others v R,*[66] it was held that where the only evidence linking a suspect with a crime was visual identification at night time, identification parade evidence or other evidence was important to test the correctness of the identification by eyewitnesses. Further, the court affirmed that there was nothing objectionable in a witness requesting parade members to shout for him so that he could satisfy himself that he did not make any mistake in identifying the particular suspect.[67] In deciding the appeal the court had this to say on the law of identification quoting the case of *Hibuya v R*[68] :-

"It is for the prosecution to elicit during evidence as to whether the witness had observed the features of the culprit and if so, the conspicuous details regarding his features given to anyone and particularly to the police at the first opportunity. Both the investigating officer and the prosecutor have to ensure that such information

---

61 *David Mwita Wanja & 2 others v R,* Nairobi Criminal Appeal No. 117 of 2005 (2007) eKLR.

62 See also *R v Mwango s/o Manaa* (1936) 3 EACA 29 and *Paul Ihuo Mburu v R,* Nairobi Criminal Appeal No. 329 of 2006, (2008) eKLR.

63 *Njihia v Republic* (1986) KLR 422 at 424.

64 *Kella v Republic* (1967) EA 809.

65 Ibid.

66 (2002) 1 EA 218.

67 See also *Hibuya v R* (1996) LLR 425.

68 *Ibid.*

is recorded during investigations and elicited in court during evidence. Omission of evidence of this nature at investigation stage or at presentation in court has, depending on the particular circumstances of a case, proved fatal this being a proven reliable way of testing the power of observation, and accuracy of memory of a witness and the degree of consistency in his evidence."

Counsel for the first appellant in the matter had contended that since the 1st appellant had a swelling, it was incumbent upon the police to get other people in the parade who had similar swellings. The court dismissed this argument and stated that the requirement as to parade members is that they should be *"as far as possible of similar age, height, general appearance and class of life"* as the suspect and not that they should be identical. Mere absence of such swelling from the parade members could not and did not vitiate the importance of the parade evidence. Further, the officer who conducted the identification parade must be called as a witness for the prosecution for the evidence of the identification to be relied upon.[69]

3.5 Search and Seizure

Search and seizure has constitutional implications under the right to privacy. Article 31 of the Constitution provides that, *'Every person has a right to privacy, which includes the right not to have their person, home or property searched and their possessions seized.'* These principles also have validation in the common law as exemplified by Lord Denning MR in the case of *Southam v Smout,*[70] where he adopted a quotation from the Earl of Chatham by stating that, *"The poorest man may in his cottage bid defiance to all the forces of the Crown. It may be frail - its roof may shake - the wind may blow through it - the storm may enter - the rain may enter - but the King of England cannot enter - all his force dares not cross the threshold of the ruined tenement. So be it - unless he has justification by law."*[71]

---

69 *Ibid*, see also *Njiru & Others v R* (2002) 1 EA 218.

70 *Southam v Smout* (1964) 1 QB 308.

71 *Ibid* at 320.

Search and seizure in the Kenyan context is anchored on the warrant and reasonable ground requirement. Thus, it can be conducted in two ways, first with a warrant and secondly without a warrant.

3.5.1 Search and Seizure with a Warrant

Section 118 of the CPC provides that where it is proved on oath to a court that anything related to an offence which has been committed, or anything which is necessary for the conduct of an investigation into an offence, is, or is reasonably suspected to be somewhere a written search warrant may be issued authorizing an officer to search the particular place and, if the thing is found, it shall be seized and taken before a court.

The provisions of Section 118 came into sharp focus in the case of *William Moruri Nyakiba & another v Chief Magistrate Nairobi & 2 others.*[72] In this case, an affidavit, without there being a formal application, was filed before the Magistrates court seeking the issue of search warrants of the premises of the applicants. The applicants moved to the High Court to have the warrants quashed *inter alia* on the grounds that the affidavit was not accompanied by any formal application and it was therefore improper for search warrants to have been issued. Ojwang' J, held that it is not necessary for there to be a formal application for one to move the court through Section118 of the CPC. All that was required was a statement on oath, and the court could issue the warrants, so long as there was a sound basis for the request.

Neither is it necessary for the application seeking a search warrant to be served upon the person to be affected by the warrant. This was affirmed in the case of *James Humphrey Oswago v Ethics & Anti-Corruption Commission.*[73] In this matter, the Petitioner, the Chief Executive Officer of the Independent Electoral and Boundaries Commission, had been summoned by the Ethics and Anti-Corruption Commission (EACC) with regard to certain investigations touching

---

72 *William Moruri Nyakiba & another v Chief Magistrate Nairobi & 2 others* High Court at Nairobi, Misc. Criminal Application No. 414 of 2006, (2006) eKLR.

73 *James Humphrey Oswago v Ethics & Anti-Corruption Commission,* Nairobi High Court, Petition No. 409 of 2013, (2014) eKLR.

on the tendering and procurement process of Election Voter Identification Device kits used in the elections of 4th March 2013. EACC then applied for search warrants to search the petitioner's various houses, which was granted, and pursuant thereto, the EACC took away various documents and electronic equipment. The petitioner filed a constitutional petition and argued that his rights to privacy had been breached as he had not been given an opportunity to be heard. He asked that the search warrants be quashed. The High Court held that there had been no violation and that the warrants were properly applied for and issued under Section 118 of the CPC. The court emphasized that such an application need not be served, as the very purpose of asking for the warrants may be lost since the information sought could be concealed or destroyed by the person affected.

A search warrant may be issued on any day, and may be executed on any day between the hours of sunrise and sunset, but the court may by the warrant authorize the police officer or other person to whom it is addressed to execute it at any hour.[74] Further, Section 120 (1) CPC, avers that whenever the place liable to search is closed, a person residing in or being in charge of the building or place shall, on demand of the police officer or other person executing the search warrant and on production of the warrant, allow him free ingress thereto and egress therefrom and afford all reasonable facilities for a search therein. If the ingress thereto and therefrom cannot be so obtained, the police officer or other person executing the search warrant may proceed in the manner prescribed by Section 22 (2) or Section 23 of the CPC which permit the police to break into and out of the place to be searched. So that the police power of search and seizure is not abused, it is necessary for sufficient reasons to be tabled before the court before a court may issue warrants. In a common law case, *R v Central Criminal Court exp. AJD Holdings,*[75] it was held that before applying for a search warrant, the police should consider very carefully the material hoped to be revealed by the search. In this case, the warrant purported to give the officers a free hand to seek and seize all documents. Probably courts ought to lean towards ensuring that warrants are strictly construed so that they do not give the police excessive latitude as to infringe on the privacy of the individual.

---

74 CPC, Section 119.

75 *R v Central Criminal Court exp. AJD Holdings* (1992) Crimm. L.R. 669 (Div. Ct).

3.5.2 Search and Seizure without a Warrant

Section 57 and Section 60 of the NPSA give a police officer the power to enter premises and stop vehicles, etc., without warrant if he has a reasonable cause to believe that the delay caused by obtaining a warrant would lead to not being able to get the particular evidence. Such believe must however be recorded in writing. [76] In conducting such search, the officer needs to produce his certificate of appointment and make a record of anything seized.[77]

In *Joseph Musomba v Attorney General*[78] the police went into the chambers of the petitioner, an advocate of the High Court of Kenya, and without warrant conducted a search and seizure, and collected assorted files of his clients. The petitioner filed a constitutional reference seeking to have the search and seizure operation declared unconstitutional and further sought payment of general damages. The court observed that there was nothing peculiar in the case so as to excuse the police from not seeking a search warrant from the court. Neither were any reasons, for first not seeking a court warrant, put down in writing. The court held that the search and seizure were not conducted in accordance

---

76 *Section 60* of the *NPSA* provides, *"(1) When a police officer in charge of a police station, or a police officer investigating an alleged offence, has reasonable grounds to believe that something was used in the commission of a crime, is likely to be found in any place and that the delay occasioned by obtaining a search warrant under section 118 of the Criminal Procedure Code (Cap. 75) will in his opinion substantially prejudice such investigation, he may, after recording in writing the grounds of his belief and such description as is available to him of the thing for which search is to be made, without such warrant, enter any premises in or on which he or she suspects the thing to be and search or cause search to be made for, and take possession of such thing.*
(2) Sections 119, 120 and 121 of the Criminal Procedure Code (Cap. 75) as to the execution of search warrant, and the provisions of that Code as to searches shall apply to a search without a warrant under this section.
(3) For purposes of conducting a search under this section; (a) the officer shall carry with him, and produce to the occupier of the premises on request by him, the officer's certificate of appointment; (b) if anything is seized under subsection (1), the police officer shall immediately make a record describing anything so seized, and without undue delay take or cause it to be taken before a magistrate within whose jurisdiction the thing was found, to be dealt with according to the law."

77 *Ibid.*

78 High Court at Kisumu, Petition No. 4 of 2012, (2012) eKLR.

with the law and fell short of the requisite standards and proceeded to award Kshs. 500,000/= as damages for the unfair search.

It is however permissible for an officer to stop an individual and if suspicion is raised, proceed to conduct a search and seizure. It matters not that the grounds for suspicion only appear after the person has been stopped.[79]

3.6 Illegally Obtained Evidence

This is evidence obtained contrary to the provisions of the Constitution and relevant statutes governing investigation of crimes. A discussion under this topic calls for a careful balance between the constitutional rights of the accused, and the society's interest in having all evidence gathered, so as to uncover the truth surrounding the commission of an offence. Some jurisdictions allow all evidence irrespective of how it is gathered (the inclusionary rule) and others apply the exclusionary rule, where illegally obtained evidence is not allowed.[80] The evidence gathered in the latter are considered the *"fruits of the poisonous tree"* hence inadmissible.

The Evidence Act and the CPC do not give an exact position as regards the status of illegally obtained evidence before the court. The general rule under common law is that evidence is admissible so long as it is relevant to the matters in issue. Thus in *Kuruma v R,*[81] the appellant was convicted regardless of the fact that an illegal search had been conducted on him. The Privy Council held that in considering whether evidence is admissible, the test is whether it is relevant to the matters in issue, and, if it is relevant, the court is not concerned

79 See *Kuria Wagachira v R* (1957) EA 808.

80 The USA is one of the jurisdictions that apply the exclusionary rule; See *Weeks v USA* 232 U.S 382 (1914); *Silverthorne Lumber Co v USA*, 251 US (1920) and *Mapp v Ohio*, 367 US 643 (1961). For discussion on the two rules see Oaks, Dallin H. (1970), *Studying the exclusionary rule in search and seizure, University of Chicago Law Review*, Vol. 37 No. 4 p665-757; Wilkey, Malcolm R (1978) *Exclusionary Rule: Why suppress valid evidence?* Judicature 62 (5): 214-232; Barnett, Randy E (1983), Resolving *the Dilemma of the Exclusionary Rule: An application of Restitutive Principles of Justice*, 32 Emory L.J p 937.

81 (1955) AC 197, (1955) 1 All E.R 236. See also *King v Regina* (1968) 2 All E.R 610.

with the method by which it was obtained, or with the question whether that method was tortuous but excusable, save for the principle that a confession can only be received in evidence if it is voluntary.

The reason for this position has been said to be that under the common law there are no constitutional rights, because no written constitution protecting fundamental freedoms exists, thus the question of adopting the exclusionary rule never arises. However, even in the common law, there have been questions to this rule.[82]

The Constitution of Kenya, 2010 has a very expansive bill of rights and it will be interesting to see the approach that will eventually be taken by the courts on whether illegally obtained evidence is admissible. The jurisprudence is still at its nascent stages, and the only case so far, is that of *Antony Murithi v O.C.S Meru Police Station & 2 others*[83] where the court applied the exclusionary rule. In this case, the petitioner, who was suspected to have committed the offence of rape, had been handcuffed and taken to hospital without explanation, forced into a small room and sat on the floor. While his legs were also handcuffed, he was assaulted with a syringe extracting blood from him. His mouth was forced open and the clinical officer with the help of the police scooped a fluid from his mouth. The court held this was against freedom from torture, and cruel, inhuman and degrading treatment, and that the acts were acts of disrespect to the petitioner. It held that the petitioner's inherent dignity, and the right to have that dignity respected and protected, were breached by the respondent thus the evidence obtained in the process couldn't be used against him.

3.7 The Investigatory Role of the Courts- Inquests.

The role of the courts is not really to investigate because we have an adversarial system. Their role is to conduct cases and make decisions. However this role is compromised by the power to hold inquests. The purpose of inquests is to hold inquiries as to sudden deaths and missing persons believed to be dead.

---

82 *R v Payne* (1963) 1 All E.R 848 and *People (A.G) v O'Brien* (1965) I.R 142.

83 *Antony Murithi v O.C.S Meru Police Station & 2 others* High Court at Meru, Petition No. 79 of 2011, (2012) eKLR.

Inquests are covered by the provisions of sections 385, 386, 387 and 388 of the CPC. Section 385 of the CPC sets out the judicial officers empowered to hold inquests. These are magistrates empowered to hold a subordinate court of the first, or second class, and a magistrate specially empowered in that behalf by the Chief Justice. Section 386 makes provision for police to investigate and report deaths to magistrates which deaths are suspected to have been caused by suicide, or by another person, or by accident, or under reasonable suspicion that another has committed an offence, or a missing person or one believed to be dead. Such deaths may be made the subject of an inquest. Under Section 387 inquests are to be held where a person dies in police custody or in prison. One cannot help but notice the obvious issue that comes to light is the conflict of interest that is apparent when an individual dies in the hands or custody of police officers as their role in inquests is also pivotal. It is also apparent that there is a lethargic approach as most questionable deaths are left uninvestigated and only the high profile cases are subjected to an inquest.

Section 388 provides *inter alia* that the DPP may direct a Magistrate to hold an inquest. This provision of the law was declared unconstitutional in the case of *Sisina & Others v AG.*[84] The High Court held that this provision of the law contravened Article 160 of the Constitution which provides that in the exercise of judicial authority, the Judiciary, shall not be subject to the control or direction of any person or authority. The court was of the opinion that Section 388 of the CPC gives the DPP power to control or direct a judicial officer, hence unconstitutional.

Although the CPC does not lay down procedures to be followed in inquests, in practice, inquests are carried out almost like normal trials. The police arrange for persons to give testimonies in court, and with the permission of the court, the family of the deceased or other properly interested or affected person, may be allowed to question them and have counsel representing them. However, unlike a trial the DPP does not have an obligation to prove any case before the court, but he should, together with the presiding magistrate, ensure that the prevailing circumstances surrounding the death of the deceased have come to be clearly known as far as may be practicable.

---

[84] High Court at Nakuru, Misc. Civil Application No. 345 of 2005 (2013) eKLR.

Upon termination of an inquest, a number of options are available to the magistrate pursuant to Section 387 (4) and (5) CPC. First, if at the termination of the inquiry, the magistrate is of the opinion that an offence has been committed by some person or persons unknown, he shall record his opinion and shall forthwith send a copy thereof to the DPP. Second, if at the termination of the inquiry the magistrate is of the opinion that no offence has been committed, he shall record his opinion accordingly. In the case of an inquiry relating to a missing person believed to be dead, Section 387 (6) as read with Section 388 (4) provide that the magistrate shall at the termination of the inquiry report the case together with his findings to the DPP and shall make recommendations as to whether or not the period regarding the presumption of death provided for by Section 118A of the Evidence Act should be reduced and if so what lesser period should, in the circumstances of the death, be substituted for the period of seven years. An inquest may be re-opened in case new evidence comes to light.[85]

In *Oforo Makupa v R*[86] a fundamental question arose as to whether the same court that held inquest can also do the trial. The Superior Court did not set aside the conviction, but frowned on the practice, by stating that when a magistrate has conducted an inquest, the subsequent criminal proceedings should, if practicable be heard by another magistrate. In essence the Magistrate would be the investigator and judge.

3.8 Commissions of Inquiry

The legal authority for the establishment and management of commissions in Kenya is the Commissions of Inquiry Act.[87] The main function of a commission of inquiry is to inquire into the conduct of any public officer or the conduct or management of any public body, or into any matter into which an inquiry would, in the opinion of the President, be in the public interest.[88] After completion of its work, it forwards its report to the appointing authority who is the President.

---

85 *Re Mitchelstown Inquisition* (1888) 22 LR Ir 279.

86 (1964) EA 301.

87 Chapter 102, Laws of Kenya.

88 Section 3 (1) of the Commission of Inquiry Act.

Pursuant to Section 10 of the Commission of Inquiry Act the Commission has power to summon and examine witnesses. Any person whose conduct is the subject of inquiry under this Act, or who is in any way implicated or concerned in any matter under inquiry, shall be entitled to be represented by an advocate in the proceedings of the inquiry or any part thereof, and any other person who desires to be so represented may, by leave of the commissioner, be so represented.

There have been a number of commissions of inquiries. In 1913, Kenya had its first commission under the colonial rule. Its mandate was to inquire into and investigate labour shortages in the colony. It established that the natives were not interested in taking up work as labourers because of the poor conditions of work. There was also the Ndung'u commission which inquired into the illegal allocation and allotment of public land.[89] This report made a number of recommendations but there has been a lack of full implementation. Another commission that is worth mentioning is the Gicheru Commission in 1990 which was formed to inquire into the death of Robert Ouko. This commission did not however get to finish its work as it was disbanded in unclear circumstances. In 2005, the Goldenberg Commission completed its report. This report implicated a number of people for further investigation and others for prosecution.[90] It is a well-known fact that most of the named people have managed to go to court and have had their names expunged from the report thus barring any prosecution. Also, in 2008, the Truth, Justice and Reconciliation Commission (TJRC) was formed to inquire into the past historical injustices in Kenya. In May, 2013 the Commission presented its report and whether or not its recommendations will be fully implemented is a matter which only time can tell.

The effectiveness of commissions of inquiry is a subject open to debate. It is often the case that their reports are never implemented or indeed made public and it arguable that in most cases, commissions of inquiry are meant to suppress public pressures, so that the executive may seem to be deeply concerned of the matter at hand and interested in resolving the issues.

* * *

---

89 Report of the Commission of Inquiry into the Illegal Allocation of Public Land.

90 Report of the Judicial Commission of Inquiry into the Goldenberg Affair.

CHAPTER 4

ARREST

4.1 Introduction

Section 2 (1) of the National Police Service Act[1] (NPSA) defines arrest to mean the act of apprehending a person for suspected commission of an offence or by the action of legal authority. In ordinary parlance, to arrest is to take away a person into police custody after suspicion of having committed an offence. Arrest is not the equivalent of being requested to attend to the police station to assist or to shed light to a suspected criminal offence as provided for under Section 52 (1) of the NPSA.[2] To arrest, is to apprehend a person for the purpose of having him answer to criminal charges that he is suspected to have committed.

Arrest is no doubt a traumatizing experience for the ordinary person and is a procedure that is susceptible to abuse. The law recognizes this and places certain safeguards on the process of arrest. The aim of these safeguards is to avoid situations where an arrested person is exposed to abuse or dehumanizing treatment.

---

1 Chapter 84, Laws of Kenya.

2 Section 52 (1) of the NPSA provides, *"A police officer may, in writing, require any person whom the police officer has reason to believe has information which may assist in the investigation of an alleged offence to attend before him at a police station or police office in the county in which that person resides or for the time being is."*

4.2 Constitutional Safeguards on Arrest

The starting point for these safeguards is Article 49 of the Constitution, 2010 which specifically grants certain rights to all arrested persons. It will be observed that as provided by Article 49 of the Constitution an arrested person is vested with certain rights which are as follows :-

(i) An arrested person must be informed of the reason for his arrest in a language that he understands.
(ii) An arrested person has a right to remain silent and he must be informed of this right in a language that he understands.
(iii) An arrested person must be informed and must be made to understand the consequences of not remaining silent in a language that he understands.
(iv) An arrested person has a right to communicate with an advocate and other person whose assistance is necessary.
(v) An arrested person cannot be compelled to make any confession or admission that could be used in evidence against him.
(vi) An arrested person must be held separately from persons who are serving a sentence.
(vii) An arrested person must be brought before a court as soon as reasonably possible but not later than 24 hours after being arrested, or if the 24 hours end outside ordinary court hours, or on a day that is not an ordinary court day, the end of the next court day.
(viii) An arrested person must at the first court appearance, be charged or informed of the reason why he needs to continue being detained, or be released.
(ix) An arrested person has a right to be released on bond on bail, on reasonable conditions pending a charge or trial, unless there are compelling reasons why he should not be released.
(x) An arrested person must not be remanded in custody if the offence is punishable by fine only or by a term of imprisonment not exceeding 6 months.

Further to the constitutional provisions, the Fifth Schedule to the NPSA, provides for Arrest and Detention Rules. The Rules reiterate the rights of the individual set out in Articles 49, 50, and 51 of the Constitution. In addition, they provide for safe-guards in relation to lock-up facilities. The Rules provide that such lock-up facilities must be hygienic and conducive for human habitation; must have adequate light, toilet, washing facilities and outdoor area; that men and women be kept separately; that juveniles and children be kept separately from adults; and such persons be kept separately from convicted prisoners.[3]

The police officer in charge of the station is also obligated to maintain a register. The register must show the name of the person; the reasons for his arrest and detention; the date and time of arrest and detention; the date and time of first appearance in court; identity of the arresting officer; the date and time for interrogations and identity of the interrogators; and, the date and time of any transfer of the detainee to another place of detention. An officer must also be appointed to be responsible for the welfare of detainees and to update the register.[4]

The Rules also provide that a person who has been arrested and detained has a right to communicate with and receive visits of members of his family; inform family members of his arrest; have access to doctors and general medical assistance; and lodge complaints against ill-treatment and the right to compensation.[5] A person can only be detained in a designated lock-up facility.[6]

A police officer who contravenes the Arrest and Detention Rules, is guilty of a disciplinary offence and may be tried for a criminal offence. [7]It is critical that the rights of an accused person are safeguarded if the criminal process is to be vested with integrity. Consequences of not complying with the constitutional and statutory provisions on arrest can invite a constitutional challenge on the criminal process and may vitiate the entire or part of the criminal proceedings. For example, a court can decline to accept a confessionary statement where the accused is kept in custody for a duration of time beyond what is provided in the

---

3 Arrest and Detention Rules, Schedule 5 of the NPSA, Rule 5.

4 *Ibid*, Rule 8.

5 *Ibid*, Rule 9.

6 *Ibid*, Rule 10.

7 *Ibid*, Rule 14.

constitution.[8] A person is also entitled to sue for damages if his rights under the constitution are violated including any contravention on the provisions on arrest.[9]

4.3 How an Arrest is Conducted

An arrest is conducted by touching or confining the body of the person to be arrested unless there is submission to custody by word or conduct.[10] If a person resists arrest, all means necessary may be used to effect arrest.[11] However, greater force than is reasonable given the circumstances should never be employed.[12]

Pursuant to the provisions of Section 22 of the CPC it is permitted for a person acting under warrant, or for a police officer to enter into a building where it is believed the suspect is in. The person residing in such place is supposed to allow free ingress. If free ingress is not allowed it is permissible for such persons to break in to effect the arrest. If the building is in actual occupancy of a woman who ordinarily does not appear in public such woman is to be given notice and access to withdraw before breaking into such building.

The Police or any other person authorized by the Police Commissioner, may search, or detain an aircraft, vessel or vehicle in which there is reason to believe that anything stolen or unlawfully obtained may be found or which is suspected to have been used in committing an offence. The police also have power to stop, search and detain a person who is reasonably believed to be conveying a stolen item or an unlawfully acquired item. The person making arrest may seize any offensive weapons found on such person and submit them to court or police. The above steps must not all be accomplished for the arrest or search to be lawful.[13]

---

8 See *Ngoya v R* (1985) KLR 309 where some inculpatory statements were rejected as the accused had been in custody in excess of twenty days.

9 See for example *M'Ibui v Dyer* (1967) EA 315 where a suit for damages was successful.

10 CPC, Section 21(1).

11 *Ibid*, Section 21(2).

12 *Ibid*, Section 21(3).

13 Section 26 CPC.

Wagachira (Kuria) v R[14] touched on the interpretation of then Section 25 of the CPC which is similar to the current Section 26 of the CPC. In this case, the appellant who was pushing a bicycle was stopped by a policeman on the suspicion that the bicycle was stolen. On being stopped the policeman checked the number on the bicycle and found that it had been altered. The appellant produced a receipt to show that the bicycle was his but the receipt was later found to be a forgery. He was charged with the offence of conveying suspected stolen property, forgery of a cash sale receipt, uttering a false document and corruption, for he had offered to bribe the police officer. On appeal, he contended that his arrest was unlawful as for the police officer to have properly exercised his powers under section 25 (now Section 26) he should not only stop, but must also search and detain the person suspected and that reasonable grounds for suspicion must exist at the time that the person is stopped. It was held that it is not necessary for the police officer to go through every stage of stopping, searching and detaining, and section 25(now Section 26), applies even if the grounds for reasonable suspicion have not appeared until after the person has stopped, or been stopped, for some other reason. The appeal was dismissed.

If a vessel is detained on reasonable suspicion that it has been used to commit an offence, the affected person is not entitled to compensation or damages for any loss occasioned by detention of the vessel.[15] If a woman is to be searched, the search should be conducted by another woman and decency must be ensured.[16]

An arrest may be effected with or without warrant.

4.3.1 Arrest without Warrant

Section 58 of the NPSA[17] and Section 29 of the CPC, provide the power to arrest without a warrant. These sections combined, cover numerous situations and it is arguable that almost all common offences are arrestable without warrant. An officer may thus without warrant, arrest one who is accused by

---

14 (1957) EA 808.

15 CPC, Section 26 (2).

16 CPC, Section 27.

17 Which gives the various situations when a police officer can arrest without warrant.

another person of committing an aggravated assault in any case in which the police officer believes upon reasonable ground that such assault has been committed; one who obstructs a police officer while in the execution of duty, or who has escaped or attempts to escape from lawful custody; one whom the police officer suspects on reasonable grounds of having committed a cognizable offence; one who commits a breach of the peace in the presence of the police officer; one in whose possession is found anything which may reasonably be suspected to be stolen property or who may reasonably be suspected of having committed an offence with reference to that thing; one whom the police officer suspects upon reasonable grounds of being a deserter from the armed forces or any other disciplined service; one whom the police officer suspects upon reasonable grounds of having committed or being about to commit a felony; or any person whom he finds in a highway, yard or other place during the night and whom he suspects upon reasonable grounds of having committed or being about to commit a felony; any person whom he finds in a street or public place during the hours of darkness and whom he suspects upon reasonable grounds of being there for an illegal or disorderly purpose, or who is unable to give a satisfactory account of himself; any person whom he suspects upon reasonable grounds of having been concerned in an act committed at a place out of Kenya which, if committed in Kenya, would have been punishable as an offence, and for which he is liable to be extradited under the Extradition (Contiguous and Foreign Countries) Act (Cap 76) or the Extradition (Commonwealth Countries) Act (Cap 77); any person having in his possession without lawful excuse, the burden of proving which excuse shall lie on that person, any implement of housebreaking; or any released convict committing a breach of any provision prescribed by section 344 or of any rule made thereunder;

The first schedule to the CPC outlines particular offences under the Penal Code and specifies those which the police can arrest without a warrant and those where he would need a warrant.

4.3.2 Arrest with Warrant

There are some offences where one cannot be arrested without an arrest warrant. These offences are set out in the first Schedule to the CPC. For example the offence of Inducing Desertion contrary to Section 49 of the Penal Code requires a warrant for arrest to be effected. Arrest warrants are issued by the court on application.[18] Arrest warrants are not only issued for suspects who are supposed to be arraigned in court to answer criminal charges. A court is at liberty to also issue arrest warrants for witnesses or accused persons who have failed to attend court. Where arrest is done in compliance to an order of the Court, the person effecting it enjoys immunity.[19]

4.3.3 The Use of Force in Arrest

Sections 61(2) of the NPSA empowers a police officer to use force and firearms in accordance with the rules on the use of force and firearms contained in the Sixth Schedule of the statute. Section 21 (2) of the CPC also allows the use of necessary force.[20] There would be no justification for example for the use of a firearm to enforce the arrest of a person who is not dangerous or who is unarmed. The force used must be proportional to the circumstances prevailing at the time of arrest. The test must be the test of a reasonable man and the burden of proving that the force used was proportional must be on the defence.

In *Kimiti v Mwenda & 3 Others*,[21] the Court of Appeal had occasion to deal with the issue of force during arrest. The deceased was driving a public service vehicle (matatu) which was hijacked by gangsters on the night of 5th March 2000. One gangster took control of the vehicle and the deceased was sandwiched in the driver's cabin. The police were alerted and confronted the vehicle at which

18 One should be careful as to not confuse it with the offence of desertion itself which an individual can be arrested without a warrant pursuant to Section 94 (2) of the NPSA which provides that upon reasonable suspicion that any police officer has deserted the Service, any police officer may arrest that officer without a warrant, and shall thereupon take him before a magistrate having jurisdiction in the area in which such person deserted or was arrested.

19 See *AG v Oluoch* (1972) EA 392.

20 Section 21 (2) of the CPC provides, *"If a person forcibly resists the endeavour to arrest him, or attempts to evade the arrest, the police officer or other person may use all means necessary to effect the arrest."*

21 *Kimiti v Mwenda & 3 Others* Nyeri Court of Appeal, Civil Appeal 129 of 2004 (2010) eKLR; See also *Muwonge v Attorney General of Uganda* (1967) EA 17 and *M'Ibui v Dyer* (1967) EA 315.

time one of the gangsters produced what looked like a pistol, which prompted the police to open fire resulting in the death of the deceased. The family sued for damages, which suit, was dismissed by the High Court. They appealed. In its analysis the Court of Appeal noted that whether or not police have used excessive force in effecting arrest is a matter of degree dependent on the peculiar circumstances of each case, and that in deciding whether liability should attach for alleged careless or negligent use of firearm by police in effecting arrest, the court should take into account, among other things, that the pursuit and arrest of dangerous and armed criminals is a hazardous operation and that it is in the public interest that the police operations are not unreasonably impeded by the decisions of the courts. Moreover, the court affirmed that the law allows the police to use all means necessary to effect arrest but even then, they are not allowed to use greater force than reasonable or necessary in the particular circumstances. In its final analysis the court stated, *"Having regard to the peculiar circumstances of this case including the fact that deceased sustained multiple gunshot wounds, we draw the inference that the police had no reasonable apprehension of danger to themselves and that the shooting to death of the deceased was unreasonable use of force, unnecessary and unlawful and liability attaches to their action against their employer the government."*

In *Bukenya v AG,*[22] the plaintiff was shot by an Army officer and he sued the Attorney General for damages. The circumstances of the case were that the plaintiff and another person, were accosted by one Komeko, an army officer, who had been informed of the presence of the plaintiff and the other person as being suspicious. When Komeko approached the two persons, one drew a pistol and Komeko shot him. The plaintiff then ran away, but after being ordered to stop and failing to do so, Komeko shot him twice in the back. Under the then Ugandan Armed Forces Act, a soldier could arrest without warrant any person whom he suspects on reasonable grounds of having committed or about to commit an offence. It was submitted on behalf of the defence that Komeko shot the plaintiff to prevent him from escaping, and that the shooting was necessary and reasonable, and that he did not use any more force than was necessary, to effect the lawful arrest of the plaintiff. The court in assessing this argument affirmed that no officer should shoot a person in cold blood should they fail to

22 (1972) EA 326 (U).

acquiesce the arrest. In the instant case, there was no reason to believe that the plaintiff was armed, as he was running away, and therefore the shooting was unlawful. The defendant was ordered to pay damages to the plaintiff.

The State as an employer of police officers may bear vicarious liability for the acts of the officers.[23]

4.3.4 Arrest by Private Person

It is not only the police who are authorized to arrest. A private person may also arrest in certain instances. The authority for the aforementioned assertion is as provided for under Section 34 of the CPC. A private person may arrest any person who in his view commits a cognizable offence, or whom he reasonably suspects of having committed a felony. The term felony is described by the Penal Code *"an offence which is declared by law to be a felony or, if not declared to be a misdemeanour, is punishable, without proof of previous conviction, with death, or with imprisonment for three years or more."*[24]

A Person found committing an offence involving injury to property may be arrested without a warrant by the owner of the property or his servants or persons authorized by him.[25] A private person who arrests a person without a warrant must take that person before a police officer or the nearest police station. If he has committed a cognizable offence, the officer shall re-arrest him. The officer can release him if he is of the opinion that no offence has been committed. In addition to private arrest, a person has obligation to assist the police or a magistrate in arresting.[26]

Just as a police officer, a private individual effecting arrest has obligation to use reasonable force.

---

23 *Muwonge v Attorney General of Uganda* [1967] EA. 17

24 Section 4, Penal Code.

25 Section 34 (2), CPC.

26 Section 42, CPC.

In *M'Ibui v Dyer,*[27] the plaintiff and two others were transporting 'miraa.'[28] For fear of bandits, they passed through a secondary road and not the normal highway route. Their vehicle broke down near the defendant's sheep farm. The defendant was awoken by his workers and informed that there was an attack on his sheep 'boma.' He drove to his sheep boma where he found his sheep scattered and drove towards the road to track down the "thieves". The defendant found the vehicle stopped and two people scrabble on it before it drove off. He saw what he thought were sheep in the vehicle which in fact were *miraa* sacks and shot twice. The vehicle stopped and three men got out and ran away. The defendant shot a third shot in the direction of the plaintiff. The plaintiff got two wounds one in his shoulder and the other in his leg. The plaintiff sued for his injuries. In assessing the case, the court held that in Kenya law, there was no distinction between the power of the police officer and of a private person to arrest without warrant on suspicion of a felony. Each is entitled to arrest without warrant. The private person does not have to prove that a felony has been committed. So long as there were reasonable grounds for the suspicion, a private person is entitled to arrest and in doing so to use such force as is reasonable in the circumstances or is necessary for the apprehension of the offender.[29] In the instant, the court held that there were reasonable grounds for suspecting that a felony had been committed. The defendant was not negligent in firing the first two shots in the air by way of warning. He was however negligent in firing the third shot in the direction of the plaintiff the amount of force being neither reasonable nor necessary. Judgment was entered for the plaintiff on his claim for damages.

In *Uganda v Muherwa,*[30] the accused being out to arrest the deceased for stealing his beans, cut him with a 'panga' on his thigh causing the deceased to bleed to death. He was charged for manslaughter. In his judgment, the judge stated that although it was lawful to effect a private arrest, one exceeding this power, in fact, does an unlawful act, and on the facts, the court found the accused guilty of manslaughter.

---

27 (1967) EA 315.

28 *Catha edulis* or khat or qat, a mild stimulant.

29 Refer to sections 21 and 34 of the CPC.

30 (1972) EA 466 (U).

4.3.5 Arrest by Magistrates

Magistrates are also empowered to effect arrest. Sections 38 and 39 of the CPC provide for the following two instances; first, when an offence is committed in the presence of a magistrate within the local limits of his jurisdiction, he may himself arrest or order any person to arrest the offender, and may thereupon, subject to the provisions of the CPC as to bail, commit the offender to custody. Secondly, a magistrate may at any time, arrest or direct the arrest in his presence, within the local limits of his jurisdiction, of any person for whose arrest he is competent at the time and in the circumstances to issue a warrant.

4.3.6 Other Persons Who May effect Arrest

4.3.6.1 Administration Police Officers

Section 27 (j) of the NPSA Act provides that the functions of the Administration Police Service shall include, *inter alia*, the apprehension of offenders.

4.3.6.2 Chiefs acting under The Chiefs' Act

The Chiefs' Act[31] in section 8 (2) provides that any chief or Assistant Chief knowing of a design by any person to commit an offence within the local limits of his jurisdiction may, if it appears to such chief or assistant chief that the commission of the offence cannot be otherwise prevented, arrest or direct the arrest of such person; and any person so arrested shall, without delay, be taken to the nearest police station. Every chief or assistant chief receiving information that any person who has committed a cognizable offence triable by any court or for whose arrest a warrant has been issued, is within the local limits of his jurisdiction shall cause such person to be arrested and to be taken forthwith before a court having jurisdiction in the matter.[32]

---

31 Chapter 128, Laws of Kenya.

32 *Ibid*, Section 8 (2).

Finally, Section 8 (4) of the Chief's Authority Act provides that every chief or assistant chief receiving information that any cattle or other livestock or other property of any description which has been stolen outside the local limits of his jurisdiction has been brought and is within such local limits, shall cause such cattle or other livestock or other property to be seized and detained pending the orders of an administrative officer, and shall forthwith report such seizure and detention to an administrative officer.

4.4 Arraignment in Court after Arrest

To arraign is to bring to court a person who has been arrested, so that he can answer to the charges.

Article 49 (f) of the Constitution, provides that an arrested person has a right, to be brought before a court as soon as reasonably possible, but not later than twenty-four hours after being arrested; or if the twenty-four hours ends outside ordinary court hours, or on a day that is not an ordinary court day, the end of the next court day. It follows that a person must be arraigned in court within 24 hours of his arrest unless the exceptions apply. If he is not going to be arraigned, he is entitled to be released on bond or bail pending a formal charge. The question that arises is what ought to happen if a person is arraigned outside the period provided by the Constitution.

Lessons on this may be taken from the experience of the former constitution, which similarly provided that a person must be arraigned in court within 24 hours, unless the offence was a capital offence, in which case he ought to have been arraigned within 14 days.[33] The decisions on this point were varied but the matter seems to have been settled by the Court of Appeal in its decision in the case of *Julius Kamau Mbugua v R,*[34] where the court reviewed the previous authorities and international practice and laid the law on the issue. The Court held that the remedy for infringement of the rights of an accused person, lay in damages, as the unlawful detention had no link or effect on the trial process

---

[33] Section 72 (3) (b) of the Constitution of Kenya, 1963 (now repealed by the 2010 Constitution).

[34] Nairobi Court of Appeal, Criminal Appeal 50 of 2008, (2010) eKLR.

itself. The accused cannot therefore be exonerated and acquitted of the crime on the basis alone, that he was arraigned in court beyond the specified period.

It is however important to understand the history behind the arguments that a trial is a nullity if the accused is arraigned in court after the prescribed constitutional period. The pioneering case to consider the question of unlawful detention before a suspect is charged in court, was that of *Albanus Mwasia Mutua v R,*[35] where the issue of unlawful detention was, for the first time, raised in a second and final appeal. Counsel representing the appellant contended that the appellant had been unlawfully detained in police custody for eight months before he was charged in court with the offence of robbery with violence under Section 296 (2) of the Penal Code, which carries a death penalty, and that such violation of the appellant's rights under section 77 of the repealed Constitution rendered the trial and the conviction a nullity. He sought the acquittal of the appellant on that ground. The Court instead, invoked section 72 (3) (b) and allowed the appeal saying:

"At the end of the day, it is the duty of the courts to enforce provisions of the Constitution, otherwise there would be no reason for having those provisions, in the first place. The jurisprudence which emerges from the cases we have cited in the judgment appears to be that an unexplained violation of a constitutional right will normally result in an acquittal irrespective of the nature and strength of evidence which may be adduced in support of the charge … The deprivation by the police of his right to liberty for a whole eight months before bringing him to court so that his trial could begin obviously resulted in his trial not being held within a reasonable time. The appellant's appeal must succeed on that ground alone".

This decision as delivered in July 2006 had immediate ramifications on the criminal justice system. The majority of appellants both in the superior court and in the Court of Appeal, invariably raised the issue of unlawful detention under the then section 72 (3) (b) of the Constitution, either by filing supplementary grounds of appeal or through separate constitutional applications. Initially, many appellants had some measure of success and many appeals were allowed with the appellants being released on the ground that there was a violation of

35 Nairobi, Court of Appeal, Criminal Appeal 120 of 2004, (2006) eKLR.

their constitutional rights to a fair trial based on the long period of detention before arraignment.

In *Paul Mwangi Murunga v R,*[36] the appellant who had been convicted and sentenced to death for the offence of robbery with violence filed a second appeal to the Court of Appeal and in the course of prosecuting the appeal, his counsel raised the issue of unlawful detention for 10 days before he was taken to court. The court made a finding that a delay of 10 days which was totally unexplained was too long and allowed the appeal on that account. In the judgment, the court stated thus regarding the burden of proof:-

"We do not accept the proposition that the burden is upon an accused person to complain to a magistrate or a judge about the unlawful detention in custody of the police... Under section 72 (3) of the Constitution, the burden to explain the delay is on the prosecution and we reject any proposition that the burden can only be discharged by the prosecution, if the person raises a complaint. But in case the prosecution does not offer any explanation, then, the court as the ultimate enforcer of the provisions of the Constitution must raise the issue".

It is important to note that in the judgment of the court in the *Murunga* matter, the case of *Ndede v R,*[37] was cited. The significance of this cited case is that it was one of the so called "Mwakenya" cases.[38] The courts at that time in history, chose to see no evil and hear no evil, and sought no explanation as to where the accused persons involved in those cases had been before being brought to court. The consequence of the silence on the part of the courts was the infamous "Nyayo House Torture Chambers". The Court of Appeal in the *Murunga* case, termed it a history about which the courts of this country can never be proud of.

In *Gerald Macharia Githuku v R,*[39] the appellant who had been convicted for capital robbery and sentenced to death complained, in the course of the appeal, of unlawful detention for three days in violation of section 72 (3) (b) of the

---

36 Nakuru Court of Appeal, Criminal Appeal 35 of 2006, (2008) eKLR.

37 (1991) KLR 567.

38 When the then Government of Daniel Moi was cracking down on perceived political dissidents. *"Mwakenya"* then was a banned publication, having been declared seditious.

39 Nairobi Court of Appeal, Criminal Appeal No. 119 of 2004, (2007) eKLR.

Constitution. The court allowed the appeal on that ground, notwithstanding that it was satisfied on the evidence, that, the appellant was guilty of the offence and the breach did not result in substantial prejudice to him.

In the High Court a similar approach was initially taken. In *Ann Njogu & 5 Others v R,*[40] the superior court strictly applied the decision in *Albanus Mutua* case. In the matter, the applicants were arrested for a non-capital offence and detained in a police station for more than 24 hours and charged in court after slightly more than 48 hours later. Their constitutional application alleging that the unlawful detention rendered the charge a nullity was allowed, the court stating that there was no known cure once it was shown that a person's constitutional and fundamental rights were violated prior to the purported institution of the criminal proceedings. In view of the court, the prosecution was null and void.

In *R v Amos Karuga Karatu,*[41] the accused was tried by the High Court for the offence of murder contrary to Section 203 as read with Section 204 of the Penal Code. The prosecution called 10 witnesses and after closing its case, the counsel for the accused relying on *Albanus Mutua* submitted that the accused should be acquitted because he was unlawfully detained for 5 months before he was charged. The superior court acquitted the accused solely on that ground, holding as follows:-

"A prosecution mounted in breach of the law is a violation of the rights of the accused and is therefore a nullity. It matters not the nature of the violation. It matters not that the accused was brought to court one day after the expiry of the period required to arraign him in court. Finally, it matters not that the evidence available against him is weighty and overwhelming. As long as that delay is not explained to the satisfaction of the court, the prosecution remains a nullity".

In *Republic v George Muchoki Kungu,*[42] a preliminary objection to a charge of murder was raised on the ground that the accused was unlawfully detained by

---

40 Nairobi High Court, Miscellaneous Criminal Application No. 551 of 2007, (2007) eKLR.

41 Nyeri High Court, Criminal Case No. 12 0f 2006, (2008) eKLR.

42 Nairobi High Court, Criminal Case No. 49 of 2007 (2008) eKLR.

police for 106 days before he was charged with the offence. The prosecution filed an affidavit explaining the delay and submitted, among other things, that murder is a serious offence; that the accused should not be released without the case being heard on merit and that releasing the accused would result in bad law and, lastly, that such release would be against the public interest. The superior court nevertheless rejected the explanation proffered and held that the proceedings were illegal, null and void as they were instituted in violation of section 72 (3) (b) of the Constitution (now repealed). The court emphatically said:-

"Upon discovery of the Constitutional violation, the court has no jurisdiction to continue hearing an illegality, and, or, a nullity. That is the basis for the court's firm holding that any proceedings instituted outside the 14 days stipulated in section 72 (3) (b) are illegal, null and void irrespective of the weight of evidence that the prosecution, might have. Put differently, the evidence, might be there with the prosecution. But the forum at which such evidence can be adduced does not legality exist due to the illegality of the proceedings when they were first instituted in violation of the constitutional provisions under section 72 (3) (b)".

However, the initial liberal attitude, of entertaining allegations of unlawful detention, raised for the first time in the course of a first or second appeal, slowly changed. This change of attitude is illustrated by the decision in *Samuel Ndung'u Kamau & Another vs. Republic,*[43] the Court of Appeal said:

"The provisions of section 72 (3) (b) (of the repealed constitution) *are framed in a way which presupposes that a complaint with regard to violation would either be raised at the trial or in an application under section 84 of the* (repealed) *Constitution, where witnesses are normally called or affidavit evidence is presented to prove or rebut a factual position. When such a complaint is raised for the first time before this court, it may not be possible to investigate the truth or falsity of the allegation. That being our view of the matter, this ground fails, more so when it does not relate to the question whether or not the 2nd appellant alone or together with other persons not before the court committed the offence he stands convicted of".*[44]

---

43 Nairobi Criminal Appeal No. 223 of 2006 (Nairobi).

44 See also *Dominic Mutie Mwalimu vs. R* Nairobi Court of Appeal, Criminal Appeal No. 217 of 2005, (2008) eKLR.

Thus gradually, the Court declined to entertain a ground of breach of section 72 (3) (b) of the former Constitution, raised for the first time in the appeal where an appellant, who being represented by a counsel, failed to raise such complaint in the trial court on the reasoning, that in such a case, the appellant must be treated to have waived his right to complain about the alleged violations of his constitutional rights before he was brought to court.[45]

In the case of *Republic vs. David Geoffrey Gitonga,*[46] the accused was tried for the offence of murder and at the conclusion of the trial, after the accused had made his defence, his counsel submitted that the trial was a nullity since the accused was detained for 140 days before he was charged in violation of section 72 (2) (b) of the former Constitution. The trial Judge declined to acquit the accused saying that a breach of section 72 (3) (b) does not render a trial a nullity but entitles an accused to compensation as stipulated in section 72 (6). The trial Judge reasoned thus:

"I am aware that contrary opinions have been expressed by others in this court. I do not share those views. I hold the considered view that such trial is not a nullity at all. These are my reasons. Firstly, the principle of nullity presupposes that the process of trial is void either because it is against public policy, law, order, and indeed, nullity is non-curable. Secondly, for a trial to be void in law it must be shown either that the offence for which the accused is being tried is non-existent, or that the authority or court seized of the matter has no authority to do so. It is a public policy of all civilized States that offenders be subjected to due process in respect of defined offences, and by duly competent courts or tribunal...A trial will be a nullity where the offence is non-existent or there is lack of jurisdiction. To say otherwise would be against both public policy and the law. The court will not act against the law nor will it go against public policy. A rapacious rapist and a serial killer will not be allowed to go scot-free because either deliberately or inadvertently, the prosecution authority has not deemed it fit to have him brought before a court within 24 hours or as case may be within 14 days".

---

45 See also *James Githui Waithaka & Another vs. Republic, Nyeri Criminal Appeal No. 115 of 2007* (unreported) and *Protus Madakwa alias Collins & Two Others vs. Republic, Criminal Appeal No. 118 of 2007* (Nairobi) (unreported).

46 Criminal Case No. 79 of 2006 (Meru) (unreported).

It was now clear that the tide had changed. A preliminary objection on grounds of long detention was dismissed in *Republic vs. Judah Kiogora Ngaruthi & Another*[47] (Emukule J) and so too in *J.K. v Republic* (Osiemo J).[48] In the latter, the superior court after making a finding that the rights of the appellant had not been violated, stated as follows:-

"The appellant having failed to assert his right from the time he appeared in court and throughout the proceedings, he must now be treated as having waived the alleged violation of the constitutional right and I reject this ground and further no prejudice to the appellant had been established.

Secondly, a declaration that the accused's right has been violated does not automatically entitle accused to an acquittal. As often said, justice must be seen to be done but the watchful eye of the public. The court must constantly balance the claim of the accused against the possibility unproven and unprovable in many cases that delay has been procured or encouraged by someone acting in the interest of accused."

In the *Julius Kamau Mbugua* case,[49] the Court of Appeal grappled with the apparent confusion, based on the authorities noted above, on what should be done in a situation where an accused has been detained beyond the constitutional period. The court found that indeed in the instant case there had been an extra judicial detention which was unlawful and stated what ought to happen in such an instance as follows :-

"Lastly, had we found that the extra judicial detention was unlawful and that it is related to the trial, nevertheless, we would still consider the acquittal or discharge as a disproportionate, inappropriate and draconian remedy seeing that the public security would be compromised. If by the time an accused person makes an application to the court, the right has already been breached, and the right can no longer be enjoyed, secured or enforced, as is invariably the case, then, the only appropriate remedy under section 84 (1) would be an order for compensation for such breach. The rationale for prescribing monetary compensation in section 72 (6) was that the person having already been unlawfully arrested or detained such

---

47 Meru High Court, Criminal Case No. 14 of 2008

48 Eldoret High Court, Criminal Appeal No. 83 of 2007.

49 *Julius Kamau Mbugua Supra* note 34

unlawful arrest or detention cannot be undone and hence the breach can only be vindicated by damages. Again, we respectfully agree with Emukule, J. that breach of Section 72 (3) (b) entitles the aggrieved person to monetary compensation only. That is the relief that this Court gave in Kihoro v Attorney General of Kenya,[50] *for breach of right to personal liberty. The alleged unlawful detention does not exonerate the appellant from the serious crime he is alleged to have committed. The breach could logically give rise to a civil remedy – money compensation as stipulated in section 72 (6). That is the appropriate remedy which the appellant should have sought in a different forum."*

It would appear from the decision in *Julius Kamau Mbugua*[51] that a violation of the right to be arraigned within 24 hours would probably not entitle the accused to nullify the charges, solely based, on account of the long period in being kept in custody.

However, it is still not explicit in the Constitution of 2010, what remedy one would be entitled to when such a violation occurs. The former constitution, under section 72 (6) provided for compensation meaning that the intention was for one to be compensated by way of damages if such a violation occurred. The 2010 Constitution does not contain an explicit remedy for damages. There is no doubt however, that where such violation occurs, one would clearly be entitled to damages, for any detention after the stipulated period, would be an unlawful detention. It is however debatable whether the 2010 constitution, as framed, intended for the right to be arraigned within 24 hours to be absolute, such that a violation was not envisaged, and that is the reason why no remedy was ever outlined, in the event of a violation. Following the *Julius Kamau Mbugua* decision,[52] it is however doubtful, though not completely settled, whether a violation of this right would nullify the proceedings.

---

50 *Kihoro v Attorney General of Kenya* (1993) 3 LRC 390.

51 *Supra* note 34.

52 *Ibid.*

4.5 Habeas Corpus

Habeas corpus simply means "produce the body". It is a remedy that is oft utilized when a person has been seized by the police but has not been arraigned in court within the stipulated period of time. Under Article 25 of the Constitution the right to an order of *habeas corpus* is an absolute right which cannot be limited. Where a person has been kept in custody beyond the time specified, any person can approach the court for an order of *habeas corpus.* Since in most instances, the incarcerated person will not be in a position to swear an affidavit, any person can swear the affidavit in support of the application for *habeas corpus.*

The writ of *Habeas corpus* is also recognized in the CPC vide the provisions of Section 389 which stipulates, that the High Court, may, whenever it thinks fit, direct that any person within the limits of Kenya be brought up before the court to be dealt with according to law; that any person illegally or improperly detained in public or private custody within those limits be set at liberty; that any prisoner detained in a prison situated within those limits be brought before the court to be there examined as a witness in any matter pending or to be inquired into in that court; that any prisoner so detained be brought before a court martial or commissioners acting under the authority of a commission from the President for trial to be examined touching any matter pending before the court martial or commissioners respectively; that any prisoner within those limits be removed from one custody to another for the purpose of trial; and that the body of a defendant within those limits be brought in on a return of *cepi corpus* to a writ of attachment.

The Rules to making an application for *habeas corpus* are in the Schedule to the CPC. In *Paul Mburu Kamau v PCIO Coast Province and Another,*[53] the applicants were arrested, apparently for murder, and the period of 14 days (provided in the former constitution) expired while they were still being held in police custody. An application for *habeas corpus* was made. The court ordered their release on terms that they deposit their passports and report to the police every week. In *Mohamed v Republic,* [54]one Mohamed was arrested by the police, then released the following day with advice to report to the police station

[53] Mombasa HCCR Application NO.8 of (2006) eKLR.

[54] (2003) KLR 344.

the next day. He did report but was locked in and not released. The applicant through his wife filed for a writ of *habeas corpus.* Etyang J. made clear that if one goes to police station for recording a statement, he cannot be arrested and confined. If arrest ensues then the person must be informed of the reasons for the arrest. He must then be arraigned in court within the stipulated time. The writ of *habeas corpus* was issued.

An interesting point arose in the case of *Mariam Mohamed & Another v Commissioner of Police & Others.*[55] In this matter the subject had been arrested by police sometime in February 2007. He was never arraigned in court and in October 2007 an application for the writ of *habeas corpus* was filed. It emerged that the subject had been detained in the police cells, but released, and later spirited away to a foreign country, apparently on suspicion of being involved in terrorist activities. The court was alive to the serious constitutional violations made but since the subject was neither within the jurisdiction of the court, nor in the custody of the respondents, it declined to issue the orders of *habeas corpus.*

4.6 Extradition

There are two statutes that deal with extradition. The first is the Extradition (Commonwealth Countries) Act[56] and the second is the Extradition (Contiguous and Foreign Countries) Act.[57] The Extradition (Commonwealth Countries) Act is an act of Parliament enacted to make provision for the surrender by Kenya, to other Commonwealth countries, of persons accused or convicted of offences in those countries, to regulate the treatment of persons accused or convicted of offences in Kenya who are returned to Kenya from such countries; and for purposes incidental thereto and connected therewith. Under this Act, an offence is an extradition offence if it is an offence against the law of a requesting country, and which is punishable under that law, with imprisonment for a term of twelve months or any greater punishment, and the act or omission constituting the offence, would constitute an offence against the law of Kenya if it took place in Kenya.

55 High Court at Nairobi, Misc. Criminal Application No. 732 of 2007, (2007) eKLR.

56 Chapter 177, Laws of Kenya.

57 Chapter 76, Laws of Kenya.

Every fugitive is liable to be arrested, detained, and surrendered to the requesting country. However, a fugitive shall not be surrendered, or committed to or kept in custody for the purposes of surrender, if it appears to the court of committal, or to the High Court on an application for *habeas corpus*, or to the Attorney-General, that -

(a) the offence of which the fugitive is accused or was convicted is an offence of a political character; or
(b) the request for his surrender (though purporting to be made on account of an extradition offence) is in fact made for the purpose of prosecuting or punishing him on account of his race, religion, nationality or political opinions; or
(c) that he might, if surrendered, be prejudiced at his trial or punished, detained or restricted in his personal liberty by reason of his race, religion, nationality or political opinions.
(d) A fugitive accused of an offence shall not be surrendered, or committed to or kept in custody for the purposes of surrender, if it appears to the court of committal, or to the High Court on an application for habeas corpus, or to the Attorney-General, that he would, if charged with that offence in Kenya, be entitled to be discharged under any rule of law relating to previous acquittal or conviction.
(e) A fugitive shall not be surrendered, or committed to or kept in custody for the purposes of surrender, unless provision is made by the law of the requesting country, or by an arrangement made with that country, for securing that he will not, unless he has first been restored or had an opportunity of returning to Kenya, be dealt with in that country for or in respect of any offence committed before his surrender, other than -

    (a) the offence in respect of which his surrender is requested; or
    (b) any lesser offence proved by the facts proved before the court of committal; or
    (c) any other extradition offence in respect of which the Attorney-General may consent to his being so dealt with.

Proceedings for committal are then supposed to be held and if the court is satisfied that the fugitive needs to be extradited, will make an order for extradition. More or less similar provisions abound under CAP 76.

In *Kunga v R*,[58] Kunga was employed by the East Africa Railways in Uganda. He was to be charged in the district court of West Acholi at Gulu with the offence of stealing by a person in the public service. The signature of the chief magistrate on the warrant was certified by the Minister of Justice who was also the Attorney General of Uganda. The Senior Resident Magistrate, Kenya, endorsed it on 25th February 1975 for execution in Kenya and shortly Kunga was arrested. He appeared before the Senior Resident Magistrate the next day and was remanded from time to time until March 18 when he was identified on oath by a corporation employee. Later he opposed his committal to Uganda on the argument that he will not receive a fair trial in Uganda. It was further argued in opposition to the extradition that the magistrate had nothing before him to show that the Ugandan authorities have any evidence or sufficient evidence against him, the seriousness or triviality of the charge was not shown for there were no particulars of charge; that the punishment for the offence was not considered, and if it had been, it would have been revealed that it was possibly death by firing squad, and the applicant was unlikely to have a fair trial in the conditions obtaining in the courts and generally in Uganda then.

The court had to consider the law on extradition and it opined that the only question was whether or not the magistrate had evidence before him which gave him authority and jurisdiction to commit the prisoner to the person named on the warrant to return to Uganda. The court appreciated that this would involve some examination of the evidence but that the court must not be a Court of Appeal from the magistrate on questions of fact. The court averred that it could interfere if there was no evidence before the magistrate upon which he could exercise his discretion whether he would commit or not, or whether the crime is alleged to be of a political character, or whether the nationality of the prisoner is material, or the crime is not within the scope of the Act.

The court noted that the warrant was issued in Uganda which is a country to which Part III of the Extradition (contiguous and foreign countries) Act applies in accordance with the Extradition (Application of Part III) Order. The

58 (1975) EA 151.

court noted that the magistrate also considered section 16 of the Act[59] and was of the view that there were no reasons to stop the arrest. The court was not satisfied that Kunga will not get a fair trial in Uganda. It reasoned that if it were, Parliament would have had Uganda deleted from the subsidiary legislation that applies in Part III of the Act. The court considered that overall, what was important was a consideration of section 16 (3), and whether in the end, the return of the prisoner to the contiguous country would be oppressive or just. In this matter, the High Court ordered the case returned to the magistrate for consideration of the argument that Kunga would be shot if found guilty.[60]

* * *

59 The following were matters to be considered under section16 i.e. whether the distance and all circumstances would make it oppressive or too severe a punishment to return the fugitive immediately. See *Re Henderson (1950) 1 All E.R 283*. Assuming the accused is found guilty the punishment of being returned is out of proportion to the offence, i.e. the charges are trivial or it appears that the proceedings will be contrary to natural justice.

60 See also *Walter Osapiri Barasa v The Cabinet Secretary Ministry of Interior and National Co-ordination & 3 Others,* Nairobi High Court Constitutional Petition No. 488 of 2013 (2014) eKLR.

CHAPTER 5

PROSECUTION OF OFFENCES

5.1 Introduction

The State has an interest in safeguarding the public interest, including, the interest of the public in having offenders prosecuted. The onus is therefore upon the State to conduct prosecutions. An offence is deemed to be a wrong against the State and it is always the State who is the complainant in a criminal case. That is the reason why every criminal case is titled *Republic v ABC*. It is the state which is the legal complainant although in ordinary parlance, it is the victim of the crime who is usually referred to as "the complainant". It follows that all prosecutions are undertaken by the State on behalf of the public. It is for this purpose that the Office of the Director of Public Prosecutions (DPP) was created; to undertake prosecutions on behalf of the State.

Once a person is arrested, it is expected that he will be charged with committing an offence within 24 hours of his arrest.[1] If he is not charged, then he has to be released forthwith. The decision of whether or not to charge an individual suspected of having committed a criminal offence, is the prerogative of the Director of Public Prosecutions (DPP), who is ultimately responsible for conducting all prosecutions on behalf of the State, save for prosecutions conducted before the courts martial. The person in charge of prosecutions before the Courts Martial is the Director of Military Prosecutions (DMP) who is appointed by the Defence Council.[2] The DMP, must be at least of the rank of Brigadier, and must be an advocate of the High Court of Kenya, of at

1 Constitution of Kenya, 2010, Article 49 (1) (f) and (g) of the Constitution of Kenya, 2010. See Chapter 4 for a full discussion on Arrest.

2 Kenya Defence Forces Act, Chapter 199, Laws of Kenya, Section 213 (1).

least 10 years standing.[3] The DMP has power to direct the military police to investigate any information or allegation of criminal conduct and exercises all powers of prosecution before the Courts Martial.[4]

The prosecution of crime not falling within the jurisdiction of the Courts Martial, is principally governed by the Constitution, and The Office of the Director of Public Prosecutions Act (ODPP Act)[5]. Good practice can also be gleaned from the non-binding *Guidelines on the Role of Prosecutors.*[6]

5.2 The Office of the Director of Public Prosecutions

The office of the DPP is established by Article 157 of the Constitution and elaborated by the ODPP Act. The DPP is appointed by the President after approval by the National Assembly. He must have the same qualifications for appointment as those required for appointment to be a judge of the High Court.[7]

The powers of the DPP in the current constitutional set-up are laid out in Article 157 of the Constitution. The same partly provides as follows :-

(6) The Director of Public Prosecutions shall exercise State powers of prosecution and may—

(a) institute and undertake criminal proceedings against any person before any court (other than a court martial) in respect of any offence alleged to have been committed;

(b) take over and continue any criminal proceedings commenced in any court (other than a court martial) that have been instituted or undertaken by

3 *Ibid*, Section 213.(2)

4 *Ibid*, Section 213.(3).

5 Act No. 2 of 2013, which commenced on 10 January 2013.

6 *Guidelines on the Role of Prosecutors,* Adopted by the Eighth United Nations Congress on the Prevention of Crime and the Treatment of Offenders, Havana, Cuba, 27 August to 7 September 1990.

7 Constitution, Article 157 (2) and (3), and Section 8, ODPP Act.

another person or authority, with the permission of the person or authority; and

(c) *subject to clause (7) and (8), discontinue at any stage before judgment is delivered any criminal proceedings instituted by the Director of Public Prosecutions or taken over by the Director of Public Prosecutions under paragraph (b).*

(7) *If the discontinuance of any proceedings under clause (6) (c) takes place after the close of the prosecution's case, the defendant shall be acquitted.*
(8) *The Director of Public Prosecutions may not discontinue a prosecution without the permission of the court.*
(9) *The powers of the Director of Public Prosecutions may be exercised in person or by subordinate officers acting in accordance with general or special instructions.*
(10) *The Director of Public Prosecutions shall not require the consent of any person or authority for the commencement of criminal proceedings and in the exercise of his or her powers or functions, shall not be under the direction or control of any person or authority.*
(11) *In exercising the powers conferred by this Article, the Director of Public Prosecutions shall have regard to the public interest, the interests of the administration of justice and the need to prevent and avoid abuse of the legal process.*
(12) *Parliament may enact legislation conferring powers of prosecution on authorities other than the Director of Public Prosecutions.*

It will be seen from the above that the DPP may do any of the following in relation to prosecutions :-

(a) Institute and undertake criminal proceedings against any person before any court (other than a court martial) in respect of any offence alleged to have been committed.
(b) Take over and continue any criminal proceedings commenced in any court (other than a court martial) that have been instituted or undertaken by another person or authority, but with the permission of the person or authority; and
(c) Discontinue, at any stage before judgment is delivered, any criminal proceedings instituted by the DPP or taken over by the DPP.

The DPP of course cannot appear in all matters in person; therefore, he has subordinates who act on his behalf either on general or specific authority.[8] Thus police officers and state counsels in the office of the DPP are agents of the DPP, and their action to prosecute, or not, is therefore considered the action of the DPP who is their principal.

In the previous constitutional set-up, the functions of the DPP were undertaken by the Attorney General (AG). In the current regime, matters relating to criminal prosecution fall squarely within the domain of the DPP and not the AG. The Office of the DPP comprises of the Director himself (the DPP), Deputy Directors, Secretary of Prosecution Services, Prosecution Counsel, technical staff and such other members of staff of the Office as may be appointed from time to time.[9] The ODPP Act, provides for an advisory board, whose principle functions are to advise the Office on recruitment and appointment of members of staff of the Office, promotions, discipline and any other matters that may be referred to the Board by the Director.[10] There is also established a Fund, pursuant to Section 45 (1) of the ODPP Act, to be known as the Prosecutions Fund, which is to be utilized for the enhancement of the operational capacity of the Office, the welfare of the personnel of the Office, and any activity approved by the Office.

5.3 The Role of the Prosecutor

The role of the Prosecutor is to represent the state in criminal matters and exercise the State's powers of prosecution. It is not the case that the Prosecutor's role is to ensure a conviction. His role is much wider in scope than merely just pressing for a conviction. As stated in *Boucher v The Queen*:-[11]

"It cannot be overemphasized that the purpose of a criminal prosecution is not to obtain a conviction; it is to lay before a jury what the Crown considers to be credible

---

8 Constitution, Art 157 (9); See also Section 22 (1) of the ODPP Act.

9 ODPP Act, Section 13 (1).

10 Section 17 (1) of the *ODPP Act.*

11 (1954) 110 CC 263 at p 270; See also *Benedetto v The Queen*, Privy Council, Appeal No. 62 of 2002.

evidence relevant to what is alleged to be a crime. Counsel have a duty to see that all available legal proof of the facts is presented; it should be done firmly and pressed to its legitimate strength, but it must also be done fairly. The role of Prosecutor excludes any notion of winning or losing; his function is a matter of public duty than which in civil life there can be none charged with greater personal responsibility. It is to be efficiently performed with an ingrained sense of the dignity, the seriousness and the justness of judicial proceedings."

Kenya employs the adversarial system of litigation, and it may be argued that in an adversarial setting, the prosecutor must take the role of an adversary and aim at winning at all costs. But this notion does not apply, as was ably stated as follows, by Justice White, in the American case of *United States v Wade*[12] :-

"Law enforcement officers have the obligation to convict the guilty and to make sure they do not convict the innocent. They must be dedicated to making the criminal trial a procedure for the ascertainment of the true facts surrounding the commission of the crime. To this extent, our so-called adversary system is not adversary at all; nor should it be. But defense counsel has no comparable obligation to ascertain and present the truth."

This position had earlier been impressed in the case of *Berger v United States*[13] where it was stated that:-

"The (prosecutor) is the representative not of an ordinary party to a controversy, but of a sovereignty whose obligation to govern impartially is as compelling as its obligation to govern at all; and whose interest, therefore, in a criminal prosecution is not that it shall win a case, but that justice shall be done. As such, he is in a peculiar and very definite sense the servant of the law, the twofold aim of which is that guilt shall not escape or innocence suffer. He may prosecute with earnestness and vigor, indeed, he should do so. But, while he may strike hard blows, he is not at liberty to strike foul ones. It is as much his duty to refrain from improper methods calculated to produce a wrongful conviction as it is to use every legitimate means to bring about a just one."

---

12 388 U.S. 218, at 256 (1967).

13 295 US 78, at p88 (1935).

Since the prosecutor's role does not involve a duty to win the case, it behoves upon the prosecutor to reveal the whole of the evidence. In *Thomas Cholmondeley v Republic,*[14] the Court of Appeal underscored the prosecution's duty at common law to disclose to the defence all relevant material which tended either to weaken the prosecution case or to strengthen the defence case.

It can be safely concluded that the role of the prosecutor is no more than laying down all the evidence of the case. He is not supposed to take a partisan position, or deem his position as akin to a contest with the accused, for which he must win. He needs to place all the evidence on the table, both for and against the accused. He is not expected to collect and present only the evidence that is in his favour, but, he must be fair to the accused as well, and ought to present evidence that is exculpatory to the accused, if such evidence is available. At the end of it all, what is expected is a fair trial, and a fair trial cannot take place if some of the relevant evidence is concealed.

5.4 Discretion to Prosecute

Article 157 (10) of the Constitution and Section 6 of the ODPP Act provide that the DPP shall not require the consent of any person or authority for the commencement of criminal proceedings. Moreover, in the exercise of his or her powers or functions, the DPP shall not be under the direction or control of any person or authority. It thus follows that, the DPP is the one who ultimately makes the decision on whether or not to prosecute an individual. However, it is important to note that in the exercise of his powers, Article 157 (11) of the Constitution, provides that the DPP must have regard to the public interest, the interests of the administration of justice and the need to prevent and avoid abuse of the legal process.

The court observed in the case of *Francis Anyango Juma v DPP and Another,*[15] that the intention of Article 157 (10) of the Constitution, is to enable the DPP to carry out his constitutional mandate without interference from any party. The court averred that it cannot direct or interfere with the exercise by the DPP, of

14 Court of Appeal, Criminal Appeal No. 116 of 2007, (2008) eKLR.

15 High Court at Nairobi, Petition No. 160 of 2012, (2012) eKLR.

his power under the Constitution, or direct him on the way he should conduct his constitutional mandate, unless there was clear evidence of violation of a party's rights under the Constitution, or violation of the Constitution itself.

The same sentiments were echoed in the case of *Chirau Ali Mwakwere v Robert M. Mabera & 4 Others*[16] where the court stated as follows :-

"The DPP is constitutionally mandated under Article 157 to order investigations on any information or allegation of criminal conduct and institute criminal proceedings against any person before any court. The office of the DPP is an independent office and this court would not ordinarily interfere in the running of that office and the exercise of its discretion provided it is within the Constitution and the law. The office of the DPP is subject to the Constitution and the Bill of Rights contained therein and in every case, the High Court as the custodian of the Bill of Rights is entitled to intervene where the facts disclose a violation of the rights and fundamental freedoms guaranteed under the Constitution."[17]

Thus although the DPP has wide discretion, the court is entitled to intervene where it is of the opinion that there is a violation of the Constitution. A violation in this instance infers that the DPP has not had regard to the public interest, the administration of justice, and/or that his actions are tantamount to an abuse of the legal process.

This position is not new or unique to the Constitution of 2010. It was actually the position even in the previous Constitutional regime although the letter of the law did not explicitly state as much. In the former Constitution, the power to prosecute was vested upon the office of the Attorney General. These powers were provided for in Section 26 of the former Constitution and the relevant provision was drafted as follows :-

16 Nairobi High Court, Petition No. 6 of 2012 (2012) eKLR.

17 *Ibid*, para 55.

S.26 (3) The Attorney-General shall have power in any case in which he considers it desirable so to do -

(a) to institute and undertake criminal proceedings against any person before any court (other than a court-martial) in respect of any offence alleged to have been committed by that person;
(b) to take over and continue any such criminal proceedings that have been instituted or undertaken by another person or authority; and
(c) to discontinue at any stage before judgment is delivered any such criminal proceedings instituted or undertaken by himself or another person or authority.

These provisions were put to test in the celebrated cases of *Githunguri v Republic*[18] where the High Court of Kenya twice had occasion to interpret the powers of the AG to commence proceedings. The facts of the case were that Stanley Munga Githunguri was charged on the 20 May 1985 with four counts alleging contraventions of the Exchange Control Act.[19] Two of the offences were alleged to have been committed in 1976 and the third in 1979. The fourth count was an alternative to the third count. A preliminary application was made by the accused, before the trial Chief Magistrate, to the effect that the charges against him had been the subject of a police investigation six years earlier, which resulted in the office of the AG deciding not to prosecute, a decision which the office had officially communicated to the applicant and certain money which was the subject of the investigations had been restored to him. This position prevailed through the terms of two AGs, and was reiterated in parliament, by one of the successive holders of that office. Githunguri thus filed a reference under section 67 (1) of the former Constitution.[20] His application was on the issue whether the AG's office had properly exercised its power under section 26 of the Constitution in reviving and prosecuting the charges against him. The

18 *Githunguri v R* (1985) 1KLR 91 and *Githunguri v R* (1986) KLR 1.

19 CAP 113 Laws of Kenya (since repealed).

20 Section 67 of the repealed Constitution provided *"Where a question as to the interpretation of this Constitution arises in proceedings in a sub-ordinate court and the court is of the opinion that the question involves a substantial question of law, the court may, and shall if a party to the proceedings so requests, refer the question to the High Court."*

trial magistrate's court allowed the application and referred the matter to the High Court for interpretation. Five questions were formulated as follows:

1. *Whether the power conferred under section 26 (3) of the Constitution is exhausted or spent when the office of the AG makes a decision not to institute or undertake any criminal proceedings against any person.*
2. *Whether the exercise of the power conferred on the office of the AG under section 26 (3) (a) of the Constitution has to be fair and reasonable, or can it be arbitrarily or oppressively exercised.*
3. *Whether it is a proper exercise of the powers conferred under section 26 (3) (a) of the Constitution to institute criminal proceedings against any person charging him with offences allegedly committed over 3 years ago and investigated about 6 years ago following a full inquiry, and after the office of the AG had then decided not to institute or undertake criminal proceedings and closed the files.*
4. *Whether the court has an inherent power and a duty to secure fair treatment for all persons who come or are brought before the Court, and to prevent an abuse of its process notwithstanding the powers conferred upon the office of the AG by section 26 (3) of the Constitution.*
5. *Whether a charge or charges against any person preferred 9 years after their alleged commission and six years after a full inquiry in respect thereof and five years after the decision of the office of the AG not to prosecute and to close the file (a) are vexatious and harassing; and/or (b) amount to an abuse of the process of Court; and/or (c) are contrary to public policy.*

The AG raised a preliminary objection seeking to strike out questions 2 to 5 which he submitted were outside the scope of the court's constitutional function. It was submitted that the manner in which the AG exercised his powers was not a matter for determination before a Constitutional court, which it was argued, had no discretion or jurisdiction to inquire whether the powers are being exercised fairly or oppressively. The High Court dismissed the objection on the ground that all the questions concerned the inherent power of the court in the interpretation of section 26 of the Constitution. The court then proceeded to hear the substantive reference. In its decision, the court quoted with approval several English authorities and texts which pointed to the conclusion that the court has inherent jurisdiction to interfere in the exercise of the power of the AG to prosecute, if it appears, that such prosecution amounts to an abuse of the process of the court and is oppressive and vexatious. However, the court affirmed that it cannot direct a prosecution; in other words the court could not direct the AG to prosecute a particular individual. It emphasized that vide the provisions of section 26 of the Constitution, the AG was given unfettered discretion to institute and undertake criminal proceedings against any person. The decision to prosecute or not was the AG's alone. He was "not subject to the direction of control of any other person or authority." This included judges and magistrates in relation to the decision to institute criminal proceedings. Nevertheless, this discretion was to be exercised in a quasi-judicial way. That is, it was not be exercised arbitrarily, oppressively or contrary to public policy.

In answer to the substantive questions, the court was of the opinion that given the facts and circumstances of the case, the prosecution of Githunguri was vexatious and harassing, an abuse of the process of the court and contrary to public policy. The court was careful not to give any direction to the AG, other than answering the five questions posed. It was left to the Chief Magistrate to proceed with the trial, unless the AG, in light of the answers decided (as the court hoped he will) to terminate the proceedings or unless the accused applied for a prerogative order.[21]

As it turned out, despite the High Court answering the questions posed in a way that was not favourable to the AG, the AG opted not to terminate the criminal proceedings but to proceed with the same. This prompted Githunguri to file a second application. This was a judicial review application, seeking an order of prohibition to prohibit the trial magistrate from further proceeding to hear the case.[22]The application was initially heard by two judges who failed to reach a unanimous decision and as such the matter was referred to the Chief Justice who ordered that the application be heard *de novo* by three judges.[23] First the court observed that although the application as filed was strictly a judicial review application, it was of the view that typically such application was alleging an infringement of a constitutional right and proceeded to consider the application as though it was so brought under the provisions of section 84

21 Note that he had not applied for an order of prohibition in this application.

22 This is the case cited as *Githunguri v R (1986) KLR.*

23 One of whom was the Acting Chief Justice himself, Madan J.

(1) of the Constitution on enforcement of protective provisions.[24]The AG, in opposing the application, *inter alia* argued that to grant the application would be tantamount to curtailing or interfering with the powers of the AG under section 26 of the Constitution; that the AG had unlimited powers to institute proceedings and he was not to be under the direction of any authority especially where there was no time limitation on when the proceedings may be instituted. The court in reaching its decision posited that the application was not challenging the powers of the AG, but rather, the mode of exercise of those powers. The court was of the opinion that given the time lapse and the promises made by previous AGs not to prosecute, the applicant would not get a fair trial and it would be appropriate for the order of prohibition to issue and duly proceeded to issue the same.

To say that the case of *Githunguri* was a turning point in Kenyan jurisprudence would be an understatement, for it was the first time that the High Court had occasion to interpret the apparently wide powers granted to the AG to institute criminal proceedings. Of significant importance, the Court emphasized that it had jurisdiction to oversee the mode of exercise of that power and had jurisdiction to interfere, if a prosecution offended the rights of the accused as established in the Constitution. In *Githunguri 1*, the court emphasized that when the AG was making a decision whether to commence proceedings or not, he was exercising a quasi-judicial function, and he needed to act in a way that was not arbitrary and in the public interest. *Githunguri 2* was also important in recognizing that an order of prohibition could issue to restrain proceedings that were vexatiously instituted by the AG. Therefore, although the provisions of section 26 of the repealed Constitution gave the AG control over the commencement of criminal proceedings, the same were subject to the supervisory powers of the High Court provided under the then section 123(8) of the said Constitution.

The case of *Githunguri* was applied in several other subsequent cases decided in the regime of the former Constitution, including that of *Macharia & Another v AG & Another*,[25] where the applicants were charged with various offences

---

24 Which gave power to the High Court to determine any allegation of violation of fundamental rights and freedoms.

25 (2001) KLR 448.

ranging from obtaining money by false pretenses to forgery. The applicants filed an application for a declaration that the institution, prosecution and maintenance of the case against them was for purposes other than that of upholding criminal law; that it was meant to bring pressure to bear upon them to settle a pending civil dispute; that it was an abuse of the criminal process of the court; was oppressive, illegitimate, and contrary to public policy; and that it was in contravention of the applicant's rights under section 77 of the Constitution. The applicants thus sought an order of prohibition prohibiting the Magistrate's court from hearing or proceeding with the criminal case. The court in assessing the application, emphasized that the AG's discretion to arraign a person in court should be exercised in a quasi-judicial way. Further, it was held that the court can declare a prosecution to be improper if, it is for a purpose other than upholding the criminal law. The court agreed with the applicant that the case was meant to bring pressure to bear upon the applicants to settle a civil debt, that it was an abuse of the criminal process of the court, and that it amounted to harassment and was contrary to public policy and ultimately contravened the rights of the applicant's under section 77 of the Constitution.

The position in the 2010 Constitution is more explicit than it was in the former constitution, that the DPP must not abuse the process of court in undertaking prosecutions.

5.4.1 The Decision to Prosecute or Not to Prosecute

It is not in all cases in which a person is suspected to have committed a crime that the DPP will prosecute. The discretion to commence prosecution rests with the DPP and ultimately, it will be the DPP who will decide whether or not to prosecute.

In arriving at a decision to prosecute, the DPP must first have regard to the evidence and ensure that there is, in his opinion, sufficient evidence that can sustain the charge and result in a conviction. He ought not to prosecute where there is no evidence, for if he proceeds to do so, clearly the prosecution would be an abuse of the criminal process. Second, the DPP must comply with the provisions in the Constitution which require him to have regard to the public interest, the interest of administration of justice and the need to prevent and avoid abuse of the legal process.[26] The prosecutor therefore needs to do a balancing act in coming to the decision whether to prosecute or not. He must weigh the potential prosecution of the suspect against the public interest and arrive at a just decision given the surrounding circumstances.

It follows that it is not in all instances where evidence is available that he must prosecute. He may consider issues such as the triviality of the offence, the relationship of the suspect with the complainant (victim), reconciliation, the age of the accused, the situation of life of the suspect, and general public interest. Thus in the case *of Otieno Clifford Richard v R,*[27] (under the former Constitution) a private prosecution was commenced against the First Lady as the AG had opted not to prosecute her for a suspected assault of a photographer. The AG thereafter took over and terminated the proceedings. Perhaps this decision was driven by the status of the suspect (being the First Lady), the nature of the offence (a misdemeanor), and it may be that the AG felt that public interest would not be served if the First Lady was arraigned in court and prosecuted for such an offence.

Ultimately the decision to prosecute will be the Prosecutor's and it is doubtful whether he can be compelled to prosecute unless it can clearly be proven that he has violated his mandate under the Constitution by his failure to so prosecute. Even then, Courts should still be extremely cautious in entertaining an application to compel the DPP to prosecute, for there could be valid reasons not to prosecute despite there being ample evidence to sustain the charge.[28] It has been argued that for the purposes of practicality and the integrity of the judicial process particularly, the independence and impartiality of the office of the DPP, would be compromised if the courts were to decide or were to be in any way concerned with decisions as to who is to be prosecuted and for what.[29]

---

26 Constitution, Article 157 (11).

27 High Court at Nairobi, Misc. Civil Application No. 720 of 2005, (2006) eKLR.

28 Constitution, Article 157 (10); Section 6 (1) of the ODPP Act*;* See also *Clifford Otieno v R (ibid).*

29 *Connelly v DPP* (1963) 3 All ER 510 at 519 (1964) AC 1254 at 1277; *DPP v Humphrys* (1976) 2 All ER 497 at 527-528, (1977) AC 1 at 46 and *Barton v R* (1980) 147 CLR 75 at 94-95, 110; *Jago v District Court* (NSW) (1989) 168 CLR 23 at 38-39, 54, 77-78; *Williams v Spautz* (1993) 2 LRC 659 at 690, (1992) 174 CLR 509 at 548 and *Ridgeway v R* (1995) 3 LRC 273 at 320, (1995) 129 ALR 41 at 82.

The prosecutor must be allowed to make the decision whether "a prosecution will promote the ends of justice, instill a respect for law, and advance the cause of ordered liberty," and to take into account "the degree of criminality, the weight of the evidence, the credibility of witnesses, precedent, policy, the climate of public opinion, timing, and the relative gravity of the offense".[30]

The 2010 constitution overtly directs the office of the DPP to have regard to the public interest, the interests of the administration of justice and the need to prevent and avoid abuse of the legal process in exercising his powers.[31]Of significant importance, the High Court has through the provisions of Article 165 of the Constitution, explicitly been given powers that would include the interrogation of the exercise of the powers of the DPP. The determination that the DPP in exercising his powers to commence prosecution is undertaking a quasi-judicial function[32] brings him squarely under the radar of the High Court vide the provisions of Articles 165 (6) and (7) of the Constitution. The High Court would have supervisory jurisdiction on the mode of exercise of the powers of the DPP and the High Court may make any order considered appropriate for the fair administration of justice. Although the orders are not specified, it is not far to see that an order of prohibition is one that may be granted by the High Court while exercising its supervisory duties. Such order may either be directed to the court handling the matter or indeed to the DPP himself. This will be so if the Court feels that the DPP, is not, as he is required to have under Article 157 (11), regard to the public interest, the interests of the administration of justice and the need to prevent and avoid abuse of the legal process.

In *Kenya Commercial Bank Limited & 2 Others v Commissioner of Police and Another,*[33] the court stated as follows on its oversight role over the powers of the DPP :-

"the office of the Director of Public Prosecutions and Inspector General of the National Police Service are independent and this court would not ordinarily

---

30 *Pugach v. Klein*, 193 F. SMpp. 630, 634-35 (D.D.C. 1961).

31 Constitution, Art 157 (11).

32 *Githunguri v R, supra,* note 18.

33 High Court at Nairobi, Petition No. 218 of 2011, (2013) eKLR.

interfere in the running of their offices and exercise of their discretion within the limits provided for by the law. But these offices are subject to the Constitution and the Bill of Rights contained therein and in every case, the High Court as the custodian of the Bill of Rights is entitled to intervene where the facts disclose a violation of the rights and fundamental freedoms guaranteed under the Constitution."

The case of *Republic v Attorney General & 3 Others Ex-Parte Kamlesh Pattni*[34] is of interest since it touched on the prosecution of the key suspect to the Goldenberg Affair.[35] The applicant sought *inter alia* an order of prohibition to issue against the DPP or other authority from prosecuting or continuing to prosecute him. The applicant was then facing a court case that was commenced in the year 2006.[36] But prior to this case, the applicant had earlier been charged in the year 1993 and other criminal cases were later initiated. All these were either terminated or dismissed, and only one, instituted in the year 1997, proceeded. As at 1999, 26 prosecution witnesses had testified. The matter was then kept on hold to pave way for the Bosire Commission of Inquiry into the Goldenberg Affair. The commission rendered its report in August 2006, after which the new case, the subject of the judicial review proceedings, was commenced. Within the same trial, a new charge sheet was drawn in the year 2012. The arguments put forth by the applicant included the point that his right to be tried within a reasonable period of time had been infringed. He further cited other impediments to the impending trial that he saw as militating against a fair trial, such as loss of memory of potential prosecution or defence witnesses; death of witnesses in the intervening period; and loss of vital documentary evidence. With regard to the notion of fair trial, the applicant argued that he stood to suffer from the long period of time that has elapsed since the events occurred in 1990/1993.

---

34 High Court at Nairobi, Civil Misc. Application No. 305 of 2012, (2013) eKLR; See also *Republic v Judicial Commission of Inquiry into the Goldenberg Affair & 2 others ex Parte George Saitoti* (2006) eKLR and *Republic v Judicial Commission of Inquiry into the Goldenberg Affair & 2 others ex Parte Eric Cheruiyot* Juridical Review application H.C. Civil Application No. 416 of 2006.

35 The Goldenberg Affair, being a scandal in which the Government is said to have lost billions of shillings in an export compensation scam in the early 1990s.

36 Nairobi Chief Magistrate's Criminal Case No. 518 of 2006.

The court held that unless trial begins and concludes without unreasonable delay, an accused person's constitutional rights are violated, not only because of the delay, but also because of other incidental consequences of delay, such as loss of memory of witnesses, witnesses falling by the wayside in one way or another, and loss of documents, among other pertinent considerations. The court observed as follows:-

"Notwithstanding the convoluted history of the charges brought against the Applicant and others, being placed at a considerable and grave risk to freedom for nearly the past two decades is astounding, by any standards. Being placed at such risk for an indeterminable period of time with no end in sight must leave the conscience of the drafters of the Constitution shattered. For it is not the treatment the Constitution contemplated for any accused person, irrespective of their status in society. Criminal trials, decrees the Constitution, should be commenced and concluded within a reasonable time."

The court held that the criminal cases involving the applicant and his co-accused had failed to meet the constitutional thresholds of a fair trial and issued orders of inhibition, barring the continuance of the case before the Magistrate's Court.

It may be that at times, the matter in issue is pending in a civil suit, and one of the parties pushes for a criminal prosecution, in respect of the same subject matter. Though it is not the law that no criminal prosecution may be commenced when the matter is pending in a civil suit,[37] in some circumstances, the commencement of the criminal matter may be deemed to be an abuse of the process of court. This is precisely what transpired in the case of *Josephine Akoth Onyango & Another v DPP & Others.*[38] The petitioner was charged in the year 2012, with the offence of forging a land transfer instrument in the year 2003. The complainant was the previous owner of the land in issue and her complaint was that the petitioner fraudulently caused the property to be transferred in her name. Prior to the institution of the criminal proceedings, the complainant had filed a civil suit, seeking among other things, orders for a declaration that the transfer of the suit land was done fraudulently, without consideration, fraud

37 Criminal Procedure Code (CAP 75), Section 193.

38 Nairobi High Court, Petition No.471 of 2013, (2014) eKLR.

and misrepresentation. The petitioner argued that the criminal trial was an abuse of the power of the DPP and would embarrass the fair trial of the civil matter. The court, although appreciating that the presence of a civil case is no bar to a criminal case, held that on the facts, the criminal trial was an abuse of the process of court and an injunction stopping the DPP from prosecution was issued, pending the finalization of the civil suit.

There is no doubt that if for one reason or the other the High Court is of the opinion that the trial has been commenced for other extraneous purposes, or that the accused will not receive a fair trial, then the Court will interfere and prohibit the institution or continuance of such criminal proceedings. The fact that the High Court can make any order implies that the court can as well prohibit the DPP from prosecuting a particular case, buttressing the submission that the DPP will never be in absolute and unbridled control of the power to commence or continue proceedings.

5.4.2 The Power to Terminate Proceedings

The power to discontinue criminal proceedings is vested in the DPP under the provisions of Articles 157(6)(c), Article 157(7) and Article 157(8) of the Constitution and Section 25 (1) of the ODPP Act.[39] In a nutshell the above provisions empower the DPP to discontinue criminal proceedings at any stage before judgment is delivered. The DPP may discontinue a prosecution commenced by him or a private prosecution that he has taken over.[40]

The CPC provided (and still provides) for two modes of termination of proceedings. These are set out in Section 82 and 87. Section 82 of the CPC gives the prosecutor power to enter a *nolle prosequi* (which is a decision by the State that proceedings shall not continue), at any stage of the proceedings before judgment, and provides that thereupon, the accused shall at once be discharged.

---

39 ODPP Act, Section 25 (1) provides that, "*The Director may, with the permission of the court, discontinue a prosecution commenced by the Director, any person or authority at any stage before delivery of judgment.*"

40 Note that he requires permission to take over proceedings commenced by way of private prosecution pursuant to Article 157 (6) (b) of the Constitution.

Such discharge is not a bar to subsequent proceedings against the accused on account of the same facts.[41] Section 82 applies to all criminal cases irrespective of the status of the court. Section 87 applies to trials in subordinate courts and gives a public prosecutor, power to withdraw charges, either with the consent of the court or on the instructions of the DPP (formerly AG). Under Section 87, if the withdrawal is done before the accused is called upon to make his defence, he shall be discharged, which discharge is no bar to subsequent proceedings, but if the application is made after the accused person has been called upon to make his defence, he shall be acquitted. The powers to withdraw charges as provided under Section 82 and 87 of the CPC are therefore not the same.

In the former constitutional regime, the initial position of the courts was that the power of the AG to enter a *nolle prosequi* under Section 82 or withdraw charges under Section 87, could not be questioned by the court, this being argued to be an exercise of a constitutional power that was squarely at the discretion of the AG. In *Rupert Nderitu & Others v AG*,[42] the trial of the accused had proceeded and a prima facie case established. The accused were then put on their defence pursuant to the provisions of Section 210 of the CPC. The AG then entered a *nolle prosequi* before the defence case was closed. The court giving effect to the provisions of section 82 of the CPC discharged the accused. The accused were later re-arrested and charged with the same offence afresh. The accused persons then filed a constitutional application arguing that since the *nolle prosequi* was entered after they had been put to their defence, they had effectively been acquitted of the charges and thus the plea of *autrefois acquit* was available to them. The application was not successful, the court giving full effect to the words of Section 82, that the AG could enter a *nolle prosequi* at any stage of the proceedings before judgment and the same was no bar to subsequent proceedings being preferred.

With time however, the tide began to change and the courts began interrogating the mode of exercise of the powers of the AG to enter a *nolle prosequi*. The turning point was the case of *Crispus Karanja Njogu v Attorney General*.[43]

41 CPC, Section 82 (1).

42 Cited in B'wonon'ga, *"Procedures in Criminal Law in Kenya,"* East Africa Educational Publishers Ltd, 1994, at p155.

43 Nairobi High Court, Criminal Application No. 39 of 2000 (unreported).

The applicant in the case was charged with the offence of making a document without authority contrary to Section 357 (a) of the Penal Code. During the pendency of the trial, the respondent and complainant, Kenyatta University, publicly admitted that investigations had shown that the allegations about making fake degrees which led to the charges against the accused applicant were untrue. The AG then applied to enter a *nolle prosequi*, which was resisted, and the matter was referred to the High Court[44] for interpretation of the terms upon which a case, such as the one facing the accused, could be terminated by entry of a *nolle prosequi*. The AG admitted that the *nolle* was being entered because the prosecution had no evidence against the applicant. The High Court affirmed that it had jurisdiction to interrogate the mode of exercise of the discretion by the AG to enter a *nolle prosequi*. The Court stated as follows with regard to the powers of the AG to enter a *nolle prosequi*:-

"We however do hold that despite the provisions of section 26 (8) of the Constitution, the powers of the AG under section 26 (3) of the Constitution are subject to the jurisdiction of the Courts by virtue of section 123 (8) of the Constitution. Where therefore the exercise of the discretion to enter a nolle prosequi does not meet the test of Constitutionality by virtue of section 123 (8) of the Constitution, then the nolle prosequi so entered will be deemed and declared unconstitutional."

In the event, the High Court was of the opinion that the exercise by the AG of the power of *nolle prosequi* had been capricious and oppressive and amounted to an abuse of the process of court. The *nolle prosequi* was thus rejected with the court making an order for the trial of the accused to proceed in full.[45]

Similar holdings were made in the cases of *George Gitau Wainaina v AG,*[46] and in *Adan Keynan Wehyliye v Republic.*[47] In the latter case, the applicant was charged with murder. After eleven witnesses had testified, the DPP applied to enter a *nolle prosequi*. The intention of the DPP in terminating the charges was to charge the applicant afresh with the same offence but now jointly with another person who had testified in the trial of the applicant. The applicant

44 Under Section 67 of the repealed Constitution.

45 Eventually the trial proceeded and the accused was acquitted under S. 210 CPC.

46 High Court at Nairobi Criminal "Revision" No. 6 of 2003 (2008) eKLR.

47 Criminal Case No. 233 of 2003 (2005) eKLR.

filed a constitutional reference attacking the entry of the *nolle prosequi* in both technical and substantive grounds. It was submitted that allowing the *nolle prosequi* would infringe the rights of the applicant to a fair and speedy trial, that the reasons given in terminating the proceedings were merely for the convenience of the prosecution in intending to hold a joint trial, and generally that allowing the *nolle prosequi* at that stage of the trial would be an abuse of the court process. In responding to these submissions the court was of the view that, at that stage of the trial, the prosecution must have been aware of the line of defence that the applicant (as accused) intended to take, and to terminate the trial at that stage and charge the applicant afresh would be prejudicial to the applicant as the prosecution would have an unfair advantage thus leading to an unfair trial.[48]

In the current constitutional set up, Article 157(6) of the Constitution empowers the DPP to terminate proceedings at any stage before judgment. However, under Article 157(8) the DPP may not discontinue a prosecution without the permission of the court. Thus the DPP must first seek leave to terminate proceedings, and if the court declines to grant such permission, the proceedings must continue. If such permission is granted, then it follows that the proceedings will be terminated and depending on the stage of the proceedings, the accused will either be discharged or acquitted. If the DPP terminates proceedings after the close of the prosecution case, then the accused must be acquitted of the charges, meaning that he cannot be prosecuted afresh as the plea of *autrefois acquit* will be available to him. Both Sections 82 and 87 of the CPC must now be held to have been modified by the provisions of Article 157(7) and (8) of the Constitution to the extent that permission must be granted by court to terminate proceedings, and secondly, that if the termination takes place after the close of the prosecution's case, the accused shall be acquitted. It is immaterial that Section 82 still provides that if the DPP enters the *nolle prosequi*, irrespective of the stage of the proceedings, the accused only obtains a discharge and may be subsequently be charged with the same offence. It will indeed be prudent that both Sections 82 and 87 of the CPC be amended to conform to Article 157 of the Constitution.

---

48 See also *Moses Miheso Lipeya v R*, High Court at Kakamega High Court Revision No. 7 of 2007 (2007)eKLR and *Billy Elias Nyonje v R*, High Court at Kakamega, Criminal Application No. 34 of 2002 (unreported).

In the former constitutional dispensation, it was debatable whether the subordinate court had any role to play or whether it had power to interrogate the reason behind the entry of a *nolle prosequi* by the AG. Although some decisions appeared to suggest that the subordinate court had discretion to either accept or decline a *nolle prosequi*[49], the law made no such provision, but there was no doubt that the High Court had power to look into whether the *nolle prosequi* was fair exercise by the AG of his prosecutorial discretion.

The 2010 Constitution has removed any doubts. Permission of the court will be required vide the provisions of Article 157 (8) and this seems to infer that the DPP will seek this permission from the trial court, irrespective of whether the trial court is a subordinate court. Inevitably, the trial court will have to make a decision on whether or not to accept the *nolle prosequi* and this will certainly involve an interrogation as to whether the entry of the *nolle prosequi* is a proper exercise by the DPP of his powers to terminate proceedings.

In *Republic v Enock Wekesa & another,*[50] decided after the Constitution of 2010, the State had applied to enter a *nolle prosequi* that was rejected by the trial magistrate court. The State filed a revision and *inter alia* argued that it is only the High Court which can question the functions of the AG with regard to entry of a *nolle prosequi.* The High Court rejected this view and held that the trial court, irrespective of whether it is a subordinate court, has power to interrogate the entry of a *nolle prosequi* and either allow or reject it under the 2010 Constitution.

It is expected that in arriving at a decision on whether or not to grant or decline permission to withdraw charges, the trial court will follow the same principles and standards that the High Court had set when interrogating the exercise by the AG of his power to enter a *nolle prosequi* in the previous constitutional regime. The approach that the High Court gave in determining whether the AG had exercised his powers properly, were basically anchored on the premise that the AG needed to act in good faith, with regard to the public interest and

---

49 See for example *Republic v Islam A. Omar & 2 Others*, High Court at Nakuru, Criminal Case No. 57 of 2007 (2007) eKLR.

50 High Court at Kitale, Misc. Criminal Revision No. 267 of 2010, (2010) eKLR.

prevent an abuse of the process of court. This it will be observed are more or less the requirements now set out in in Art 157 (11) of the Constitution.

5.5 Private Prosecutions

A private prosecution refers to a prosecution that has been instituted by persons, other than the office of the DPP or those authorized to prosecute on behalf of the public. The mechanism provided by a private prosecution has been hailed as a useful constitutional safeguard against capricious, corrupt or biased failure or refusal of police forces and the office of DPP to prosecute offenders against the criminal law.[51] Private prosecution allows a person aggrieved by the failure of the DPP to commence prosecution, to himself proceed to prosecute the suspected offender.

The Constitution of 2010 does not explicitly mention a private prosecution. The same can however be inferred by a reading of Art 157 (6) (b) which sets out that the DPP shall have power to take over and continue any criminal proceedings commenced in any court (other than a court martial) that have been instituted or undertaken by another person or authority, with the permission of the person or authority. The term "other person or authority" can only mean a person who is not a public prosecutor, hence a private prosecutor. The ODPP Act, is more direct as it provides that any person may institute a private prosecution.[52]

The DPP can take over such proceedings but with the permission of the person or authority who instituted such proceedings. If taken over, the DPP can opt to proceed with it or to terminate such proceedings, just as he would have power to do so, if the proceedings were instituted by his office. The right to private prosecution was also envisaged under the repealed Constitution at section 26 (3) (b).The AG was however empowered to take over such proceedings as he wished and he did not have to seek the permission of the private prosecutor unlike the position in the present Constitution.

---

51 *Gouriet v Union of Postal Office Workers* (1978) AC 435.

52 ODPP, Act Section 28 (1).

5.5.1 Instituting a Private Prosecution

Unlike a public prosecution, a private prosecution is not simply instituted by filing an already drawn up charge to the court for a plea to be taken. First the private prosecutor must seek permission from the court to commence the private prosecution[53] and the prosecution cannot proceed if leave is denied. In the case of *Clifford Otieno v R*[54], it was stated that it is good practice and an important safeguard, if the application for leave to commence the prosecution, were served on the accused person and the accused be allowed to address the court if he so desires to do so.

A person so permitted to commence a private prosecution may prosecute in person or through an Advocate. Section 89 of the CPC provides for the manner of drawing a complaint and Section 90 for summons or warrants of arrest and these aptly apply to private prosecutions. Any person who institutes private prosecution shall, within thirty days of instituting such proceeding, notify the DPP in writing of such prosecution.[55]

5.5.2 Principles to be Applied in Granting Leave to Prosecute

There are considerations that the court should take into account before granting permission to prosecute. In *Kimani v Kahara,*[56] the court was of the view that the following factors are important before a private prosecution is commenced i.e. it must be demonstrated that -:

(i) The DPP or other public prosecuting bodies or persons have failed to commence a prosecution.
(ii) The complaint must disclose an offence known to law.
(iii) *Locus Standi* to the effect that the complainant has must have suffered personal injury or damage.

---

53 CPC, Section 89.

54 *Supra*, note 27.

55 ODPP Act, Section 28 (2).

56 (1985) KLR 79 at 86.

The first two requirements are obvious, for if the public authorities have commenced a prosecution, then there would be no purpose to institute a private prosecution. One can also only be prosecuted for an offence known in law. If in the opinion of the magistrate no offence is disclosed, the magistrate can decline to give permission to prosecute as was the scenario in the case of *Jopley Constantine Oyieng v R.*[57]

The jurisprudence points at the need to first make a report to the DPP and exhaust the public prosecution machinery before embarking on a private prosecution. In *Floriculture International Limited and Others,*[58] cited in the case of *Clifford Otieno v R,*[59]Kuloba, J. held that:-

"For all these reasons criminal proceedings at the instance of a private person shall be allowed to start or to be maintained to the end only where it is shown by the private prosecutor;

(1) that a report of the alleged offence was made to the Attorney General or the Police or other appropriate public prosecutor, to accord either of them a reasonable opportunity to commence or take over the criminal process, or to raise objection (if any) against prosecuting; that is to say, the complainant must firstly exhaust the public machinery of prosecution before embarking on it himself; and

(2) that the Attorney General or other public prosecutor seized of the complaint has taken a decision on the report and declined to institute or conduct the criminal proceedings; or that he has maintained a more than usual and reasonable reticence; and either the decision or reticence must be clearly demonstrated; and

(3) that the failure or refusal by the State agencies to prosecute is culpable and, in the circumstances, without reasonable cause, and that there is no good reason why a prosecution should not be undertaken or pursued; and

(4) that unless the suspect is prosecuted and prosecuted at the given point of time, there is a clear likelihood of a failure of public and private justice; and

(5) the basis for the locus standi, such as, that he has suffered special and exceptional and substantial injury or damage, peculiarly personal to him, and that he is not motivated by,

---

57 *Jopley Constantine Oyieng v R,* Criminal Appeal No. 45 of 1988 (unreported).

58 High Court Misc. Civil Application No. 114 of 1997 (unreported)

59 *Supra,* note 27.

malice, politics, or some ulterior considerations devoid of good faith, and

(6) *that demonstrable grounds exist for believing that a grave social evil is being allowed to flourish unchecked because of the inaction of a pusillanimous Attorney General or Police force guilty of a capricious, corrupt or biased failure to prosecute, and that the private prosecution is an initiative to counter act the culpable refusal or failure to prosecute or to neutralize the attempts of crooked people to stifle criminal justice."*

The point was also impressed in the case of *Amwona & Others v KBL*[60], (again cited in the *Clifford Otieno* case).[61] Emukule J. stated as follows:-

"In our custom and practice, where an offence is alleged to have been committed, or that there is a conspiracy in the air to commit a crime, an offence, cognizable in law, the first public right of defence is to hie and hasten to report the matter to the nearest Police Station. That is the exhortation of "Utumishi Kwa Wote" that is spread all over the city "to help us fight crime." ***If there is no response from the Police, or the Police appear reluctant to take up the matter, the next course of action is to report or write to the AG who has power*** *under section 26(4) of the Constitution(now repealed) to require the Commissioner of Police to investigate any matter which, in the AG's opinion, relates to any offence or alleged offence or suspected offence, and the Commissioner is bound to comply with that requirement and is further bound to report to the Attorney General upon such investigation. If the Plaintiff has exhausted those channels and to his dismay, neither the Police, nor the Attorney General take up his complaint he/she is legally entitled to seek permission under section 88(1) of the CPC, to institute what is commonly called a "private" or a "citizen's" prosecution."*

From the above principles, it needs to be appreciated therefore that a private prosecution is a fallback position which ought only to be entertained when the DPP has failed to act, as the essence of a private prosecution is not to allow persons to usurp the position of the DPP in prosecuting.

The private prosecutor also needs to demonstrate *locus standi*. Generally, it is accepted that a private prosecutor should not prosecute on behalf of the public interest. To so prosecute on behalf of the public is to usurp the powers of the DPP. One therefore needs to demonstrate a personal interest before being

---

60 High Court, Misc. App. No 19 of 2004.

61 *Supra*, note 27.

allowed to privately prosecute.[62] As noted in the *Kahara* case,[63] no provision is made in the CPC for a private prosecution in the High Court or for an appeal by a private prosecutor. This is because a private prosecutor does not prosecute on behalf of the public interest.

It was stated in the case of *Gregory v Nottingham*[64] that private prosecutions would generally exclude serious criminal matters and that it largely applies where limited private interests are involved. On this account the private prosecutor must not set himself in competition with the DPP, in the conduct of prosecutions. Further the court noted that where the DPP has previously instituted proceedings and thought it fit to terminate them, it is imprudent for a private prosecutor to file new proceedings under a private prosecution. However, an open window was left to a private prosecutor who disagrees, for good cause, such as bad faith or corruption, to challenge the decision of the DPP to terminate proceedings, but such person must apply directly to the High Court.

It is important to note that once a private prosecution has been permitted, the prosecution is conducted by the private individual as representing the State in the prosecution and the private prosecution should never be confused for a civil suit. It is always the State who is the complainant, as every criminal offence is deemed to be an assault against the State, and a criminal trial is always a trial being conducted by the State, even where the prosecutor is a private individual and not from the Public Prosecutor's office. It is therefore improper to title a private prosecution as one would title a civil suit as was the case in *Riddlesbarger v Robson.*[65] It was emphasized in the said case that the correct title should be *R through Rufus Riddlesbarger (*Prosecutor) *v Brian John Robson* (Accused). A properly titled case was *Republic through Devji Kanji v Davendra Valji Halai.*[66]

Permission is a key element in every private prosecution although in instances where the prosecution has continued, it may be implied that permission was

---

62 See *Gregory & Another v Republic through Nottingham & 2 Others* (2004) 1 KLR 547.

63 *Supra,* note 56 at p86.

64 *Supra,* note 62.

65 *Riddlesbarger v Robson* (1959) EA 841.

66 *Republic through Devji Kanji v Davendra Valji Halai* (1978) KLR 178.

granted.[67] It would follow that once the complaint is allowed the Magistrate has to formally draw up the charges. There seems to be no bar to the charges being drawn by the Private Prosecutor and adopted by court. Once the charges are drawn, a summons requiring the presence of the accused would issue for his attendance and the taking of plea. The matter would thereafter proceed as any other criminal trial. It should be kept in mind that the procedure for instituting private prosecution proceedings has not changed even with the coming into force of the Constitution of 2010. The procedures in the previous constitutional dispensation still prevail as was held in the case of *Aluochier v Stephen Kalonzo Musyoka & 217 Others.*[68]

5.5.3 Who May Institute a Private Prosecution?

There are no limitations as to the persons who may institute private prosecutions so long as the condition on *locus standi* is met. However, vexatious litigants are barred from conducting private prosecutions without the written consent of the Attorney General (now DPP). This is provided for in section 4 of the Vexatious Proceedings Act.[69] Section 2 defines a vexatious litigant as one who has been declared as such by the High Court on grounds that he has habitually and persistently and without any reasonable grounds instituted vexatious proceedings.

5.5.4 Control of Private Prosecutions

The current constitution provides that the DPP may take over a private prosecution with the permission of the person who commenced the prosecution. The private prosecutor can decline the offer by the DPP and proceed with the matter. However, if he surrenders the matter to the DPP, he thereafter loses control of the case and the DPP is free to either continue with the case or to withdraw it, as he deems fit. The position that prevailed in the former constitutional regime was that the AG could take over any private prosecution

67 *Ibid.*

68 Nairobi High Court, Petition No. 339 of 2013, (2013) eKLR.

69 (CAP 41) Laws of Kenya.

without first seeking permission from the private prosecutor and deal with it as he deems fit. The experience was that the AG would take over and terminate such proceedings.[70]

Though private prosecutions are provided for, it is not common to find such prosecutions. Private prosecutions by their nature are not easy to conduct and are expensive to the prosecutor. This is because the prosecutor must investigate the matter with his own resources, avail witnesses with his own resources and pay for legal representation. There is also the risk of being condemned to pay costs in case of an acquittal although costs may be awarded in case of a conviction.[71]

* * *

70 *Clifford Otieno v R*, supra note 27.

71 CPC, Section 171.

CHAPTER 6

CHARGES

6.1 Introduction

A criminal trial is commenced by way of filing of a charge or charges against the suspect who now becomes the accused. These are filed in the appropriate court registry. The term "Charge" has two connotations; one the document that is filed and secondly the content thereof, i.e., the offence that the person has been charged with. The document that contains the charges is popularly referred to as the "Charge Sheet." A person cannot be charged for an act or omission which at the time it was committed was not an offence in Kenya or was not a crime under international law.[1] Every accused person is entitled to a fair trial and one of the ingredients of a fair trial is the right to be informed of the charge, with sufficient detail to answer it.[2]

Under Section 134 of the Criminal Procedure Code (CPC)[3] every charge is required to contain two elements. The first is the statement of the specific offence(s); the second is the particulars, to give reasonable information as to the nature of the offence charged. A charge or information[4] is sufficient if it meets these two requirements. The statement of the offence sets out the law, and the sections of the law, which are alleged to have been contravened by the accused person. The particulars of the offence usually provide a brief detail of

---

1 Constitution of Kenya, 2010, Article 50 (2) (n).

2 *Ibid.* A similar provision existed under Section 77(2) (b) of the former constitution.

3 Chapter 75, Laws of Kenya.

4 "Charge" is the term used for charges before the subordinate court, whereas "information" is the term used for charges before the High Court.

how, where and when, the offence was committed.[5] It is a requirement that the charge be in writing[6] and therefore one cannot be charged in court orally. A charge can be said to similar to pleadings in civil cases. The very essence of a charge is to first, bring to the attention of the court, the offence allegedly committed by the accused person and secondly, to bring to the attention of the accused person, the allegations against him so as to enable him prepare a defence.

The rule of the thumb is that charges should be clearly framed in a simple language so that the accused person, who in normal circumstance, is a lay man, may know what he is accused of. A proper reflection of the law, will enable the accused person put up his defence. This goes to satisfy one of the basic tenets of a good criminal system: to allow the accused person to defend himself before a conviction and sentence may be passed upon him.[7]

It is the Republic which prefers charges on behalf of the public and therefore all charges are brought in the name of the Republic. Every criminal charge will therefore be the Republic against the accused. Crimes are assumed to be wrongs against the State and that is the reason that they are brought in the name of the Republic. Although there is always the person who is aggrieved by the commission of the offence, popularly called the complainant, that person is merely a complainant by fact i.e. the *de facto* complainant. The legal complainant is always the State. This is the case even where the person who has brought the charges is a private individual acting under the right of private prosecution. He still prosecutes on behalf of the State. Most, though not all of the charges are preferred by the Police.[8]

---

5 CPC, Section 137.

6 *Ibid.*

7 *R v University of Cambridge* (1723) 1 stra, 557 cited in the case of *John v Rees & Others (1969)* 2 All E.R 274, where it was succinctly adumbrated *"Even God himself did not pass sentence upon Adam before he was called upon to make his defence."*

8 Some departments or government agencies prefer charges on their own such as the National Social Security Fund, the National Health Insurance Fund, County Governments, and the Anticorruption Authority.

6.2 Joinder of Charges/Counts

Charges are usually framed in the form of "counts". A count constitutes a single offence alleged to have been committed. It is permissible for several offences to be charged and tried together (i.e. there may be a joinder of counts) whether they be felonies or misdemeanors[9] so long as;-

they are founded on the same facts; or form part of a series or offences of the same or a similar character.[10]

The rules as to joinder of counts need to be specifically followed. Thus either one or the two specified elements that would allow for a joinder have to be present. If offences are tried together, and they are not founded on the same facts, or do not form part of a series of offences of a similar character, then there would be a misjoinder of counts. Separate trials need be held in such a situation. Where they are so charged, a description of each offence must be set out in a separate paragraph of the charge, the so called "counts".

To demonstrate a joinder of charges, let us take the simple example of several traffic offences. Let us assume that ACC is driving a motor-vehicle while he is under the influence of alcohol; and the vehicle is defective and overloaded. Let us further assume that he is stopped by a traffic police officer, but he fails to stop. He is eventually apprehended, but in the course of arrest, assaults the police officer. From the above facts, ACC, has respectively committed the offences of driving under the influence of drink[11], driving a defective motor-vehicle[12], driving an overloaded motor vehicle[13], failing to stop[14], and assault of a police officer[15]. There is no doubt that these offences are derived from the same facts, or at least, form part of a series. They can therefore be tried together in one trial.

---

9 Felony meaning an offence punishable with death or imprisonment for 3 years and above; any other offence is a misdemeanor. See S.4 Penal Code, Chapter 63, Laws of Kenya.

10 CPC, Section 135.

11 Traffic Act, Section 85.

12 *Ibid*, Section 55.

13 *Ibid*, Section 56.

14 *Ibid*, Section 51(c).

15 Penal Code, Section 253(b).

There are five distinct offences committed, and therefore ACC, will be charged with five counts. If a joinder of counts was not permitted, it would mean that a separate trial would have to be held for each particular offence, irrespective of whether the evidence was the same. That would mean five distinct trials against ACC, and it would also mean that the witnesses be recalled for each trial to repeat the same evidence. A joinder of counts is therefore used not only to save time, but more so for convenience, for all the five offences can be tried in one trial. This ensures that the one trial can be utilised to simultaneously try several offences alleged to have been committed over the same facts, same series, or are of the same character.

The court is however at liberty to order that a person be tried separately for each offence if it feels that the accused may be embarrassed in his defence by reason of being charged with more than one offence, in the same charge, or that it is fair for other reasons that the offences be tried separately. This would indeed be the correct thing to do if the counts are so numerous as to render the charge sheet "overloaded" or "overburdened."

In *Omboga v R*[16], the appellant, an accounts clerk with the judiciary, was charged in the magistrate's court with two counts: fraudulent false accounting contrary to section 331 of the Penal Code, and stealing by a person employed in the civil service contrary to section 280 of the Penal Code. In the first count, he was charged with receipt of money and that he knowingly furnished a false statement of Kshs.749/= received by him. In the second count it was framed that he stole a total of Kshs.749/= which came into his possession by virtue of his employment. Evidence was given by five persons that on various dates they paid money for court fees and were either given receipts for lesser amounts or no receipt at all. He was convicted. At his first appeal, the judge noted that the first count was defective, in that the appellant was alleged to have made a number of false entries and he should have been charged separately for each false entry. He however held that no prejudice or failure of justice resulted. The judge did not comment on the second count. On second appeal to the Court of Appeal, the court was of the view that the first count which charged in omnibus form a general allegation of fraudulent false accounting extending over a period of a year was incurably bad. To prove the charge, the prosecution adduced evidence

16 (1983) KLR 340.

of a series of separate acts, each one of which could, and should, have formed the subject of a separate charge. As the charge was framed, the appellant could not possibly have known what offence was being charged against him. The second count was equally defective. These were a series of offences, committed on different dates, each one of which should have been the subject of a separate charge. The court held that the defects caused prejudice to the appellant with the result that the appeal was allowed.

In *Obanda v R,*[17] the appellant was convicted of three counts of corruption contrary to section 3 (1) of the Prevention of Corruption Act,[18] by the magistrate's court. There was an alternative to the first count, a charge of demanding with menace contrary to section 302 of the Penal Code, on which the magistrate made a finding that it was proved beyond reasonable doubt but did not convict, which was the correct course to do. In the course of appeal the Court of Appeal considered the question of joinder. It stated thus *"two different offences may constitute a series and their joinder is possible even if they do not arise out of the same acts or part of a system of conduct but one requirement is that a sufficient nexus must exist. This would exist if the evidence of one is admissible in the trial of the other. An alternative rule is that the two or more offences should exhibit such similar features that they could conveniently be tried together in the general interest of justice which would take account of the interest of the accused, witnesses and police…If there are some special features which make joinder prejudicial or embarrassing to the accused or the offences are too numerous or complicated, the magistrate should in his discretion sever them and order separate trials."*[19]

In the instant the court held that the offences to which *Obanda* pleaded not guilty before the trial magistrate, were not too numerous or complicated, and there was no special feature about them, which prejudiced him or embarrassed him, or his advocate, so there was no call for them to be severed. The appeal was dismissed.

---

17 (1983) KLR 507.

18 Chapter 65 Laws of Kenya.

19 *Supra*, note 17 at p 521.

In *Ochieng v R,*[20] the appellant was a clerk in the accounts office in the provincial headquarters in Kisumu. His duties involved the receiving of invoices from transporters providing services to the police department and preparing payment vouchers against those invoices. He was charged with forty-four counts alleging forgery, fraudulent false accounting and uttering and stealing by a person employed in the public service, all covering twelve transactions over a period of nearly six months. Eleven of the twelve transactions comprised at least three offences, namely, forging of an invoice from a transporter, forging a payment voucher to match it and stealing the sum stated in those documents. The appellant was convicted on eleven counts of forging invoices, eight of forging payment vouchers and four of stealing by a public servant. His first appeal to the High Court was allowed in respect of two counts only, and he filed a second appeal to the Court of Appeal. In the course of determining the appeal, the court had occasion to give opinion on the number of counts that may be laid in one charge sheet. The court stated obiter that it was undesirable to charge an accused person with so many counts in one charge sheet. That alone may occasion prejudice. It is proper for the court to put the prosecution to its election at the inception of the trial as to the counts, upon which it wishes to proceed. Usually, though not mandatory, no more than twelve counts should be laid in one charge sheet. The others can be withdrawn under section 87 (a) of the CPC which will entitle the prosecution to bring them again if necessary. Moreover, the possibility of embarrassment and prejudice to the defence cannot be excluded when there are numerous counts, because of the danger of an assumption, that because the accused faces so many charges, there must be substance in some of them. In the instant case, the court however held that no prejudice was occasioned.

In the English case of *R v Novac & Others,*[21] the point was put forth as follows:-

"We cannot conclude this judgment without pointing out that, in our opinion, most of the difficulties which have bedeviled this trial, and which have led in the end to the quashing of all convictions except on the conspiracy and related counts, arose directly out of the overloading of the indictment. How much worse the difficulties would have been if the case had proceeded to trial on the original indictment,

---

20 1985 (KLR) 252.

21 *R v Novac & Others* (1977) 65 CAR 107, at 118.

containing 38 counts, does not bear contemplation. But even in its reduced form, the indictment of 19 counts against four defendants resulted, as is now plain, in a trial of quite unnecessary length and complexity."

Earlier in *R v Hudson and Hagan,*[22] the court addressed the matter of joinder of counts in the following manner, *"The court has on many occasions pointed out how undesirable it is that a large number of counts should be contained in one indictment. Where prisoners are on trial and have a variety of offences alleged against them, the prosecution ought to be put on their election and compelled to proceed on a certain number only. Quite a reasonable number of counts can be proceeded on, say, three, four, five or six, and then, if there is no conviction on any of those, counsel for the prosecution can consider whether he will proceed with any other counts in the indictment. If there is a conviction, the other counts can remain on the file and need not necessarily be dealt with unless this court should for any reason quash the conviction and order the others to be tried. But it is undesirable that as many counts as were tried together in this case should be tried together..."*

6.3 Joinder of Persons

It is allowed for more than one person to be joined in one charge and such persons may be tried together. It is not the position that a person must be tried alone for the offence he has committed, even where the offence was committed jointly. It is permissible for the following persons to be tried together[23] –

(i) *Persons accused of the same offence committed in the course of the same transaction.* (for example two gangsters).
(ii) *Persons accused of the offence, and persons accused of abetment or attempt to commit the offence.* (Here you have the principal offender and another who for example assists the offender. For example A may steal an item, then B who was not involved in the stealing, aids him to escape).
(iii) *Persons accused of more offences than one of the same kind committed by them jointly within a period of 12 months.* (This is a case of several offences but committed jointly. For example a gang of four gangsters may have

22 *R v Hudson and Hagan* (1952) 36 CAR 94 at p95.

23 Sections 136 (a) - (f), CPC.

committed three separate robberies together. For these to be tried in one trial, the incidences must have occurred within a period of 12 months).

(iv) *Persons accused of different offences committed in the course of the same transaction.* (This situation may arise where there are several offenders but not all commit the same offence. They can all be tried together so long as the individual offence (s) is committed in the same transaction. For example a prison officer may aid a prisoner to escape. The prisoner will be charged with the offence of escaping from lawful custody whereas the prison officer will be tried with a separate offence of aiding a prisoner to escape. They are different offences committed by different people but in the course of the same transaction, i.e. the escape from prison).

(v) *Persons charged with committing an offence under Part 26-30 of the Penal Code*[24]*, can be tried alongside persons accused of receiving or retaining property which came into their possession by virtue of being transferred from the first accused persons, or of abetting or attempting to commit either of the last offences.* (For example one person may steal and another, who was not involved in the stealing, later retains such property. The two can be tried together).

(vi) *Persons accused of an offence relating to counterfeit coin under Part 36 of the Penal Code can be charged alongside persons accused of another offence under that part relating to the same coin, or of abetting or attempting to commit such an offence.*

In *Ngoya v R,*[25] the six appellants were jointly charged in the magistrate's court with three counts of robbery with violence, one of burglary and one of shop-breaking. All these offences were alleged to have been committed on the night of 30/31 May 1979 by a gang of robbers armed with firearms. In the same charge sheet, the 4th, 5th and 6th appellants were further jointly charged, together with another man, with two further counts of robbery with violence. The offences were alleged to have been committed on the night of 23/24 June 1979. On the 9th June 1979, the 2nd and 3rd appellants were arrested being suspected of having been in the gang of May 30/31 and were in custody when the second attack of 23/24th June occurred. They were not therefore charged with the attack of May 30/31. They were convicted of the offences and their appeals to the High Court

---

24 These parts of the Penal Code cover offences related to theft, stealing, robbery and extortion, burglary and housebreaking, and obtaining by false pretences.

25 (1985) KLR 309.

dismissed. In the Court of Appeal, the court considered the question of joinder of persons and charges. The court noted that the first appellate court (the High Court) was of opinion that Section 136 (c) of the CPC covered the case.[26] The Court of Appeal differed with this view and was of opinion that section 136 (c) could not apply as the offences were not committed by all the accused jointly. The 2nd and 3rd appellants were in custody when the offences of 23/24 June were committed and they could not have participated, such that, those offences could not have been committed by the 2nd and 3rd appellants jointly with the 4th, 5th and 6th appellants. The Court of Appeal was of the opinion that however, the offences committed on both occasions were committed by the same gang, although not consisting of the same persons in both occasions, in that on both occasions the same weapons were used and the offences formed part of a series of offences of the same or similar character and thus the appellants were properly charged together under section 135 (1) of the CPC.[27]

6.4 Framing of Charges

The provisions with regard to how a charge is supposed to be drawn are found in Section 137 of the CPC. It provides for the rules of framing charges. First we should recall that the charge must contain the statement of the offence and the particulars thereof. There is no specific form which is acceptable. But whichever form is given it must follow the following rules.

(i) Every charge must commence with the statement of offence.
(ii) The statement of offence shall describe the offence shortly in ordinary language and reference to the section creating the offence.
(iii) After the statement of offence, the particulars of the offence should be set out in ordinary language.

---

26 Section 136 (c) of the CPC provides, *"Persons accused of more offences than one of the same kind (that is to say, offences punishable with the same amount of punishment under the same section of the Penal Code or of any other Act or law) committed by them jointly within a period of twelve months may be joined in one charge and tried together."*

27 Meaning a joinder of counts, *supra* paragraph 6.2 above.

(iv) The forms in the 2nd Schedule (of the CPC) are the prescribed forms for drawing charges but variations can be made according to the circumstances of each case.
(v) Where the charge contains more than one count, the counts must be numbered consecutively.
(vi) If there are alternative charges, the same should be set out in the alternative.
(vii) The description of property in a charge should be in the ordinary language and indicate with reasonable clearness the property referred to. It is not necessary to name the person to whom the property belongs to nor its value.
(viii) If the property is of more than one person it is enough to state that the property is owned by that person and others. If it is owned jointly as in a club, it is enough to provide the name of the joint body as the owner i.e. you can use the collective name without naming the individuals.
(ix) If property is of the public, it can be described as the property of the Government.
Coins, bank notes and currency, may be described as money.
(x) The Accused person must be described sufficiently to identify him. It is not necessary that his name be the correct name; it is also not necessary to state his abode, style or occupation. If his name is not known and he cannot be sufficiently described, he can be termed as an "a person unknown".
(xi) If an instrument or document is referred to in the charge, it is enough to describe it by the usual name.
(xii) The place, time, thing, or matter referred to in a charge should be described in ordinary language.
(xiii) In charges of intent, it is not necessary to state the person who was intended to be defrauded or injured, unless the enactment provides so.
(xiv) Figures and abbreviations may be used.
(xv) For offences between section 280-283 (of the Penal Code), it is enough to specify the gross amount of property in question and the dates between which the offence was committed without specifying the exact times or exact dates.
(xvi) Where a previous conviction is to be charged it is to be provided in a statement at the end of the charge.

6.5 Effect of Misjoinder of Counts or Persons, and Defects in the Charge Sheets

It is not always the case, that a misjoinder of either charges or persons, will vitiate the trial. So too a misjoinder of counts, or persons. The trial will only be vitiated if the defects have occasioned a miscarriage of justice.[28] This is provided for by Section 382 of the CPC which is drawn as follows:-

S. 382 Subject to the provisions hereinbefore contained, no finding, sentence or order passed by a court of competent jurisdiction shall be reversed or altered on appeal or revision on account of an error, omission or irregularity in the complaint, summons, warrant, charge, proclamation, order, judgment or other proceedings before or during the trial or in any inquiry or other proceedings under this Code, unless the error, omission or irregularity has occasioned a failure of justice:

Provided that in determining whether an error, omission or irregularity has occasioned a failure of justice the court shall have regard to the question whether the objection could and should have been raised at an earlier stage in the proceedings.

The court has to assess whether any prejudice has been caused. If there is no prejudice, then a conviction will not be reversed, solely on account of the misjoinder.[29] In *Malebe v R*,[30] the three appellants were charged jointly on separate counts, in one charge sheet, with the offence of stealing by servant. The particulars of the joint charge sheet alleged that the offences were committed on separate dates. The items alleged to have been stolen were different and the appellants were alleged to have stolen them on unknown dates between different months. Moreover, the appellants were not charged jointly as having had a common intention. They were convicted and each sentenced to 8 months imprisonment. They appealed against both conviction and sentence. The court in assessing the charges attacked the joint charge against the several persons, as they were alleged to have committed separate offences on different dates, and held that the same amounted to a misjoinder, and such charge was defective. There should have been a separate charge for each person and separate counts

28 See *Avone v R* (1969) EA 129.

29 CPC, Section 382.

30 (1982) KLR 320.

for each alleged offence committed on different dates; in other words, the two ought to have been charged separately. The misjoinder occasioned a miscarriage of justice since the accused did not know what charges were against them jointly or separately and when they were committed. The trial was declared a nullity.

A similar conclusion was arrived at in the case of *Kubanisi v R.*[31] The court was of the opinion that the lack of particulars in a charge sheet, in the circumstances, led to a miscarriage of justice. In the said case, the appellant was charged with the offence of attempting to commit a felony contrary to section 389 of the Penal Code. The particulars were that "*On ... (He) attempted to commit a felony contrary to section 389 of the Penal Code.*" The court held that the charge was bad for uncertainty because it did not state the felony that was alleged to have been attempted. In *James Omari Nyabuto & another v Republic,*[32] it was argued that the charge against the appellants was defective in that it omitted to state that the appellants had been "jointly charged" or "jointly with others not before court". The Court of Appeal agreed that there was a defect but hastened to add that they were not satisfied that the omission or the irregularity in the charge had occasioned the appellants any failure of justice.

In the case of *J.M.A v R,*[33] the appellant, *J.M.A*, was on 3rd June, 2003, presented before the Senior Resident Magistrate's Court, at Nanyuki with a charge sheet charging him with the main count of defilement of a girl aged under fourteen years contrary to section 145 (1) of the Penal Code, the particulars of which read as follows:

"*J.M.A: On the 27th day of May, 2003 in Meru Central District of the Eastern Province, had carnal knowledge of K. N.R a girl under the age of fourteen years.*" The appellant faced an alternative count of indecent assault on a female contrary to section 144 (1) of the Penal Code, and the particulars thereof read as follows: "*J.M.A: On the 27th day of May, 2003 in Meru Central District of Eastern Province, indecently assaulted K.N.R a girl under the age of fourteen years by touching her private parts.*"

---

31 (1965) EA 572. But see *Njunga v R* (1965) EA 773.

32 Court of Appeal at Kisumu, Criminal Appeal No. 194 of 2008, (2009) eKLR.

33 *J.M.A v R* Court of Appeal at Nyeri, Criminal Appeal No. 348 of 2007, (2009) eKLR.

On first appeal, the superior court, relying on a Court of Appeal decision,[34] held that the conviction of the appellant on the main charge was wrongful as the charge was fatally defective since the particulars in the charge did not allege that the act of having carnal knowledge was 'unlawful'. For that reason the court quashed the appellant's conviction on the main count of defilement of a girl under fourteen years of age and set aside the sentence of life imprisonment which had been imposed on him by the trial court. The court, however, held that the evidence supported the alternative count of Indecent Assault on a female contrary to section 144 (1) of the Penal Code. Accordingly it entered a conviction against the appellant for that offence, and thereafter sentenced him to a term of 15 years imprisonment with hard labour. The sentence was ordered to run from the date the appellant was convicted of the defilement charge. He appealed to the Court of Appeal. The particulars of the alternative count did not, also, include the term "unlawful". Section 144 (1) of the Penal Code as it then stood provided as follows: *"Any person who unlawfully and indecently assaults any woman or girl is guilty of a felony and is liable to imprisonment with hard labour for five years with or without corporal punishment."* The Court of Appeal noted that clearly both the main and alternative counts were defective to the extent that in both of them the term "unlawful" was not included in the particulars of the respective counts. However, in the opinion of the court, it was not in all cases in which a defect detected in the charge on appeal will render a conviction invalid. It referred to Section 382 of the CPC and held that the irregularities did not prejudice the appellant. The appeal was accordingly dismissed.

It therefore follows that a mere defect in the charge sheet will not necessarily nullify a conviction. The test of Section 382 of the CPC must be met, that is, the defect must have occasioned a miscarriage of justice.

6.6 Duplicity in Charges

The law sets out that every charge must be identified separately and its particulars provided. This is the "count" as we have seen earlier in the chapter. Every count should charge its one offence unless it is permitted by the law for a count to

[34] *Achoki v R* (2000) 2 EA 283.

charge more than two offences.[35] Where a count charges two offences it is described as being bad for duplicity. Such a charge may be subject to challenge, and if it has occasioned a miscarriage of justice, a conviction based on a charge that is duplex may be set aside. However, if there is no miscarriage of justice, a conviction even based on a charge that is bad for duplicity may be allowed to stand following the provisions of Section 382 of the CPC.

Thus in *Seidi v R*,[36] the court declined to set aside a conviction on a charge that was clearly duplex. In this case, the appellant was charged with four counts. First, causing death by reckless or dangerous driving; second, using a motor vehicle on the road with defective tyres; third using a motor vehicle on the road with defective brakes; and fourth, carrying passengers without a licence. He was acquitted on the third count but convicted on the rest. He appealed on conviction on counts 1 and 2. The facts of the case were that the appellant was driving a Land Rover[37] which was loaded with both goods and passengers. The car got a tyre burst, which was replaced, but the replacement tyre itself burst, causing the car to be involved in an accident. As a result three people died and twelve were injured. He was charged with the above counts. The charge was defective in that it did not clearly set out the particulars of the charge, and the facts on which the prosecution relied, as constituting reckless or dangerous driving. It also joined in one count the charge of causing the death of three separate persons and the injuries of twelve others. The court held that the joinder of the three deaths and twelve injured persons was however not prejudicial to the appellant. It was also noted that the facts relied to constitute the charge, included the condition of the vehicle and the speed at which it was driven, and these were omitted from the charge. The court was similarly of the view that the appellant was fully aware of the substance of the case he had to meet, and the defects in the charge, did not occasion a failure of justice. The defects were therefore curable under section 382 of the CPC.

---

35 For example, Housebreaking and Burglary as prescribed in the 2nd Schedule to the CPC.

36 (1969) EA 280.

37 A notoriously versatile 4 wheel drive vehicle.

A matter in which the court thought that there was a clear miscarriage of justice was the case of *Saina v R.*[38] In this case, the appellant was charged in a single count with the offences of shop breaking and theft, and as an alternative, the offence of handling stolen property. The alternative charge was also contained in the single count. He was convicted of the main count. On appeal it was held that each offence must be set out in a separate count and failure to do so was an incurable illegality. The court particularly singled out the alternative charge being contained in the single count as an incurable defect. Each offence ought to have been set out in a separate paragraph.

6.7 Filing Charges in the Alternative

Pursuant to the provisions of Section 137 of the CPC a charge can be framed in the alternative. If this is so, it must be clearly indicated that one charge is alternative to another. In such situation, the charge sheet has the "main charge/s" and the "alternative charge." The effect of having a main and alternative charge is that an accused person cannot be convicted for both offences, unlike the position, where the charges are in separate counts. If the accused is found guilty of the main charge, then it follows that there is no need of making a finding on the alternative charge.[39] If however the accused is acquitted on the main charge, the trial court must then assess whether the alternative charge is proved, and if so, proceed to convict the accused on the alternative charge.

This raises the question: why should charges be drafted in the alternative? The simple and straightforward answer to this is that there may be uncertainty as to whether the facts point to one offence or the other. In practice, it is common in cases where one is found with stolen property for charges to be drafted in the alternative. This is due to the fact that, the prosecutor may not be sure whether the person found with the property is the one who stole, or was merely handling stolen property, which is an offence in itself. The prosecutor may therefore frame a charge of stealing and an alternative charge of handling stolen property. As has already been stated above if the accused is found guilty of stealing, in this instance, then there would be no need to make a finding on the alternative

---

38 (1974) EA 83.

39 *Wainaina & Others v R* (1973) EA 182.

charge of handling stolen property. If he is acquitted of the main charge, then the court must move to the alternative charge and determine whether the same has been proved. If it has, then the accused will be convicted of the alternative charge of handling stolen property.[40]

In *Wainaina v R*,[41] the appellants were charged with incitement to violence, and in the alternative, with creating a disturbance in a manner likely to cause a breach of peace. It was proved that they had been part of a hostile crowd of hundreds, and all of the appellants had thrown stones at the police while speaking or shouting, although only in respect of three of them were the words identified. The magistrate found that the throwing of stones in these circumstances amounted to incitement to violence and also the lesser offence which he said was merged in the greater. On appeal it was held that having made a finding of guilt on the first charge, the magistrate should have made no finding on the alternative charge.[42]

A question may arise whether a defective main charge may support an alternative charge, an issue which arose in the case of *BMO v Republic.*[43] In this case, the appellant moved to the superior court and argued that the three main counts of defilement were incurably defective and they ought not to have been relied on to convict him. The defect in the charges was that they omitted to describe the acts of carnal knowledge as "unlawful". During the main trial, the learned trial magistrate had rejected the submission that the main charge of defilement was defective merely for omission of the word "unlawful". He found that the appellant could not be said to have misunderstood the nature of the charges and the omission did not occasion any failure of justice. No finding was made on the alternative charges, rightfully so, since the main charges were sustained. On appeal, the appellant argued that the charges as drawn were defective. It was further argued that this being the case, the evidence adduced in support of that charge dissipated with it, and could not be referred to as a foundation for a finding on the alternative counts.

---

40 *Bennault Oinamo v R* (1976) KLR 159.

41 *Supra* note 39.

42 Note that under Section 171 CPC, a trial court can convict on a lesser offence though not charged. See Chapter on Judgment.

43 *BMO v Republic* (2010) eKLR.

The learned Judge upon examining the provisions of Section 145(1) of the Penal Code agreed with the appellant that the main counts were incurably defective. The Judge quashed the convictions based on those counts and set aside the sentences. On the argument that the alternative charge therefore had to fail on that account, the court disagreed and stated as follows:-

"the practice of charging offences in the alternative is one of abundant caution and that is why no finding is made on such charges once there is ample evidence to support the main charge. If the main charge is not proved, either because it is defective or because the evidence on record does not support any element of the offence, the evidence does not evaporate into thin air! It may be examined to see if it supports a minor and cognate offence and if it does prove such offence beyond doubt, a conviction will follow. Many a times only the main charge in offences such as Murder, Robbery or Rape, for example, will appear on record. But it cannot be argued that if the evidence establishes minor and cognate offences such as manslaughter, theft or indecent assault respectively, the court cannot convict for those offences on the ground that they were not charged. So too with defilement. Indecent assault is a minor and cognate offence and was for consideration if the main charge was unsustainable. Section 179 of the CPC allows for such procedure.[44]

6.8 Filing of Conspiracy and other Charges

Conspiracy charges inevitably involve charging an accused for "conspiring" to commit an offence. By its very definition a conspiracy connotes the involvement of more than one person in the crime since it is not possible for one to conspire alone. Ordinarily, if the act that the accused were conspiring to commit has been done, the accused would be charged with the completed offence rather than to charge on a conspiracy. Since a person must have conspired alongside another, difficulties can arise when one of the accused persons is acquitted. Can the other accused then be convicted or must he be set free?

This issue arose in *Mulama v R*[45] where the appellate court frowned on the practice of charging on conspiracy charges instead of the specified complete

---

44 For a more elaborate discussion, see Chapter 11 on Judgment.

45 (1976) KLR 24.

offences. The matter had earlier arisen in acute fashion in the Ugandan case of *Uganda v Milenge.*[46] Several accused were charged jointly on five counts with various offences; the first count being of conspiracy to defraud, which first count, covered substantive offences in the four remaining counts. The magistrate ruled that the accused would be embarrassed if they had to defend all five counts and ordered the prosecution to elect either to proceed with the count of conspiracy alone and withdraw the other four counts or alternatively, withdraw the count of conspiracy and proceed on the other four counts. The State appeal to the High Court was dismissed and a further appeal was made to the Court of Appeal. It was held that the magistrate had a discretion to order a separate trial of the conspiracy charges and that this discretion was exercised correctly. This is intended to avoid an accused from being embarrassed in his trial.

It makes sense to charge on the separate complete offences rather than to charge on a conspiracy. The risk is that in the conspiracy charges, if one person is found not guilty, then, irrespective of the weight of evidence, the other co-accused must be set free, for one cannot conspire alone. When the complete offences are charged, it matters not that one co-accused is set free, for in this instance, each person has to answer to the separate charge individually. There is indeed little point of charging the conspiracy charge alongside the complete charge unless there are special reasons for doing so.

In *Uganda v Nikolla,*[47] N. and M. were jointly charged with "willfully and unlawfully" committing adultery. It came out at trial that although N did not know that M was married at the time he married her, (since M had not been legally divorced), N and M had committed adultery. The court held that it is undesirable in adultery cases that both the man and woman should be charged, unless they are likely to plead guilty, but if charged, there should be separate counts because the *mens rea* in each case is different.[48]

---

46 (1970) EA 269.

47 *Uganda v Nikolla* (1966) EA 345.

48 See also *Ayor v Uganda* (1968) EA 303 and *Charles Benon Bitwire v Uganda* Cr. Appeal No.23 Of 1985.

6.9 Charges in Common Intention

In *Kioko v R,*[49] the appellant, one Willy Nzioka Nyumu, was convicted of murder and sentenced to death. He had been accused alongside one Kioko and it was alleged that the two jointly killed the deceased. The two had been drinking prior to going to the home of the deceased where Kioko had gone to demand repayment of a debt from the deceased. When at the deceased homestead, they set upon him with weapons and the deceased died as a result. Kioko pleaded guilty to the reduced offence of manslaughter and was convicted and sentenced to seven years. The appellant's trial proceeded to full trial on the original charge of murder. After a hearing, the appellant was convicted of murder and sentenced to death. He appealed. The appellate court was of the opinion that since Kioko had been convicted of the lesser offence of manslaughter, the charge of murder against the appellant ought to have been amended for he could no longer be charged with having murdered the deceased jointly and in the course of a common design with Kioko, who was convicted only of manslaughter. A *nolle prosequi* should have been entered and a fresh information should have been filed. The conviction for murder was substituted for one of manslaughter.

6.10 Charges against Companies

In *Nterekeiya Bus Service v R,*[50] it was held that unincorporated bodies cannot be charged as they do not have a legal personality. On the other hand, companies can be charged but must be represented in court by an individual. In *Prabhulal v R,*[51] the appellant was a director of a limited company and was charged with unlawfully employing Miss. K, also a director of the company, knowing that she had no permit or was not exempted from the necessity of obtaining a permit. The charge sheet was made out in the name of the director/ West End Clothing Ltd. The court held that the charge was defective in not naming the director to be charged as the company had six directors, thus the description of the accused in the charge was clearly not reasonably sufficient. However, the court held that the defect was cured when the appellant appeared and pleaded to the charge.

---

[49] (1983) KLR 289.

[50] (1966) EA 333.

[51] (1971) EA 52.

A company may be charged as it is a person in law. However, it must be appreciated that a company is an abstract entity, and a human being has to answer to the charges on behalf of the company. Moreover, if there has to be punishment especially that of imprisonment, the company cannot be jailed, but a human being has to take that place in jail. That is the reason why the person to be charged on behalf of the company needs to be specified, so that it is clear who exactly is intended to be prosecuted and for what commission or omission.

6.11 Uncertain or Vague Charges

In *Kubanisi v R*[52] the charge was framed in the following terms:

Statement of offence: "Attempted to commit an offence C/Sec. 389 Penal Code."

Particulars: "Wandera Reuben Kubanisi on 29th January, 1965 at 8 pm at Bungoma Railway station in Bungoma District of Western province attempted to commit a felony cont. sec. 389 P.C.

The court held that this charge is bad for uncertainty because it did not state the felony that was alleged to have been attempted. The court added that contractions such as "cont.", "sec", and "P.C." should not be used in framing the particulars of a charge.

However, where the defect is not fatal, a conviction will not be set aside as was stated in the case of *Njunga v R.*[53] In this case, the appellant, driving a disguised car, took the police in a wild chase but successfully apprehended. Under the driver's seat of the car was a *Simi* (sword). He was charged with the offence of being armed by day with the intent to commit a felony contrary to section 308 (1) (d) of the Penal Code. The felony was however not disclosed. The trial magistrate convicted him. On appeal, the High Court was of the view that in such cases, the felony which the accused is alleged to have intended

52 *Supra,* note 31.

53 (1965) EA 773; See also *Nahashon Marenya v R* Nairobi H.C. Criminal Appeal 786 of 1982.

should be stated in the charge, and if there is doubt as to the particular felony intended, different felonies can be stated alternatively. The defect in the charge in this instance (where no felony was mentioned), would however not have been fatal to the conviction, had it been obvious from the evidence what the felony intended was said to be. The intended felony in the instance was robbery, but that intention was brought about by inadmissible evidence. It is only for this reason, rather than for the reason that the charge was defective, that the appeal was allowed.

6.12 Non – Existent Charges

In *Maitha & Another v Republic,*[54] the appellants were convicted of stealing and burglary and of being in possession of an offensive weapon "contrary to section 11 (1) and 56 Legal notice no 264/63." During the investigation for an offence of burglary, the police had found in the 1st appellant's house an iron bar which they claimed was an offensive weapon. The court held that the possession of an offensive weapon would only have been an offence if the appellant had the offensive weapon in the street or public place. Further, the charge was incurably defective. Legal Notice No. 264/63 did not create an offence and it did not have sections 11 (1) and 56. The case of *Uganda v Keneri Opidi,*[55] was cited and the facts of the case are prudent to set out. The accused person pleaded guilty firstly for failing to display an "L" plate and secondly, for being a learner driver, driving while not being accompanied by a competent driver. The first count was laid under "section 9 (b) of the Traffic Ordinance," and the second under "section 9 (a) and 12 of the Traffic ordinance 1951." It was contended that in support of a revisional order against conviction and sentence that the counts were manifestly wrong in law in that the first charge should have been laid under section 9 of the Traffic Regulations and that it was probable that the framers of the charges meant section 9 (b) of the Traffic regulations. The court held, in respect of the first count, there being no section 9 (b) of the Traffic ordinance (only section 9 which however did not create an offence) the particulars set out as constituting an offence clearly of themselves could

54 *Maitha & Another v Republic* (1989) KLR 206.

55 (1965) EA 614; see also *Abdul Rasur G. Sabur v R* (1958) E.A. 126 (U) and *Musoke v Uganda* (1972) EA 137.

not create an offence. Further, that the error was a fundamental one of law, in that the accused was charged with a non-existent offence, and such error was not curable by Section 347 of the CPC.[56]The court observed that, it was not competent for a court to speculate on the intention of the framers of the charge, but must be guided in determining such intention, by the expressions contained in the record of proceedings[57] and finally, it being impossible to ascertain from the record whether the second count was laid under the *Traffic ordinance* or *Traffic Regulations*, the charge was bad.

However, in *Sabur v R,*[58] the appellant was charged with committing a traffic offence contrary to section 39(1) instead of being charged under section 40(1) of the Traffic Ordinance of 1951.[59] On appeal it was held that since the particulars of the offence were adequate to inform the appellant of the offence with which he was charged, there had been no failure of justice, and the defect was curable.

It would appear that again, the test, will be whether the defect is one which was capable of causing a miscarriage of justice in the circumstances of the case. If the offence which the accused is charged is clear, and can only fall under a particular section of the law, without doubt or ambiguity, it is arguable that the citation of the wrong provision of the law in the charge sheet, will cause no miscarriage of justice. But where, one has to speculate, then it is not clear

---

56 Similar to the Kenyan, Section 382, CPC.

57 In this regard, the State had submitted that the particulars set out in the first count of the charge constituted an offence under section 9 (b) of the *Traffic regulations* as distinct from the Traffic ordinance, and that it is probable that by section 9 (b) of the *Traffic ordinance,* the framers of the charge meant section 9 (b) of the *Traffic Regulations.* To which the court was categorical that, this may probably be so, but this being a statutory offence the charge must be strictly interpreted and the court cannot proceed on probabilities. Further that, a submission of this kind is dangerously close to being a matter of mere speculation.

58 (1958) EA 126 (U).

59 Section 39(1) of the Traffic Ordinance, 1951 provided, *"No person shall drive a motor vehicle of any class or description on a road at a speed greater than the maximum prescribed for such a vehicle in the Second schedule to this ordinance."* Whereas Section 40 (1) of the Traffic Ordinance, 1951 provides, *"Any person who drives or aids, abets, counsels or procures any other person to drive a motor vehicle at a speed in excess of a speed limit lawfully imposed shall be guilty of an offence and shall be liable on conviction to a fine not exceeding Sh. 1,000/- or to imprisonment for a period not exceeding three months."*

what charge the accused is facing, in which case, there will clearly be prejudice to the accused, and he must be given the benefit of the defect in the charge.[60]

6.13 Amendment of Charges

A charge can be amended at any stage of a trial before the close of the case for the prosecution, but strict compliance must be made to the provisions of Section 214 of the CPC. This section provides safeguards necessary to prevent a miscarriage of justice in that;

(i) The court shall call upon the accused person to plead afresh to the altered charge;
(ii) The accused may demand that the witnesses or any of them be recalled and give their evidence afresh or be further cross-examined by the accused or his advocate.
(iii) Depending on the circumstances of the case, the court may adjourn the trial for such period as may be reasonably necessary.[61]

One of the leading cases on this point is *Yongo v R.*[62]In this case, the appellant was charged with creating a disturbance in a manner likely to create a breach of peace contrary to section 95 (1) of the Penal Code. The charge stated that the appellant had committed the offence on 1st August 1982[63] by uttering the words, *"Moi's Government is finished and he won't come back to power"*. The key prosecution witness, a Mr. Robert however, stated that the appellant had said, *"No, we need a change in government."* In cross examination the witness stated, *"The accused said we needed change in the government."* The second prosecution witness testified that the Robert had told him that the accused had said *we need change in the government.* The court then proceeded to amend the charge so as to make the words alleged to have been uttered by the appellant read, *"We need a change in government."* The amended charge was then read to the appellant

60 See also *Matu s/o Gichimu v Rex* (1951) 18 EACA 311.

61 *Sebugenyi v R* (1959) EA 411 (u).

62 (1983) KLR 319.

63 The day of the attempted coup to overthrow the government of President Daniel arap Moi. The coup was unsuccessful.

and he maintained his plea of not guilty. The prosecution then closed its case. The Court of Appeal had no difficulty in overturning the conviction. It held that there had to be a record of compliance with Section 214 of the CPC. In the instant, there was no record that the appellant had been informed of his right to recall witnesses. The court was of the view that this failure occasioned prejudice to the appellant and overturned the conviction.

In the Court of Appeal decision in *Njuguna v R*,[64] the appellant was charged and convicted of the offence of robbery with violence contrary to Section 296 (2*)* of the Penal Code. The particulars of the offence were initially stated that the appellant and others had used actual violence upon one Murage, but after all witnesses had testified on behalf of the prosecution, the charge was amended to state that the appellant and his colleagues wounded Murage during the robbery. In amending the charge, the trial magistrate merely drew the appellant's attention to the amendment and recorded the appellant as saying he had understood. On appeal, the appellant challenged this procedural flaw on the part of the trial magistrate, arguing that the magistrate was under a duty to ask him whether he wanted to have the witnesses who had previously testified to be recalled to testify afresh or for further cross-examination. It was held by the Court of Appeal that pursuant to Section 214 of the CPC, a trial court has no option but to read an amended charge to an accused person. The trial court is further required to inform the accused person to have the previous witnesses recalled, either to give evidence afresh, or to be further cross-examined by him. The Court of Appeal emphasized that the right to hear witnesses give evidence afresh is a basic right going to the root of a fair trial, and it is the duty of the trial court, to show in the records that the accused person was informed of that right, and to record further, what the accused person said in answer to that information. The court held that this failure was not one that was curable by Section 382 of the CPC.

In *Daniel Chege Kamundia & 2 others v R,*[65] the appellants were charged with the offence of robbery with violence. In the course of proceedings, the charges

---

64 *Njuguna v R* (2007) 2 EA 370; See also *Wilson Washington Otieno & Another v R* (1986-92) 2 KAR 251.

65 Nairobi Criminal appeals nos.722, 723 and 724 of 2003, (2006) eKLR.

were amended but the accused persons were not advised of their rights under Section 214 of the CPC. The High Court stated as follows:-

"The intention of the draftsman in making this law was to protect an accused person during his trial to ensure that he gets a fair hearing. Failure to put on record that the learned trial magistrate had complied with the provisions aforesaid and the failure to comply meant that the Appellants were denied an opportunity to re-call and cross-examine the witnesses. That also meant that the nature of the charges the Appellants faced had changed at a late stage of the proceedings and the prosecution had introduced two new counts against the 2nd Appellant and one new count against the 1st and 3rd Appellant. It cannot be said that the Appellants did not suffer any prejudice. Had they been allowed to recall the witness for further cross-examine the learned trial magistrate may well have formed a different view of the evidence and may have arrived at a different conclusion. We find that the non-compliance with the provisions of section 214 of the CPC occasioned a failure of justice and that the proceedings which followed were a nullity. The convictions entered in this case are accordingly quashed and the sentence set aside."

It is not the duty of the accused to state whether he wishes to recall any witnesses. The duty is on the court to inform the accused of this right and ensure that his answer is placed on record. In *Abdi Karim Mohamed & Another v R*,[66] the accused had been charged with the offences of being in possession of a firearm, and of being in possession of ammunition, without a firearms certificate contrary to sections 4(2) (I) and 4(2) (b) of the Firearms Act. In the course of trial the charge sheet was amended to alter the serial number of the firearm in question. After the charge was amended, it was read to the accused persons who all pleaded not guilty to it. The prosecution then closed its case. The appellants were then duly convicted of the offences and *inter alia* appealed on the ground that in their rights were violated as there was no compliance to the provisions of Section 214 of the CPC. In opposing the appeal the state counsel submitted that it was the duty of the Appellants to indicate whether they would require to re-call any of the prosecution witnesses after the amendment of the charge. The High Court in this appeal stated thus:-

66 Nairobi HCC Criminal Appeal nos. 387 and 400 of 2004(2006) eKLR.

"It is the trial Court's duty not only to comply with the proviso but to also make a note of it in the record that the same was complied with. This duty lies on the court whether or not the accused person is represented by Counsel."

The appeal was allowed and the appellants set free.

However, it is not in all instances that the conviction is quashed. In *Kababi v R,*[67] the magistrate failed to call upon the accused to plead to the amended charge. The appellant had been charged with causing death by dangerous driving. Three deaths were alleged in one count. [68] However, no objection was raised at the appellant's trial by his counsel to the fact that there was only one count. The charge was amended during the course of the trial and notwithstanding the mandatory requirements of Section 214 (1) of the CPC the magistrate did not call upon the appellant to plead to the amended charge; nor did she inquire whether the defence wanted any witness recalled. The appellant's counsel indicated however, that she had no objection to the amendment. The appellant was convicted and he appealed. The appeal was dismissed on the ground that counsel hadn't objected to the single charge and it couldn't have occasioned any miscarriage of justice. Further although Section 214 of the CPC was mandatory, failure to comply with them didn't necessarily render the conviction a nullity; each case had to be viewed according to its circumstances and in the present case there had not been any possibility for a miscarriage of justice.

6.13.1 The Time When an Amendment to the Charge Can be Carried Out

Section 214 (1) of the CPC is instructive to this end. It provides that an amendment can only be carried out before the close of the prosecution's case. The logic for this provision seems to be that after the close of the prosecution's case the defence will reveal their case and strategy, thus to allow an amendment at this point, is likely to prejudice the accused person as the prosecution would now amend the charges and align the evidence to counter his/her defence. The

67 (1976-80)1 KLR 1616.

68 In *Atito v Republic* (1975) EA 278, it was held that for every death, there should be a separate count.

following question then arises: What if an amendment is made after the close of the prosecution's case?

In *Sebugenyi (William) v R*,[69] the appellant was convicted by a magistrate of watching or besetting the shop of one Odeke, with a view to preventing him from selling goods. The charge originally drafted alleged a "besetting" only and the learned magistrate amended the charge so as to charge the appellant with "watching or besetting," thus following the words of the section. It was argued that owing to the late stage at which the amendment was done an injustice would be caused to the appellant. The requirements of the CPC were however strictly complied with as the appellant was called upon to plead to the amended charge. An adjournment was granted to enable his advocate to consider the implications of the amendment. After the adjournment the advocate stated that he did not wish any of the witnesses to be recalled and that he did not wish to call any additional witnesses. In these circumstances the court failed to see how an injustice would have been committed.[70]

A charge ought not to be amended at the judgment stage. In *Dalmar Musa Ali v R*,[71] the original charge brought against the appellant was abduction contrary to section 142 of the Penal Code; and the particulars were that with intent to marry, he took away *F. A. A.*, against her will from a Primary School to the Refugee Camp. It is on that basis that the learned magistrate heard the case, but as he *was in the course of writing his judgment*, it apparently occurred to him that the charge had not been formulated as it should have been and the following modification to the charge formed part of the judgment:

"I therefore order that the charge be amended to read as defilement c/s. 8(4) of [the] Sexual Offences Act (Act No. 3 of 2006), in that between 16th June, 2006 and 2nd July, 2006 the accused had carnal knowledge of PW1, a girl below [the age of] 18 years...He knew PW1 was below the [age of] 18 years, as he said he knew she was born in 1990, and I [find] the accused guilty of the offence of defilement..."

Ojwang J. had no hesitation in allowing the appeal and put it thus:-

---

69 (1959) EA 411 (U).

70 See also *Sauzier (Benjamin) v R* (1962) EA 50.

71 Nairobi Criminal Appeal No.58 of 2007, (2008) eKLR.

"Not only is there apparently no legal provision to support alteration of a charge during the final stage of writing judgment, but such action would clearly undermine the procedural safeguard accorded the accused, to plead to the new formulation of the charge, or to recall witnesses. The trial in the instant case, therefore, had not been conducted in accordance with the law, quite apart from its having been intrinsically unfair to the appellant herein. The proceedings and judgment of the trial Court will hereby be quashed."

A similar violation of Section 214 of the CPC occurred in the case of *Wagner & 2 Others v Republic.*[72] In the matter, the 1st appellant had been charged with three principal counts of defilement under Section 8(1) as read with Section 8(4) of the Sexual Offences Act.[73] He was also charged with three alternative counts. He was sentenced to 15 years on each of the main counts. It emerged that the trial court had unilaterally at the time of writing judgment, amended the charge sheet. The trial magistrate was of the opinion that the ages of the complainants were 13 and 14 years at the time of the offence. He therefore proceeded to amend the charge to read that the offence was contrary to Section 8(3) of the Sexual Offences Act, in place of Section 8(4) as originally charged.[74] It was the view of the trial court that the error had not prejudiced the appellant and was curable under the CPC. The conviction was set aside on appeal. The court affirmed that Section 214 of the CPC was couched in mandatory terms and that a charge sheet can only be amended before the close of the prosecution case and on giving ample opportunity to the accused.

The case of *JNM v Republic*[75] is also worthy of mention. The appellant was charged with committing an indecent act with a child under Section 11(1) of the Sexual Offences Act. The trial magistrate received evidence of six witnesses. He examined and analyzed the evidence and was convinced that an offence of incest under Section 20 (1) of the Sexual Offences Act had been proved. When

---

72 *Jon Croydon Wagner & 2 Others v R,* Nairobi Criminal Appeals No. 404, 405 & 406 of 2009, (2011) eKLR.

73 Section 8(4) covers defilement of a minor aged between 16 and 18 years and the sentence is a minimum of 15 years.

74 Section 8(3) covers defilement of a minor aged between 12 and 15 years and the sentence is a minimum of 20 years.

75 High Court at Garissa, Garissa Criminal Appeal No. 66 of 2012, (2013) eKLR.

writing his judgment, he amended the charge from the original offence of committing an indecent act with a child, and substituted it with the offence of incest, under section 20 (1*)* of the same. He proceeded to convict the appellant under the substituted offence and sentenced him to life imprisonment. On appeal it was held that Section 214 of the CPC was flouted by amending the charges at the stage of delivering his judgment. The appeal succeeded and the conviction was quashed. In place thereof the High Court convicted the appellant on the initial charge of committing an indecent act with a child.

It is however important, to note that, it is not in all cases that a violation will be held to affect the judgment. The nature, type and extent of the amendment need to be considered and weighed against the prejudice that would be caused to the accused. In the case of *Josphat Karanja Muna v R,*[76] the Court of Appeal had occasion to deal with an appeal where *inter alia* the accused raised the ground that the charge was amended yet he was not given an opportunity to recall the witnesses as required by Section 214 of the CPC. In dealing with this submission, the court was of opinion that the spirit of Section 214 of the CPC is to afford an accused person opportunity to recall and cross-examine witnesses where the amendments would introduce a fresh element or ingredient into the offence with which an accused person is charged.[77] It certainly was not meant to be invoked every time an amendment is made even if such an amendment is only to introduce a correction of name or of a word. Here the name Ben Chege Gikonyo was amended to read Ben Cheche Gikonyo. The court refused to accept that the non-compliance with the provisions of Section 214 of the CPC resulted into injustice to the appellant. The court's view was that the amendment was very minor, and the fact that the accused was not given opportunity to recall the witnesses for cross-examination, did not cause him any prejudice.[78]

---

76 Court of Appeal at Nyeri, Criminal Appeal No. 298 of 2006, (2009) eKLR.

77 See also *Chengo v R* (1964) EA 122 (T).

78 As emphasized in *Musoke v R* (1972) EA 137, the overriding interest is that justice be done to the accused.

6.14 Charges and Limitation of Time

The general position in criminal law is that there is no limitation of time within which charges must be filed unless otherwise prescribed by statute. The only specific limitation period in our statutes is contained in Section 219 of the CPC which provides: - "*Except where a longer time is specially allowed by law, no offence the maximum punishment for which does not exceed imprisonment for six months, or a fine of one thousand shillings, or both, shall be triable by a subordinate court, unless the charge or complaint relating to it is laid within twelve months from the time when the matter of the charge or complaint arose.*"

Thus the limitation period only applies to offences in which the maximum penalty is months of imprisonment or a fine of Kshs. 1,000/=, or both. The limitation is also restricted to a trial in the subordinate court.

However, it does not mean that an accused cannot allege an unfair trial, if he is charged a long time after the offence is said to have been committed. Lapse of time can bring with it numerous circumstances that may prejudice a trial. There is no rule cast in stone and each case must be considered according to its own surrounding circumstances. Time was indeed one of the factors considered in the case of *Stanley Munga Githunguri v Republic,*[79] where the court determined that the trial of Githunguri, would be an unfair trial given the surrounding circumstances. The same position was also taken in *Republic v Attorney General & 3 Others Ex-Parte Kamlesh Pattni*[80], where the court noted, "*Notwithstanding the convoluted history of the charges brought against the Applicant and others, being placed at a considerable and grave risk to freedom for nearly the past two decades is astounding, by any standards. Being placed at such risk for an indeterminable period of time with no end in sight must leave the conscience of the drafters of the Constitution shattered. For it is not the treatment the Constitution contemplated*

[79] *Githunguri v R* (1986) KLR 1. For a more elaborate discussion on this case, see Chapter 5.

[80] *Republic v Attorney General & 3 Others Ex-Parte Kamlesh Pattni* Nairobi High Court, Miscellaneous Civil Application No. 305 of 2012, [2013] eKLR; See also *Republic v Judicial Commission of Inquiry into the Goldenberg Affair & 2 others ex Parte George Saitoti* [2006] eKLR and *Republic v Judicial Commission of Inquiry into the Goldenberg Affair & 2 others ex Parte Eric Cheruiyot* Juridical Review application H.C. Civil Application No. 416 of 2006.

for any accused person, irrespective of their status in society. Criminal trials, decrees the Constitution, should be commenced and concluded within a reasonable time."

Thus, although no limitation period is prescribed, charges need to be preferred within a reasonable time, and reasonable time has to be construed depending on the circumstances of the case.

* * *

CHAPTER 7
PLEA

7.1 Introduction

Once a person is arrested, he is taken to court to answer to the charges preferred against him. The action of answering the charges in a court of law is what is referred to as the taking of a plea. In some offences, a plea can only be taken after consent of the Director of Public Prosecutions (DPP) is obtained. In such instances, the plea will be deferred until such time that consent to prosecute is obtained. A plea can also be deferred for various purposes e.g. to affirm the mental status of the accused, or to first accord him legal representation. A person can also object to taking a plea for example where there is a constitutional matter that the accused needs to first have resolved. In the taking of a plea, the accused is asked to answer to the charges.

7.2 Types of Plea

It will be noted from a reading of Section 207 of the CPC[1] that a person has various pleas available to him. These are as follows:-

Plea of *"Not Guilty"* – This is where the accused does not admit the charge. In this instance, the trial has to proceed in full to ascertain his guilt. If an accused remains silent a plea of Not Guilty will be entered.

---

1 Criminal Procedure Code, Chapter 75, Laws of Kenya.

Plea of *"Guilty"* – In this instance, the accused admits the charge and there is therefore no need of a trial. The only issue that the court will determine is sentence.

Plea of *"Autrefois convict"* – This is a plea by the accused that he has previously been convicted of the same offence. If the accused makes this plea, the court must first try whether the plea is true or not. If it finds that the plea is false, the accused will be required to plead to the charge. The plea of *autrefois convict* is a plea based on the legal requirement that an accused should not be put to "double jeopardy". A person cannot be accused of an offence to which he has already been tried and convicted otherwise the criminal process would go on *ad infinitum*. If he has already been convicted of the offence, he cannot be tried afresh for it.

Plea of *"Autrefois acquit"* – This is a plea by the accused that he has previously been tried of the same offence and acquitted of it. Again the law requires that the court first determine if this is the position, and if it is, then the accused cannot be tried a second time to safeguard on double jeopardy.

Plea of Presidential Pardon – The President has the power of pardon and if it has been exercised, the accused person cannot be made to answer to the same charges that he has been pardoned of.

The pleas of *autrefois acquit* and *autrefois convict* are grounded in the Constitution which provides under Article 50 (2) (o) that a person has a right not to be tried for an offence in respect of an act or omission for which the accused person has previously either been acquitted or convicted. It is not common to have these pleas raised in court, for it is rare to have a person tried twice for the same offence, after conviction or after being acquitted. An interesting situation however arose in the case of *Goddy Mwakio v R.*[2] The appellant in this case had been charged with the offence of making a false statement contrary to section 329 (a) of the Penal Code. Before plea, objection was taken to the charge sheet on the ground that the matters in the charge sheet were pending in a civil suit. The trial magistrate rejected the charge under Section 89 (5) of the CPC, which gives court power to reject a charge which does not disclose an offence, saying

---

2 Court of Appeal at Nairobi, Criminal Application No. 8 of 2010, (2011) eKLR.

that the issues and facts relating to the making of the false statement could be canvassed in the pending civil case, and, further that, it was incorrect, illegal and improper for the prosecution to prefer charges. The applicants were later in another trial, charged before the Chief Magistrate, Kibera with the offence of falsification of Register contrary to section 361 of the Penal Code. After the plea was taken and after the applicants had pleaded not guilty, a preliminary objection to the charge was raised and a plea of *autrefois acquit* raised. It was submitted that a court of competent jurisdiction had already rejected the charge. The Chief Magistrate ultimately dismissed the objection holding, among other things, that a discharge under Section 89 (5) of the CPC, was no bar to further prosecution of the applicants on the same charge or slightly amended charge and that the plea of *autrefois acquit* was not available to the applicants. The applicants sought a revision of this decision in the High Court which was rejected. They appealed to the Court of Appeal and sought a stay of the proceedings in the trial court. One of the matters that the court had to consider is whether the appellants had a valid ground of appeal. The Court of Appeal was of the view that the plea of *autrefois acquit* was not available to the applicants and the application for stay was rejected.

7.3 Failure to Take Plea

What if for one reason or another, no plea is taken and the trial proceeds? This situation arose in the case of *Murage & Another v R,*[3] where the appellants were charged with the offence of robbery with violence and were found guilty. Their appeal to the High Court was dismissed. They appealed to the Court of Appeal *inter alia* on the ground that no pleas had been taken and thus the entire proceedings were a nullity. The record of the trial court indeed showed that the two appellants had not been asked to plead to the charge. The question that arose was whether the appellants had received a satisfactory trial. It was held that the irregularity in not taking plea had not occasioned a failure of justice since the trial had proceeded on the basis that the accused had pleaded not guilty to the offence. The court was of the view that the fact that pleas were

---

3 (2006) 2 EA 218.

not taken was an irregularity which was curable under the provisions of section 382 of the CPC.[4]

7.4 Recording of Plea

The method of recording a plea is set out in section 207 of the CPC, for trials in subordinate courts and Section 274 of the CPC for trials in the High Court. The requirements are more or similar and to avoid duplication, lessons can be taken from Section 207. The same provides as follows:-

S.207 (1) The substance of the charge shall be stated to the accused person by the court, and he shall be asked whether he pleads not guilty, guilty or guilty subject to a plea agreement;

(2) If the accused person admits the truth of the charge otherwise than by a plea agreement his admission shall be recorded as nearly as possible in the words used by him, and the court shall convict him and pass sentence upon or make an order against him, unless there appears to it sufficient cause to the contrary: Provided that after conviction and before passing sentence or making any order the court may permit or require the complainant to outline to the court the facts upon which the charge is founded.

(3) If the accused person does not admit the truth of the charge, the court shall proceed to hear the case as hereinafter provided.

(4) If the accused person refuses to plead, the court shall order a plea of "not guilty" to be entered for him.

(5) If the accused pleads –

(a) that he has been previously convicted or acquitted on the same facts of the same offence; or

(b) that he has obtained the President's pardon for his offence, the court shall first try whether the plea is true or not, and if the court holds that the evidence adduced in support of the plea does not sustain it, or if it finds that the plea is false, the accused shall be required to plead to the charge.

---

4 See also *Joseph Victor Achoka & 2 Others vs Republic*, Court of Appeal at Kisumu, Criminal Appeal No. 201 of 2005, (2006) eKLR.

It is important that the plea of the accused is recorded correctly. On one hand, if an accused wishes to plead guilty, it would be unfair to record a plea of "not guilty" and have the accused go through the rigours of a trial, to an offence that he does not object to. On the other hand, it is even more unjust for an accused who does not admit an offence to have a plea of guilty recorded. This scenario was witnessed in a rather interesting manner in *Agnes Wairimu Mburu v Republic.*[5] The appellant was the complainant in a criminal matter before the Senior Resident's Magistrate's Court at Githunguri in which the accused, one PKN, was convicted and discharged under section 35 (1) of the Penal Code.[6] The appellant was not amused by the discharge and flew into a rage and hauled abuses at the presiding magistrate, accusing her of corrupt dealings, whereupon the magistrate ordered her immediate arrest. The appellant was arrested, locked up and subsequently charged in the same court. She was charged with the offence of being disrespectful to a judicial proceeding contrary to section 121 (a) of the Penal Code. The appellant entered a plea of not guilty to the charge. However, in a rather unorthodox manner the trial magistrate proceeded as though the appellant had entered a plea of guilty, and sentenced her. She appealed. The appellate court observed that while recording plea, it was noted that "accused denies the charge." It was therefore incomprehensible for the court to proceed as if a plea of guilty had been entered. The appellate court declared the proceedings a nullity and quashed both conviction and sentence.

It follows that, it is more probable for challenges to plea to arise where the plea recorded is one of "Guilty" rather than where the plea recorded is one of "Not Guilty". This is because, where one pleads "not guilty", the trial must proceed and at the end, one will either be convicted or acquitted on the evidence. It is rare for one to complain for having been taken through a trial in which he wanted to plead guilty. Inevitably, most, if not all, the authorities touching on recording of pleas, are cases where the plea recorded was one of "guilty."

5 High Court at Nairobi, Criminal Appeal No. 90 of 2002, (2006) eKLR.

6 Penal Code, Chapter 63, Laws of Kenya.

The leading authority on how a plea should be recorded remains the case of *Adan v R.*[7] The appellant was charged with the offence of stock theft contrary to Section 278 of the Penal Code. His plea was recorded in the following words;

"It is true I stole that bull. It was in the boma with others and I stole it. I was arrested with it."

This was entered as a plea of guilty and a conviction was recorded. On appeal, the court stated that an accused person should not be convicted on his plea unless it was certain that he really understood the charge and had no defence to it. The court noted that the danger of a conviction on an equivocal plea is obviously greatest where the accused is unrepresented, or is of limited education, and does not speak the language of the court. It is for this reason that the law requires that where a plea appears to be one of guilty, it must be recorded in the words of the accused. The court further emphasized that the word *"guilty"* should be treated with the greatest caution as it is a technical expression which has no word corresponding exactly to it in any of the languages in Kenya.[8] It does not follow for instance that every language has the same word as the English word to "steal". A further precaution is adopted, as noted by the court, by requiring the prosecution to outline the facts of the alleged offence after the recording of the plea and before the entry of a conviction and of asking the accused if he agreed with it or wished to comment on it.[9] Indeed it was stated that a plea should not be taken unless the prosecution has the facts and that an adjournment between the plea and the statement of facts ought never to be necessary and is most undesirable.

The court then proceeded to set the law and practice that should be followed in a plea of guilty as follows:-

"When a person is charged, the charge and the particulars should be read out to him, so far as possible in his own language, but if that is not possible, then in a language

7 (1973) EA 445; See also *Onkoba v R* (1989) KLR 395; *Gathitu v Republic* (1985) KLR 1; and *Kariuki v Republic* (1984) KLR 809.

8 See *Brarufu Gafa v R* (1950) 17 EACA 125 and *M'Mwendwa v R* [1957] EA 429.

9 This is not explicit in the law (which actually requires the facts to be read after the conviction but before the sentence) but the Court of Appeal approved of the practice.

which he can speak and understand. The magistrate should then explain to the accused person all the essential ingredients of the offence charged. If the accused then admits all those essential elements, the magistrate should record what the accused has said, as nearly as possible in his own words, and then formally enter a plea of guilty. The magistrate should next ask the prosecutor to state the facts of the alleged offence and, when the statement is complete, should give the accused an opportunity to dispute or explain the facts or add any relevant facts. If the accused does not agree with the statement of facts or asserts additional facts which, if true, might raise a question as to his guilt, the magistrate should record a change of plea to "not guilty" and proceed to hold a trial. If the accused does not deny the alleged facts in any material respect, the magistrate should record a conviction and proceed to hear any further facts relevant to the sentence. The statement of facts and the accused's reply must, of course, be recorded."[10]

The statement of facts was stated to serve two purposes: First, it enables the magistrate to satisfy himself that the plea of guilty is really unequivocal and that the accused has no defence; and second, it gives the magistrate the basic material on which to assess sentence. It not infrequently happens that an accused, after hearing the statement of facts, disputes some particular fact or alleges some additional fact, showing that he did not really understand the position when he pleaded guilty. It is for this reason that it is essential for the statement of facts to precede the conviction. In the instant case, no statement of facts was read out to the accused. It could not therefore be ruled out that had the plea been more thoroughly examined, it might have been changed to one of not guilty and thus it was held that the conviction was not safe.

In *Baya v R*,[11] the two appellants were originally jointly charged with murder contrary to Section 204 of the Penal Code. However, at a later date, the information for the joint charge of murder was amended by substituting the offence of manslaughter contrary to Section 202 as read with section 205 of the Penal Code, in place of the offence of murder. The first appellant in reply to the charge said *"We killed him, but that was not intentional"*. There was no record that the other appellant had replied to the charge in his own words. The trial judge then proceeded to enter a plea of guilty to the charge of manslaughter

10 *Supra* note 7, at p 446.

11 (1984) KLR 657; See also *Matu s/o Gichimu v Republic* (1951) 18 EACA 311.

in respect of both appellants. The facts as read, included the assertion that the appellants broke open the door of the deceased, entered the house and using a huge club, beat the deceased on the head inflicting fatal injuries. However, both appellants disagreed, and said that deceased was outside the house. The appeal of each was against sentence but the court was of the view that the plea of guilty was equivocal. The Court of Appeal pointed out that there ought to have been strict compliance with Section 207 CPC.

The court emphasized that there had to be strict compliance with Section 207 of the CPC which would have entailed an explanation of the charge and all its essential ingredients in the vernacular of the appellants or some other language that they understood. In this case, the first appellant did not state if he admitted or denied the charge. His reply to the charge was also equivocal and did not amount to a plea of guilty to the charge. On his reply *"we..."* the court stated that it was wholly undesirable for an accused person to use the plural when replying to a charge. There was such ambiguity in the plea of the first appellant that it ought to have been taken as a plea of "Not Guilty". As to the second appellant, there was nothing to show that he had pleaded to the charge. There was therefore no ground whatsoever for entering a plea of guilty in respect of the second appellant. The court therefore quashed the convictions and ordered a retrial.

Note that following the above decisions, the particulars of the offence, must be read. In case there is a plea of guilty, the facts must also be read. It is not enough for the prosecutor to state, as is common in our courts, *"facts as per charge sheet"*. This cannot be argued to be in compliance with the proper procedure for recording of a plea of guilty. The charge sheet only contains brief particulars of the offence but not the facts in detail. The accused after listening to the detailed particulars may very well refute the same which would mean that the plea of guilty is equivocal. This was affirmed in the case of *Ombena v R.*[12] This was a second appeal to the Court of Appeal. The two appellants were jointly charged with five counts, of selling price controlled goods, at a price exceeding the maximum price contrary to section 26 (1) of the Price Control Act, and with one count of failing to display a price list. They were convicted of their own pleas on all the six counts. Their appeals to the High Court were

12 (1981) KLR 450.

summarily rejected and they made a further appeal to the Court of Appeal against the summary rejection. The plea was recorded as follows: *"Interpreter – English/Dholuo by Mr. Nyamori. Charge read over and explained. Pleas:*

Accused 1: I admit the charges

Accused 2: I admit the charges

Court Pleas of guilty.

Prosecutor: Facts as per charge sheets, Charge read over and explained.

Accused 1: The charges are true.

Accused 2: The charges are true.

Order: Accused are convicted of the charges as laid on their own pleas of guilty."

The Court of Appeal, in assessing the plea, first set out that it was not desirable for a trial court to record only one plea in respect of more than one count. The accused ought to answer separately to each count and the words of each answer should be separately recorded, otherwise, the court cannot always be sure that the accused has both understood and applied his mind to each count. Secondly, the court commented that the statement *"facts as per charge sheet"* were not sufficient. The facts needed to be read over to the accused. In the instant, the summary rejection of appeal was reversed and the appellants acquitted.[13]

If a conviction is based on a plea of guilty, it must be demonstrated that the plea was unequivocal. The plea as recorded must not be capable of any other interpretation, other than a plea of guilty. Thus in a case of assault if the accused in response states *"I did give her injuries on her body"* and in mitigation states *"I only pushed her"* then the plea is not equivocal.[14] Any derogation would mean that the plea is equivocal and a plea of not guilty should be entered. It is for

---

13 See also *Judy Nkirote v R*, High Court at Meru, Criminal Appeal No. 48 of 2010 (2013) eKLR.

14 *Bukenya vs Uganda* (1967) EA 341.

the court to make an assessment, given the circumstances, whether the plea is equivocal or not. Whenever there is a doubt as to the equivocality of the plea, the court should enter a plea of "Not Guilty".

In *R v Ndede,*[15] the Court of Appeal faulted the trial court for entering a plea of guilty in a case where the accused had been held in custody for 30 days. In the said case, the accused was charged with the offence of being a member of an unlawful society contrary to section 6 (a) of the Societies Act, and with a second count of taking an unlawful oath, contrary to section 61 (b) of the Penal Code. He pleaded guilty to the offences, and was convicted, but later appealed to the High Court on both conviction and sentence. His appeal to the High Court was dismissed as the court thought that the plea was unequivocal. In the Court of Appeal, part of his grounds of appeal included the argument that the court ought to have taken note of the fact that he had been in custody for 34 days before being arraigned in court. The Court of Appeal in allowing the appeal stated that in interpreting section 207 (2) of the CPC the court is not always obliged to convict the accused on his plea of guilty as there may be sufficient reasons to the contrary. Thus if for example, there is evidence that the accused has been assaulted while in custody and has fresh wounds, or that the accused appears confused or does not understand the charge, these may be sufficient reasons to decline to convict on an apparent plea of guilty. In the instant case, the Court of Appeal held that the trial court and the first appellate court were wrong in failing to determine the voluntariness of the plea, especially since he had been held incommunicado for thirty days. The appeal was allowed.

Situations may occur where the charges are drawn in the alternative. In *Tumbeine Nyaru v Republic,*[16] the appellant was charged with stealing stock contrary to section 278 of the Penal Code. In the alternative, he was charged with handling stolen property contrary to section 322 (2) of the Penal Code. On being asked to plead in a language which was either English or Kiswahili, he simply said 'True.' No plea of guilty was entered but facts were stated. The facts would tend to show that the plea 'True' might apply to either of the alternative offences of stealing stock or handling the same. The accused then replied, 'facts

15 (1991) KLR 567.

16 High Court at Machakos, Criminal Appeal No. 19 of 2005, (2006) eKLR.

are correct.' It was held that the plea was not unequivocal as it was not clear as to which charge the court dealt with. The conviction therefore could not stand.

Where charges are drawn in the alternative and the accused pleads guilty to the main charge, there is no point of having him enter a plea to the alternative charge.

7.5 Language in Plea

The language used, not just in a plea, but in the whole trial is critical. It however has a very significant place in determining whether the plea of the accused is equivocal. It follows that the accused may get mixed up with the language, and his plea when translated and recorded in English, may connote something different to what he intends to state. The language of the High Court is English and that of the sub-ordinate court is English and Kiswahili.[17] As a matter of practice, courts in Kenya record the proceedings in English although the actual trial may be conducted in Kiswahili. It may be the case that the accused understands neither English nor Kiswahili, in which case, interpretation must be provided in a language that the accused understands.[18]

An accused person has a constitutional right to a fair trial and one of the ingredients of this right is the right of an accused *"to be informed of the charge, with sufficient detail to answer it."*[19] The Constitution also provides for the right of an accused to have the assistance of an interpreter, without payment, if the accused cannot understand the language used at the trial.[20] The right to understand proceedings is therefore a constitutional right, for which there cannot be any derogation, and must be strictly adhered to. An accused will only understand proceedings if the same are either conducted in a language that he understands, or are interpreted to him, into his own language, or at least to a language that he understands. The Court of Appeal stressed the importance of

17 CPC, Section 198 (4).

18 *Ibid*, Section 198 (1).

19 The Constitution, 2010, Article 50 (2) (b).

20 *Ibid*, Article 50 (2) (m).

this requirement in the case of *Irungu v R*,[21] that the right to an interpreter is a constitutional right. In this case, the accused was charged with the offence of robbery with violence, was convicted and sentenced to death. He appealed to the High Court *inter alia* on the grounds, that he was denied an interpreter, and that he did not understand the proceedings. His appeal to the High Court failed, with the court reasoning that since he had participated actively in the trial, he must have comprehended the language, especially where he had given his own defence in Kiswahili. He successfully appealed to the Court of Appeal. It was held that in the trial of an accused person, the court must ensure not only that the charge is explained to the accused in a language that he understands, but that the court is further enjoined to ensure that the evidence given during trial, is interpreted to the accused, in a language the accused understands. These the court emphasized are legal requirements. They are constitutional rights of an accused person, and cannot be waived in the belief that the accused understands the language of the court, particularly when the accused has stated that he was not good in English or Kiswahili. It is the court's duty to ensure that the accused's right to interpretation is safe-guarded and to demonstratively show its protection. The court referred to the provisions of section 198 (1) of the CPC,[22] and section 77(2) (b) of the former Constitution[23] which it considered had been violated by the trial court and set free the appellant.

We have seen that the plea must be recorded as nearly as possible in the words used by the accused. Where interpretation is required, in the course of taking a plea of guilty, this should be recorded together with the name of the interpreter and the language used. It would appear that if the accused does not plead guilty, then the issue of the language used during the taking of plea may not be material. In the case of *Josphat Karanja Muna v R*,[24] the Court of Appeal stated obiter, that since the accused pleaded not guilty, the language used in taking

---

21 (2008) 1 EA 126.

22 Section 198 (1) of the CPC provides, *"Whenever any evidence is given in a language not understood by the accused, and he is present in person, it shall be interpreted to him in open court in a language which he understands."*

23 Sections 77(2) (b) of the 1963 Constitution provided:- *"Every person who is charged with a criminal offence shall be informed as soon as reasonably practicable, in a language that he understands and in detail, of the nature of the offence with which he is charged."*

24 Court of Appeal at Nyeri, Criminal Appeal No. 298 of 2006, (2010) eKLR.

plea was immaterial, as he was not prejudiced, whether or not he understood the language. It would appear that it would also not be necessary to record the language used in defence, as that is the language that the accused understands as noted in the *Muna* Case.[25]

Sign language must now be appreciated to be one of the recognized languages. Before its widespread recognition, challenges did arise in cases where the accused was deaf and mute as indeed happened in the case of *R v Bubu*.[26] The accused, a deaf mute, was charged with the offence of stealing and after trial, he was ordered to be detained at the Governor's pleasure in accordance with the provisions of section 169 (1) (a) of the CPC.[27] The Attorney General applied to the High Court for a revision. It was noted that the accused was charged before two different magistrates. Each was satisfied that he could understand the nature of the charge and denied it and accordingly a plea of "not guilty" was entered on both occasions. On the first occasion, communication is said to have been in signs but the record did not disclose who interpreted the signs. On the second occasion, it appeared to have been the magistrate himself who illustrated the charge by miming. After the first witness had testified, the magistrate recorded *"I fear cross-examination is out of the question since accused is both deaf and dumb. Nevertheless, I believe he knows what is happening in court."* At the end of the case for the prosecution, the magistrate recorded: *"Again by various citings I have been able to remind the accused of the charge. He obviously hotly denies the charge but cannot really conduct a proper defence."* The question in the revision was whether the magistrate, having found that the accused understood the charge, and having expressed the belief that he knew what was happening in court, was justified in sentencing him to be detained at the Governor's pleasure. The court held that the magistrate was correct in the course that he followed as the accused could not understand the proceedings.

The case of *Bubu* was obviously decided in light of the circumstances prevailing at that time. At the moment, there can be no doubt that the deaf mute has a

---

25 *Ibid.*

26 (1959) EA 1094.

27 Same as current Section 167 of the CPC, which provides that when a person though not insane, cannot understand the proceedings, and he is convicted, he is to be detained at the President's pleasure.

language of his own, the sign language, which is capable of interpretation to court. It would therefore be difficult to say that the deaf/mute is incapable of understanding proceedings.

7.6 Plea of Guilty in Joint Offences

In some cases especially those where there are multiple accused persons, one of whom could not be guilty without the other, extra caution should be taken in accepting a plea of guilty from one person where the other denies the charges. This is especially so in charges of affray, conspiracies, adultery or joint offenders. A difficulty of this nature did arise in the case of *Kioko v R.*[28] Two accused persons had been jointly charged with murder but one pleaded guilty to manslaughter. The trial of the other proceeded on the original charge of murder and he was convicted. The appellate court was of opinion that since Kioko had been convicted of the lesser offence of manslaughter, the charge of murder against the appellant ought to have been amended, for he could no longer be charged with having murdered the deceased jointly and in the course of a common design with Kioko who was convicted only of manslaughter. The conviction for murder was substituted for one of manslaughter.

In the case of *R v Ishmael*,[29] one Shabani and Ismael were jointly charged with the offence of affray. Shabani pleaded guilty but Ismael did not. Shabani was convicted on his own plea of guilty. The trial for Ishmael proceeded but she was acquitted as there was no evidence of a fight. It takes two to make a fight and since Ismael was acquitted, then it followed that the conviction of Shabani was unsound, and the court proceeded to quash it on a revision. The court held the word "fight" in section 87 of the Penal Code under which the charge was preferred (as it existed at that point in time) implied a combat of two or more persons. Thus, if Ishmael was not guilty of taking part in a fight, then Shabani's action in assaulting her, were not an affray, but an assault. Consequently, the conviction was unsound. The court stated obiter, that when a court is faced with the situation where one of the two accused charged with affray pleads guilty, the proper course to take is to enter a plea of not guilty on behalf of both accused.

---

28 *Kioko v R* (1983) KLR 289. Also discussed in Chapter 6.

29 *R v Ishmael* (1968) EA 609 (T).

The same situation ought to apply to charges such as conspiracy, or where two people are accused jointly. If one of the accused pleads "not guilty", the court ought not enter a plea of guilty on the other accused.

7.7 Plea of Guilty in Serious or Capital Offences

In murder cases, a plea of guilty should only be accepted in the clearest of circumstances.[30]In *Kusenta v R,*[31] the first appellant had a plea of guilty entered and was then tried with the second appellant. Both were convicted although the second appellant claimed to have acted under duress. After originally pleading not guilty, the trial was adjourned and the appellants arraigned six months later before another judge. At this session the first appellant pleaded as follows *"Yes I killed him intentionally after Chilewa had asked me to kill the deceased".* This was entered as a plea of guilty by the judge. The Court of Appeal pointed out that this was erroneous for two reasons; first, a plea of guilty to a murder charge should only be accepted in the clearest of cases. Here the appellant was claiming to have acted in response to a request. This was a qualification to his statement that he had killed intentionally, making his plea equivocal, and a plea of not guilty should have been entered. Secondly, only a person who has pleaded not guilty can be tried; yet the first appellant who was recorded as having pleaded guilty, was tried together with his fellow co-accused as if he had pleaded not guilty. However, given the circumstances, the case had continued as if there was a plea of not guilty hence no prejudice to the accused.[32]

However, it is not the law that a plea of guilty on a capital offence cannot be accepted. The accused always has a choice to plead guilty, even in a capital offence, and the court should enter such plea if satisfied that it is completely unequivocal. Such a situation arose in the interesting case of *Onkoba v R.*[33] The appellant was charged with robbery with violence and convicted of his own plea of guilty, and sentenced to death. When he was first arraigned in court, the

---

30 The same principle can be argued to apply to other serious offences which carry severe penalties such as the death penalty.

31 (1975) EA 274.

32 See also *Mufumu v R* (1959) EA 625.

33 (1989) KLR 395.

charge was read to him and he pleaded not guilty. He was remanded, and on his second appearance, he sought for the charges to be read afresh after which he pleaded guilty to the offence of robbery with violence. The magistrate pointed out to him that there was a mandatory sentence of death, and he said that he understood, and still wished to plead guilty because as he said, *"I committed the offence"*. The matter was adjourned and on his next appearance, the magistrate again asked the appellant if he realized that the death sentence was mandatory, and whether he wished to maintain a plea of guilty. The appellant said, *"Yes, I still wish to plead guilty because I know that I am guilty"*. The facts were then given by the prosecutor. After the facts were read (partly being that he entered a house, slit the throat of the house maid, then stole various items), the appellant qualified some of these facts and the magistrate rightly so, entered a plea of not guilty and fixed the matter for hearing. At the mentions that followed, the appellant said in English, *"I still wish to admit the offence of robbery"*. The court pointed out that he had qualified the facts, but the appellant next said that his qualification was not the proper position of the matter. The court again reminded him that if he was convicted, he would be sentenced to death and the appellant said that he understood that and was prepared for it. The court asked him if he still pleaded guilty and he said *"Yes, I do."* The magistrate then read the facts as he had recorded them previously and the accused said, *"Yes, I admit them as true."* The magistrate thus convicted and sentenced him to death and in his notes made a comment that the accused has pleaded guilty despite his warnings that he would be sentenced to death. He appealed against his conviction. The court dismissed the same, holding that the plea was clearly unequivocal in the circumstances.

Difficulties can also arise in cases like those of 'possession of stolen property'[34] where one can only be convicted if he fails to offer an explanation for the possession. In *Koech v R,*[35] the appellant was charged with having in his possession 13 gramophone records which the police alleged that they reasonably suspect had been stolen. The appellant, on being asked to plead to these facts, said *"it is true; I admit the charge as read out to me."* He was thereupon convicted and sentenced. On appeal it was held that an accused under such charge could not be guilty until the court has rejected his explanation as to possession.

---

34 Penal Code, Section 303.

35 (1968) EA 109.

It was further held, that an accused who admits all the assertions of fact in regard to his possession, must then be asked for a satisfactory explanation, and on failing to give one may be convicted. Further, the court observed that if an accused admits all the assertions of fact but proffers an explanation, the accused statement should be treated as a plea of "Not guilty" and the prosecution be required to lead all their evidence. Moreover, it was observed that the misdemeanour created by the section, lies not merely in the possession or conveying of goods, which initially the police and later no doubt the court, reasonably suspect to be stolen or unlawfully obtained. The offence is not committed until the accused, "having been charged" with such possession, does not give any account to the satisfaction of the court of how he came by the suspected goods. In the final analysis, the court concluded that the appellant had not confessed to any offence at all, and it was quite wrong to convict him. Instead, the appellant should have been asked if he wished to put forward an explanation of his possession which, though it may not be true, he should have been allowed to advance.

7.8 Plea of Guilty in Absence of Accused

Strictly speaking, the accused needs to attend to his case and take plea. However, there are limited instances where the presence of the accused may be dispensed with, and his plea of guilty may be accepted, if in writing or through his advocate. These situations are covered by Section 99 of the CPC.[36]In *Manager, Tank Building Contractors V R*[37] the court held on appeal, that the conviction had to be set aside as the attendance of the appellant had not been expressly dispensed with. The appellant was accused of offences under the Factories Ordinance. He was served with summons and instructed an advocate to appear for him, but his own attendance at the trial was not expressly dispensed with.

---

36 Section 99 (1*)* of the CPC provides, *"Subject to the following provisions of this section, whenever a magistrate issues a summons in respect of an offence other than a felony, he may if he sees reason to do so, and shall when the offence with which the accused is charged is punishable only by fine, or only by fine or imprisonment not exceeding three months, or by fine and such imprisonment, dispense with the personal attendance of the accused, if the accused pleads guilty in writing or appears by an advocate.*

37 (1968) EA 143 (T).

The advocate appeared and pleaded guilty on his behalf. On appeal (against sentence) the court was of opinion that the plea ought not to have been accepted as this was not one of the cases in which his attendance could be dispensed with and the court had not by its discretion dispensed with his attendance. This case also points out that an advocate should not plead on behalf of his client unless in situations where the attendance of the accused has been expressly dispensed with. Plea should always be taken by the accused himself. However, *obiter*, the court noted that there was nothing wrong, except in cases of grave offences, in a plea of guilty being recorded against an accused whose attendance is not dispensed with, but who pleads guilty in writing and appears by advocate.[38]

7.9 Change of Plea

It was earlier thought that once a plea of guilty is entered, the matter as to the guilt of the person is finalized, the court only having the jurisdiction to pass sentence but not to overturn the plea. This was indeed the situation in *Okello v R*.[39] The appellant was charged with giving false information contrary to section 6 of the Public Service Commission Act, and after his conviction on his own confession, the magistrate allowed the accused to change his plea to "not guilty" and set aside the conviction. The case was remanded for re-trial and on the second trial the appellant again pleaded guilty, and again, after conviction, attempted to change his plea. The second magistrate refused to set aside the conviction and the sentence. The appellant appealed. On appeal it was held that the magistrate in the first hearing, having convicted the appellant on his own confession, had deprived himself of all powers, save the power to sentence. The case was remitted to the first magistrate for hearing on sentence.

Similarly, in *Kibilo v R*,[40] the appellant was charged with "handling one bull" contrary to the Penal Code. He was recorded saying *"it is true I handled this bull which I knew had been stolen."* The magistrate convicted the appellant and remanded him to custody for record and sentencing, at which time the prosecutor gave a version showing a dishonest handling, whereas the appellant

38 See *Wakelin v Rex*, (1951) 18 EACA 185.

39 (1969) EA 378.

40 (1971) EA 101.

gave a version showing an honest handling. The magistrate felt that he was bound by authority, and could not allow a change of plea after conviction, but before sentence. He appealed. On appeal it was held that the magistrate was correct in not allowing a change of plea after conviction. However on the facts the charge was defective and the plea equivocal and a retrial was ordered.

Finally, in *Kinyua v R,*[41] the appellant was charged with three counts of robbery. He pleaded guilty. Thereafter, the appellant wished to change his plea after it had been recorded but before he had been sentenced. The magistrate refused on the ground that the plea was unequivocal. On appeal the court impressed that the trial court was *functus officio* once the conviction had been recorded. It could not revisit the issue, the only matter left being sentence.

The reasoning behind this chain of authorities was that once a court had convicted a person on his own plea of guilty, it became *functus officio.* These authorities followed the position in England, as held in the case of *R v Guest.*[42] *R v Guest* was followed in the aforementioned cases of *Okello, Kibilo* and *Kinyua,* where the High Court declined to reconsider the legal position and affirmed the decision in *R v Guest* despite being put to notice that *R v Guest* had been overturned by the House of Lords in its decision in the case of *S. (an infant) v Manchester City Recorder,*[43] where by a unanimous decision the judgment in *R v Guest* was overruled and it was held that a court was not *functus officio* until sentence had been given and up to that stage a trial court had a discretion to allow the change of plea. The matter resurfaced in the Court of Appeal in the case of *Kamundi v R,*[44] and the court seized the opportunity to straighten the legal position and align it with the view held in the *Manchester City Recorder* case. In the case of *Kamundi,* the appellant was charged along with four others for the offence of robbery with violence. There were four counts, but one was withdrawn, and the accused persons pleaded guilty to the other three counts. It was recorded that the appellant, who was the fifth accused, pleaded guilty and a plea of guilty was entered, but no facts were read. The matter was then adjourned for the prosecutor to produce the criminal records of the accused persons. When

41 (1973) EA 201.

42 (1964) 3 All ER 385.

43 (1969) 3 All ER 1230.

44 (1973) EA 540.

the court resumed, the appellant was now represented by counsel and counsel applied to alter the appellant's plea of guilty on the ground that the plea was ambiguous. The court held that the plea was unequivocal and not ambiguous, and further that the court had no power to quash or set aside its own conviction, and refused to allow the appellant's application to change plea. He appealed. In the appeal, the court considered past authorities especially with regard to the decision in *R v Guest*. It pointed out correctly that under statute, there was no provision providing for a change of plea, but equally, there were no provisions to prevent a plea being changed before the court becomes *functus officio*. The court stated that the trial court must have discretion to allow a change of plea before it has finally disposed of the case. The court reasoned that, "*It is common practice to allow the accused person during the course of trial to change his plea of not guilty to one of guilty and we can see no reason why the court should not have similar powers to change a plea of guilty to one of not guilty.*"[45] On the question of when a magistrate's court becomes *functus officio,* the court agreed with the reasoning of the House of Lords in the *Manchester City Recorder* case,[46] that this can only be when the court disposes of a case by a verdict of not guilty or by passing sentence or making some order finally disposing of the case. The court proceeded to note that the power to change plea must however be judiciously exercised. In the instant case, the appellant had not been given opportunity to agree with the facts nor was his application to change plea considered by the magistrate. The court was of the view that it would be unsafe to allow the conviction to stand and ordered a re-trial.

Once there is a change of plea, there should be no further reference to the change at subsequent proceedings. In *Sagia v R*,[47] the appellant had been convicted of murder resulting from the reckless use of firearms. The trial had proceeded against the appellant on a charge of murder although earlier with consent of the prosecution the appellant may have pleaded guilty on a charge of manslaughter. The facts of the case were that the appellant a member of the Administration Police intervened to stop a disturbance in Mbeere market, in South Nyanza District. There was a scuffle and three fingers of his right hand were cut. He ran to the chief's camp nearby, obtained a riffle and ammunition,

45 *Ibid*, at p 545.

46 *S. (an infant) v Manchester City Recorder* [1969] 3 All ER 1230.

47 (1973) EA 538; See also *Oguyo v R* (1986-89) EA 430.

ran back to the market, and there fired a number of shots. Two of these shots wounded a man in one shop and killed the deceased in another shop. In the address to the assessors the judge, with reference to the firing of shots into the shop causing the death, and no doubt in reference to the earlier intention of the appellant to plead guilty to manslaughter, stated, *"It appears not to be seriously disputed by the defence because this man pleads guilty to manslaughter."* The Court of Appeal held that fact that the appellant had offered a plea of manslaughter was totally immaterial and no reference should have been made to it and that no admission made or words used by an accused person in answer to a charge can be considered in derogation of a plea of not guilty.

7.10 The Consequences of Failure to Correctly Take a Plea

If the plea is not taken as provided, the accused has an avenue to appeal. Ordinarily most appeals will be from those who oppose the recording of a plea of guilty, for if the plea recorded is one of 'not guilty', there will be a full trial and the accused will be found guilty of the offence on the basis of the evidence provided and not by virtue of his plea. Faced with an appeal, the appellate court, if it holds that the plea of guilty was not unequivocal, may either remit the case for retrial or set free the appellant depending on the circumstances.[48] Thus in *Judy Nkirote v Republic*,[49] the appellant was charged before Chief Magistrate's Court Meru with one count of being in possession of *Chang'aa* (an illicit traditional alcoholic brew) and convicted on her own plea of guilty. She appealed, arguing that her plea was unequivocal on the basis that the language was not recorded and that the prosecution did not provide any facts. The appellate court held that the plea was not properly taken, as the facts were never read out, the prosecutor only announcing that "facts as per charge sheet." It declined to order a retrial as the "chang'aa" had been destroyed and therefore there would be no exhibit.

48 For a more elaborate discussion, see Chapter 13 on Appeals.

49 *Supra* note 13; Contrast with *R v Vashanjee L Dosssani* (1946) EACA 150.

7.11 Plea Bargaining and Plea Agreements

Plea bargaining refers to the situations where an accused person offers to plead guilty to a lesser offence in lieu of being prosecuted for a more serious offence. For a long time, plea bargaining in Kenya had been practised informally in our courts. This was especially so in charges of Murder, where an accused person would offer to plead guilty to the lesser offence of manslaughter in return for the charge of murder being dropped.[50] There were no formal rules of engagement and no statutory provisions to cover such situations. An accused would informally make the offer, and the prosecutor would make a decision on whether to accept or reject the offer, mostly taking into consideration the weight of evidence that he had. If the evidence was uncertain as to the guilt of the accused on the charge of murder, he would consider accepting a guilty plea on the lesser charge of manslaughter. The prosecutor would then advise the court that they are willing to reduce the charge of murder to manslaughter, after which the charges would be amended or redrawn, and the accused asked to plead to the amended charge. In most instances, he would readily plead guilty to the lesser charge pursuant to the informal agreement. He would then be convicted on his own plea of guilty and sentenced.

This informal way of plea bargaining has now changed through amendments to the Criminal Procedure Code (CPC), effected in the year 2008, and which set out a detailed procedure for plea agreements. The procedure is not set out in the new Sections 137A to 137 'O' of the CPC. The CPC now defines a plea agreement as an agreement entered by the prosecutor and the accused or his representative, being a negotiation with the result that the charge may be reduced to a lesser included offence, or the charge may be withdrawn, or other charges stayed or a promise made not to proceed with other possible charges. A plea agreement may also provide for the payment by an accused person of restitution or compensation.

50 See for example, *Kupele Ole Kitaiga v R*, Court of Appeal at Nakuru, Criminal Appeal No. 26 of 2007, (2009) eKLR.

It has been made clear, pursuant to Section 137 N of the CPC that plea agreements cannot be entered in offences under the Sexual Offences Act,[51] and offences of Genocide, War Crimes or Crimes against Humanity. In these, the person has to answer to the specific offence and there is no avenue for a plea bargain. It is probably because of the repulsiveness and distressing nature of these offences that there is no avenue for a plea bargain. A plea agreement is only supposed to be entered into after an accused person has been charged, or at any time before judgment. Section 137 B provides that a plea agreement on behalf of the Republic shall be entered into by the Director of Public Prosecutions or officers authorised by him or other person authorized by law to prosecute.

An offer for a plea agreement may be initiated by either the prosecutor or an accused person or his legal representative.[52] The court must be notified by the parties of their intention to negotiate a plea agreement.[53] The court must not participate in plea negotiation between a public prosecutor and an accused person.[54] This is to maintain the impartial nature of the role of the court. There is a requirement for the prosecutor to consult with the police officer investigating the case before entering into a plea agreement. The prosecutor is also to have due regard to the nature of the case and the circumstances relating to the offence in addition to considering the personal circumstances of the accused person and the interests of the community. The prosecutor, unless the circumstances do not permit, ought to afford the victim or his legal representative the opportunity to make representations regarding the contents of the agreement.[55] These provisions aim to safeguard the interests of the victim of the crime so that the prosecutor does not unilaterally enter into a plea agreement without consultations.

A plea agreement must be in writing, and shall be reviewed and accepted by the accused person, or explained to the accused person in a language that he understands. If the accused person has negotiated with the prosecutor through

---

51 Chapter 62A, Laws of Kenya, which covers offences such as rape, defilement, and indecent assault.

52 CPC, Section 137 C (1).

53 *Ibid*, Section 137 C (2).

54 *Ibid*, Section 137 C (3).

55 *Ibid*, Section 137 D.

an interpreter, the plea agreement must contain a certificate by the interpreter to the effect that the interpreter is proficient in that language, and that he interpreted accurately during the negotiations and in respect of the contents of the agreement. The plea agreement must also state fully the terms of the agreement, the substantial facts of the matter and all other relevant facts of the case and any admissions made by the accused person. It must be signed by the prosecutor and the accused person or his legal representative and must be signed by the complainant, if a compensation order[56] has been included in the agreement.[57]

Before the court records a plea agreement, the accused person must be placed under oath and the court is to address the accused person personally in court, and must inform the accused person of, and determine that the accused person understands the right to –

(i) plead not guilty, or having already so pleaded, to persist in that plea;
(ii) be presumed innocent until proved guilty;
(iii) remain silent and not to testify during the proceedings;
(iv) not being compelled to give self-incriminating evidence;
(v) a full trial;
(vi) be represented by a legal representative of his own choice, and where necessary, have the court appoint a legal representative;
(vii) examine in person or by his legal representative the witnesses called by the prosecution before the court and to obtain the attendance and carry out the examination of witnesses to testify on his behalf before the court on the same conditions as those applying to witnesses called by the prosecution.

Other matters also ought to be explained to the accused before his plea on the negotiated agreement may be recorded. These include an explanation that by accepting the plea agreement, the accused is waiving his right to a full trial. The nature of the charge that he is pleading to also ought to be explained alongside the maximum possible penalty, any mandatory minimum penalty, any applicable forfeiture, any possible order of compensation, and that by so

56 Compensation is contemplated by Section 175 (2) (b) of the CPC.

57 CPC, Section 137 E.

pleading guilty, he is waiving his right to appeal except the right to appeal against sentence.[58]

The prosecutor is supposed to lay before the court the factual basis of the plea agreement and the court must determine and be satisfied that there exists a factual basis of the plea agreement. The court shall, before recording a plea agreement, satisfy itself that at the time the agreement was entered into, the accused person was competent, of sound mind and acted voluntarily. Where the court accepts a plea agreement it shall enter the factual basis of the plea on record and the agreement shall become binding upon the prosecutor and the accused. The agreement shall become part of the record of the court. [59]

Where a plea agreement is accepted by the court, the court shall proceed to convict an accused person accordingly. Upon conviction, the court may invite the parties to address it on the issue of sentence. In passing a sentence, the court shall take into account; the period during which the accused person has been in custody; a victim impact statement, if any, made in accordance with Section 329 C; the stage in the proceedings at which the accused person indicated his intention to enter into a plea agreement and the circumstances in which this indication was given; the nature and amount of any restitution or compensation agreed to be made by the accused person, and a probation officer's report.[60]

A court is entitled to reject a plea agreement, and where the court rejects a plea agreement, it shall record the reasons for such rejection and inform the parties accordingly. The plea agreement shall thereafter become null and void and no party shall be bound by its terms. The proceedings giving rise to the plea agreement shall be inadmissible in a subsequent trial or any future trial relating to the same facts and a plea of not guilty shall be entered accordingly.[61] The rejection by the court of a plea agreement is not subject to appeal or review. [62]

---

58 *Ibid*, Section 137 F.

59 *Ibid*, Sections 137 G and Section 137 H.

60 *Ibid*, Section 137 I.

61 *Ibid*, Section 137 J.

62 *Ibid*, Section 137J (4).

Where a plea agreement has been rejected by the court and a plea of not guilty consequently entered, the prosecution may proceed to try the matter afresh before another court. However, the accused person may waive his right to have the trial proceed before another court. Once a plea agreement is rejected by the court, there shall be no further plea negotiation in a trial relating to the same facts.[63] An accused person is entitled to withdraw any plea of guilty pursuant to a plea agreement, before the same is recorded, or prior to sentence.[64]

The sentence passed by a court pursuant to a plea agreement is final, and no appeal lies there from, except as to the extent or legality of the sentence imposed.[65] There is however avenue for the DPP or accused person to apply to have a plea agreement set aside on the grounds of fraud or misrepresentation.[66] The court may set aside such conviction and sentence in which case the trial should proceed as usual on the original charge.

* * *

63 *Ibid*, Section 137 J (2) and (3).

64 *Ibid*, Section 137K.

65 *Ibid*, Section 137L.

66 *Ibid*, Section 137L (2).

CHAPTER 8

BAIL

8.1 Introduction

Bail is a constitutional right which is set out in Article 49 (1) (h) of the Constitution, 2010. It is provided that an arrested person has the right to be released on bond or bail, on reasonable conditions, pending a charge or trial, unless there are compelling reasons not to be released.

There are various forms of bail which can be categorized into four as follows.

(i) Bail pending arrest (Anticipatory Bail).
(ii) Police Bail.
(iii) Bail pending Trial.
(iv) Bail pending Appeal.

8.2 Anticipatory Bail

Anticipatory bail or bail pending arrest, is the form of bail that one is granted by a court when the applicant anticipates that he will soon be arrested and possibly placed in police custody. If the court accepts to release the applicant on bail pending arrest, then the applicant will not be at a risk of being incarcerated pending formal charges being preferred against him. He will be enjoying his liberty, and the worst that can happen to him is for formal charges to be brought against him in court, but not to be confined in police custody. It is a sort of a "safety cover" to stop an impending placement in police custody.[1]

This form of bail will however not be granted in all instances. The applicant needs to demonstrate that his rights to liberty have been threatened or that his rights are at risk of being threatened.

The right to anticipatory bail had been in doubt in the previous constitutional regime as there was no explicit statutory and constitutional provision providing for the same. However, the High Court laid the matter to rest, and affirmed that this right was available, in the case of *W'Njuguna v R.*[2] In this case, the applicant filed an application *inter alia* under Sections 84 of the former Constitution and Section 123 of the CPC.[3] *Inter alia,* he sought a declaration that his fundamental rights and freedoms have been breached, in that he had been subjected to arbitrary search and entry, his right to liberty and security had been transgressed, and most importantly, that the remedy of anticipatory bail was constitutionally provided for and that the same was lawfully available to him. It was argued by the applicant that under Section 84 of the (former) Constitution, any person had direct access to the High Court when any of his fundamental rights and freedoms were being infringed, or were in danger of being infringed, and that the High Court had power to issue any order it deemed fit in the circumstances. It was argued that the right of anticipatory bail was available despite the fact that it was not explicitly provided for in the Constitution. The applicant further argued that since his right to liberty under section 72 of the (former) Constitution had been breached, he had a right to seek anticipatory bail as his liberty was under threat.

The State in response argued that the right of anticipatory bail was not provided for in the Constitution and thus could not be granted, and that in instances

---

1 *James Maina Wanjohi v R* Nairobi High Court, Miscellaneous Criminal Application No. 706 of 2007, (2007) eKLR.

2 (2004) KLR 520.

3 Section 123 of the CPC provided and still provides for the general right to bail pending trial and Section 84 of the former Constitution provided for the general right to apply to the High Court for redress where a person alleged an infringement of his constitutional rights.

where anticipatory bail had been granted, the same had been done erroneously. It was argued that what was provided for was only police bail, bail pending trial and bail pending appeal. The State referred to various past decisions in which the remedy was held not to be available. In coming to its decision, the High Court appreciated that Section 123 of the CPC related to bail after arrest pending trial, and observed that there was no specific provision affording the right of bail pending arrest, or anticipatory bail. However, it held that the right could be envisaged vide section 84 of the (former) Constitution, as pursuant to that provision, the court had power to grant any order deemed appropriate to safeguard the fundamental rights and freedoms of an individual. The court held that the right to anticipatory bail could be availed where one was being constantly harassed by the police or was in fear of being unjustifiably arrested.

The court reasoned that it mattered not that the remedy was not specifically provided for in the statutes, for not to grant it, would be an antithesis of the spirit of the constitution and that it would otherwise be a tragedy that the court could not grant the order where there was imminent infringement of one's constitutional rights. In the instant case, the applicant had a history of being incarcerated on several occasions for no apparent or justifiable reasons. The court held that the right to anticipatory bail could be available where there are serious breaches of the rights of an individual by the organs of the State. The court reckoned that for it to wait for Parliament to act before making available certain rights, it would be shirking its responsibility of protecting fundamental rights and freedoms. It did not mean that where statute is silent then the court was a toothless watchdog. The court affirmed that if the police are contravening or are likely to contravene the liberty of a citizen for ulterior purposes, the right to anticipatory bail could be granted and proceeded to grant the same.

In *Cherere Mwangi v R,*[4] the court stated that an applicant had to demonstrate that his constitutional rights and freedoms, had been, or were likely to be breached. In this case, the applicant had deponed that he had done some survey work for a client who being unhappy with his work had reported him to the police and he had been continuously harassed by the police since then. The court was satisfied that there was reasonable apprehension of a breach of his freedom of liberty and granted bail.

---

4 Nairobi High Court Miscellaneous Application No.553 of 2004, (2004) eKLR.

The importance of demonstrating that one's fundamental rights and freedoms are being breached or are in danger of being breached for an applicant to be successful, was affirmed in the case of *Kimetto v R.*[5] In the said case, the applicant sought anticipatory bail. He had sold a motor-vehicle that he himself had bought from a car dealer. It turned out that the motor-vehicle had similar plates to another vehicle and he was summoned to the police station for an explanation. He filed an application for anticipatory bail. The court was of the view that the applicant had not demonstrated how his fundamental rights had been breached and declined to grant the orders sought. The judge stated that, *"It cannot be gainsaid that the constitution bestows upon every Kenyan citizen a right to liberty. It is however important for one who moves the court under the Bill of Rights, to demonstrate how his rights have been curtailed."* In its view, the court could not curtail the police from conducting their investigations and there had been no breach of any fundamental rights given the facts of the case.

In the 2010 Constitution, just as in the former constitution, there is no precise provision that gives one the right to anticipatory bail. The only explicit provision to bail is contained in Article 49 (1) (h) which refers to bail pending a charge or trial. Apart from this, there are no other provisions in the Constitution directly touching on the issue of bail.

In the previous constitution, the provision touching on bail were contained in section 72 (5) of the Constitution which provided as follows:-

"If a person arrested or detained as mentioned in subsection (3) (b) is not tried within a reasonable time, then, without prejudice to any further proceedings that may be brought against him, he shall, unless he is charged with an offence punishable by death, be released either unconditionally or upon reasonable conditions, including in particular such conditions as are reasonably necessary to ensure that he appears at a later date for trial or for proceedings preliminary to trial."

It is not clear whether the interpretation of "pending charge or trial" in the current Constitution would extend to cover anticipatory bail. It could very well be argued that the words "pending charge" would cover anticipatory bail. But

5 *Zakayo Kimutai Kimetto* v *R*, Eldoret High Court, Miscellaneous Application No. 12 of 2006, (2006) eKLR.

even if this is not the interpretation to be given to sub-article (h), the power to grant anticipatory bail would be covered by Article 22 (1) of the Constitution,[6] which is couched in fairly similar terms to the former Section 84 of the repealed Constitution, which the High Court had used as a basis for providing the relief of anticipatory bail.[7]

This was indeed the approach that the court took in the case of *Mailu v Republic & 2 others.*[8] The court held that there was no specific provision on grant of anticipatory bail pending arrest or charge. It stated however that the High Court had jurisdiction to consider such applications under Article 22 of the Constitution which affords every person the right to institute proceedings claiming that a right or fundamental freedom in the Bill of Rights has been denied, is being violated, infringed or threatened. The court further stated that under Article 165 of the Constitution, the High Court has jurisdiction to hear and determine applications for redress, violation or infringement of, or threat to, a right or fundamental freedom in the Bill of Rights.

The applicant in the application had sought anticipatory bail claiming that he was under threat of an illegal arrest. He claimed that the issues under which he was anticipating arrest arose from business dealings with the claimed complainant. However, the court declined to grant anticipatory bail as in the circumstances of the matter, there had been no demonstration of an infringement of the applicant's constitutional rights. One therefore needs to demonstrate an infringement or threatened infringement of his constitutional rights before being granted anticipatory bail. It is not enough for one to approach the court

---

6 Article 22 (1) of the Constitution provides, *"Every person has the right to institute court proceedings claiming that a right or fundamental freedom in the Bill of Rights has been denied, violated or infringed, or is threatened."*

7 *W'Njuguna v R,* supra note 2. *Section 84 (1)* of the *repealed Constitution* provided, *"Subject to subsection (6), if a person alleges that any of the provisions of sections 70 to 83 (inclusive) has been, is being or is likely to be contravened in relation to him (or, in the case of a person who is detained, if another person alleges a contravention in relation to the detained person), then, without prejudice to any other action with respect to the same matter which is lawfully available, that person (or that other person) may apply to the High Court for redress."*

8 *Eric Mailu v R,* Nairobi High Court Miscellaneous Application No. 24 of 2013, [2013] eKLR.

because he is merely apprehensive that he will be arrested and neither should an application for anticipatory bail attempt to curtail the investigatory powers of the police.[9]

Since the application must demonstrate an infringement or threatened infringement of a constitutional right, the court that has jurisdiction to grant anticipatory bail is the High Court, for it is the High Court which is empowered by the Constitution to hear applications alleging infringement of constitutional rights. [10] The request to be made to the court ought to purely be a request for anticipatory bail and not to ask the court to arrest the applicant and thereafter furnish the applicant with bail.[11]

The procedure to be adopted in filing such an application is debatable in absence of explicit provisions on this right. In *Wafula v Republic,*[12] an application for anticipatory bail was rejected as it was brought by way of a Notice of Motion. The court was of the view that the applicant ought to have moved the court by way of a Petition under the Bill of Rights as set out in the Constitution.[13] This problem of procedure did not commence with the Constitution of 2010; it was present even in the previous constitutional regime. In *Kantaria v R*[14], the application for anticipatory bail was made by way of a Miscellaneous Chamber Summons application. The judge held that the application was fatally defective, the reasoning being that since such applications must allege a breach of the rights provided by the constitution, then the procedure to be adopted ought to

9 *Erastus Waweru Githunga v Attorney General & Another*, Nairobi High Court Miscellaneous Application No. 126 of 2005, (2005) eKLR.

10 Subject to Article 165 which restricts the jurisdiction of the High Court on matters falling within the jurisdiction of the Industrial Court and the Environment and Land Court. See Chapter 2 for a more elaborate discussion on jurisdiction.

11 See *Mradula Suresh Kantaria v R*, Nairobi High Court Miscellaneous Application No. 265 of 2005 (2005) eKLR.

12 Eldoret High Court Miscellaneous Application No. 136 of 2012, (2012) eKLR.

13 This decision is arguably bad, in light of the provisions of Article 159 (2) (d) of the Constitution which provides that courts should not pay undue regard to procedural technicalities.

14 *Supra* note 11.

be the same procedure that one adopts when seeking relief on any allegation of breach of the constitution, which was then by way of Originating Summons. [15]

Similarly in *Kinyua v R,*[16] an application for anticipatory bail, filed in the year 2007 and brought by way of Notice of Motion, was dismissed as being fatally defective. The court was of the view that the applicant ought to have moved the court by way of Petition, that being the provided procedure for filing of applications alleging a breach of fundamental rights and freedoms.[17] However, in the case of *Wanjohi v R.*[18] an application for anticipatory bail brought by way of Notice of Motion was allowed without the procedure being an issue. So too in the case of *Mbaluka v R*[19] although the court stated obiter that the application was wrongly filed by way of Notice of Motion.

The insistence on procedure is probably misplaced. Although the procedure for filing applications seeking redress where there is an allegation of breach of the constitution are set out, those rules anticipate a situation where the State will respond and the matter will proceed *inter partes.* However, most applications for anticipatory bail are heard and determined *ex parte* and it will be pointless to insist on the elaborate procedure which is tailored for hearing of applications *inter partes.* Any sort of application ought to do, so long as it is clear from the face of the application, that what is being sought for is an order for anticipatory bail. In any event, the 2010 Constitution, under Article 159 (2) (d) directs the courts not to be strictly bound by rules of procedure. It will therefore be out of place for a court to reject an application for anticipatory bail simply because the elaborate procedures through which one seeks redress for a breach of the Bill of Rights is not followed. The cases of *Kantaria*[20] and *Wafula*[21], (especially that

---

15 Under Rule 11(a) of the 2001 Constitution of Kenya (Protection of Fundamental Rights and Freedoms of an Individual), Practice and Procedure Rules.

16 High Court, Criminal Application No.669 of 2007 (2007) eKLR.

17 Following Legal Notice No. 6 of 2006 (so called "Gicheru Rules" for that was the name of the then Chief Justice) which provided for Rules for making applications for enforcement of fundamental rights and freedoms.

18 *Supra* note 1.

19 Machakos High Court Miscellaneous Criminal Application No. 71 of 2009 (2009) eKLR.

20 *Supra* note 11.

21 *Supra*, note 12.

of *Wafula* since it was decided after the promulgation of the 2010 Constitution and therefore the provisions of Article 159 (2) (d) of the Constitution applied) are arguably not good authorities.

8.3 Police Bail

Section 53 (1) of the National Police Service Act (NPSA)[22] provides that a police officer investigating an alleged offence may require any person to execute a bond subject to the condition that the person shall duly attend court when required to do so.[23] This section is a replica of section 23 of the repealed Police Act.[24] When a person is arrested, it does not mean that he has to be kept in police custody before being arraigned in court. He may be released on bond by the police and required to attend further at the police station or the court on a day specified. This provision is in line with the spirit of the Constitution which aims at safeguarding the liberty of an individual. Article 49 (1) (h) of the Constitution, does provide *that an arrested person has a right to be released on bond or bail, on reasonable conditions pending a charge or trial, unless there are compelling reasons.* Indeed there would be no need for the police to keep a person in custody pending his arraignment in court unless there are reasons to do so. Such reasons would arguably be similar to the reasons that a court would consider when assessing an application for bail pending trial. If such conditions do not exist, it would be improper for the police to insist on keeping a suspect in custody thus curtailing his right to liberty for no reason.

8.4 Bail Pending Trial

The right of one to be released on bail pending trial is a right that is granted by the Constitution. The existing stipulations touching on bail are found in Article 49 (1) (h*)* which provides as follows:-

---

22 National Police Service Act, 2011, Chapter 84 Laws of Kenya.

23 The former CAP 84 before repeal in 2011 by the NPSA.

24 The former Chapter 84, Laws of Kenya, which was repealed by the NSPA.

49. (1) (h) An arrested person has the right to be released on bond or bail, on reasonable conditions, pending a charge or trial, unless there are compelling reasons not to be released.

The Constitution is therefore clear that an accused person has a right to be released on bond or bail pending trial. The terms of bond or bail are supposed to be reasonable. The right to be released on bond/bail can only be denied to the accused if there are "compelling reasons" that would entitle the court to exercise its discretion in refusing to grant bail/bond.

In the case of *Republic v Danson Mgunya & Another,*[25] Mohamed Ibrahim J, stated that the burden should be on the prosecution and not the accused person to prove, or at least demonstrate the existence of the "compelling reasons." The Constitution does not however define what "compelling reasons" are and it is left to the discretion of the court to consider the circumstance of each case and come up with a decision on whether "compelling reasons" exist that would entitle the court to deny an accused the right to be released on bail. There are some considerations and principles that have evolved over time which courts have ordinarily looked at, and it is arguable that if any of the established considerations exist, then the court would be entitled to deny bail.

In *Republic v Dorine Aoko Mbogo & Another,*[26] the judge correctly posed the following question and proceeded to answer it. *"Under the new Constitution, the question which therefore readily comes to mind is what are the compelling reasons or circumstance why an accused person should not be admitted to bond or bail?"* The court in this instance stated obiter that the "compelling reasons", could cover the same instances under which bail could be denied in the previous constitution. Under the previous regime, bail was not available where one was charged with an offence that was punishable by death. Exceptions could however be made for child offenders by dint of the provisions of the Children Act which allowed bail to be granted to child offenders. Bail was indeed granted in the 2006 case of *Oscar Iyaite v Republic*[27] where the child faced charges of murder.

---

25 Mombasa High Court, Criminal Case No. 26 of 2008, [2010] eKLR.

26 Nakuru High Court, Criminal Case No. 32 of 2010 (2010) eKLR.

27 High Court at Bungoma, Crim. Misc. 34 of 2006 (2006) eKLR.

The constitutional provision declaring that bail was not available to capital offenders was Section 72 (5) of the repealed constitution which provided as follows :-

"If a person arrested or detained as mentioned in subsection (3) (b) is not tried within a reasonable time, then, without prejudice to any further proceedings that may be brought against him, he shall, unless he is charged with an offence punishable by death, be released either unconditionally or upon reasonable conditions, including in particular such conditions as are reasonably necessary to ensure that he appears at a later date for trial or for proceedings preliminary to trial."

These provisions were complemented by section 123 (1) of the CPC which provided (and still provides) that:-

"When a person, other than a person accused of murder, treason, robbery with violence, attempted robbery with violence and any related offence is arrested or detained without warrant by an officer in charge of a police station, or appears or is brought before a court, and is prepared at any time while in the custody of that officer or at any stage of the proceedings before that court to give bail, that person may be admitted to bail:

Provided that the officer or court may, instead of taking bail from the person, release him on his executing a bond without sureties for his appearance as provided hereafter in this Part."

It will be discerned that under the repealed Constitution, bail was not available to persons accused of a capital offence. This has however changed under the current regime as Article 49 (1) (h) of the 2010 Constitution, does not rule out bail for any offence. Bail is therefore available to all accused persons irrespective of the offence. This indeed was affirmed in the decision of the High Court in the case of *Danson Mgunya*.[28] In the said case, the accused persons had been charged with murder in the year 2008. Owing to the provisions of section 72 (5) of the repealed Constitution they were held in custody as they could not be released on bail, murder being a capital offence.[29] After the promulgation of

---

28 *Supra,* note 25.

29 Penal Code, Sections 203 and 204.

the present Constitution on 27th August 2010, the two accused persons seized the opportunity provided by Article 49 (1) (h), and filed an application to be released on bail. The court assessed the current provisions touching on bail and obiter felt that they need to be more elaborate. It was noted that statute does not provide any guidelines on how to assess an application for bail. Nonetheless the court quoted with approval the Nigerian case of *Alhaji Mujahid Dukubo Asari v Federal Republic of Nigeria,*[30] where Justice Ibrahim Tanko Muhamad set out the following principles as being material to assessing an application for bail pending trial;

(i) The nature of the charges
(ii) The strength of the evidence which supports the charge
(iii) The gravity of the punishment in the event of conviction
(iv) The previous criminal record of the accused if any
(v) The probability that the accused may not surrender himself for trial
(vi) The likelihood of the accused interfering with witnesses or may suppress any evidence that may incriminate him
(vii) The likelihood of further charges being brought against the accused.
(viii) The probability of guilty
(ix) Detention for the protection of the accused
(x) The necessity to procure medical or social report pending final disposal of the case.

Ibrahim J, in assessing these considerations however felt that provisions (ii) and (viii) should be exercised with caution in Kenya as one is presumed innocent until proven guilty. They could probably be used when an accused has been put on his defence, or where there are exceptional circumstances. The court further quoted with approval the obiter dictum of Justice Niki Tobi in the same case where it was stated that:-

"The main function of bail is to ensure the presence of the accused at the trial ... Accordingly, this criteria is regarded as not only the omnibus one but also the most important. As a matter of law and fact, it is the mother of all the criteria enumerated above."

---

[30] *Alhaji Mujahid Dukubo Asari v Federal Republic of Nigeria* S.C. 20a/2006.

In making decision on whether or not to grant bail in the *Danson Mgunya* case, the court noted that the two accused persons had been arraigned in court two and a half years after the murder. Throughout that period of time, they were fully at liberty and never escaped. Neither were they under threat by the public. They were senior citizens and it was inconceivable that they could abscond. The court therefore granted bond in the sum of Kshs. 3 million for each accused with two sureties each for a like amount.

The essence of bail pending trial is to safeguard the liberty of the accused as the accused is always entitled to the presumption of innocence unless proved guilty.[31] As emphasized by Ibrahim J in the *Mgunya* case, *"Liberty is precious and no one's liberty should be denied without lawful reasons and in accordance with the law. Liberty should not be taken for granted."* Warsame J observed in the case of *R v Muneer Harron Isamail & 3 Others,*[32] that *"Any person who is held in custody pending trial suffers the same dent on his liberty as one serving a sentence of imprisonment after conviction. By keeping an accused person in custody until tried, convicted and sentenced, bail protects against the dilution of the presumption of innocence. This presumption encapsulates against detention before lawful conviction…"*

8.4.1 Assessing Compelling Reasons

Bail can only be denied where there are compelling reasons. The following factors may be considered by a court as comprising of compelling reasons.

8.4.1.1 The probability that the accused may not surrender himself for trial

Bail is granted to allow a person enjoy his liberty before conclusion of the trial. If the accused will not appear at trial then bail ought to be denied, since the accused will never face trial. The court may make an assessment of various factors in reaching the conclusion that the accused is most likely to abscond. If the accused has a history of not appearing in court after being granted bail, the

31 Constitution, Article 50(2) (a).

32 Nairobi High Court, Criminal Revision Case No. 51 of 2009, [2010] eKLR.

court may consider such history, as pointing to the intimation that the accused may not appear at his trial if granted bail. The gravity of the offence although categorized as a reason in itself, is corollary to the concern that the accused will not appear at his trial. The reasoning here is that if the offence is grave and carries severe penalty, say death, then the accused would be more inclined not to appear at trial, than if the offence is a misdemeanor with a light penalty. In the case of *Mary Wambui Kinyanjui v R,*[33] bail was denied to the applicant. The applicant had been granted bond in a previous case but she had jumped and failed to appear. She was subsequently charged with the instant offence, separate from the earlier one, in which she had jumped bail. Bail was denied by the trial court and she made an application to the High Court. The court declined to grant the same *inter alia* owing to the fact that she had jumped bail granted in the previous trial. In any event if bail was cancelled in the previous case, there would be no point in granting the same in a subsequent matter running parallel to the earlier one.

8.4.1.2 The gravity of the offence and penalty upon conviction

This as we have seen above is related to the probability of the accused to surrender himself for trial. The point was indeed made in the previous constitutional regime in the controversial case of *Watoro v R,*[34] where in assessing an application for bail pending trial (which had been denied in the trial court), Porter J, stated that *"the seriousness of the offence has a clear bearing, which the court ought to bear in mind, on the factors influencing the mind of an accused facing a charge in respect of the offence as to whether it would be a good thing to skip or not…."* The applicant had been charged with the offence of sedition which carried a sentence of 10 years. The court considered that this offence was grave enough to deny bail and proceeded to decline to award bail. Of course it is highly debatable whether this case fell in the category of very grave offences, as a maximum sentence of 10 years does not sound much, and the case needs to be read in the context of the political situation prevailing at that time. The point that was made in the said case is however valid, that the seriousness of the offence and gravity of the sentence are factors that may be considered in denying bail.

---

33 High Court at Nairobi, Misc. Crim. Application No.353 of 2006, (2006) eKLR.

34 (1991) KLR 281.

In the more recent decision of *R v Mbogo & Another,*[35] it was stated that "… *(these serious offences) are offences which are by their reprehensiveness, not condoned by society in general. It would thus hurt not merely society's sense of fairness and justice, and more so, the kin or kith of the victim, to see a perpetrator of murder, treason or violent robbery (committed or attempted) walk to the street on bond or bail pending his trial. A charge of murder, treason, robbery with violence (committed or attempted) would thus be a compelling reason for not granting an accused person bond or bail.*

However, the consideration of the seriousness of the charge must be weighed with other circumstances, so that if the other circumstances outweigh the consideration of the gravity of the offence, then bail ought to be granted. The constitution provides that bail is available for every offence and therefore each case must be assessed according to its own circumstances. Thus in *Mgunya,* bail was allowed in a case of murder, and so too in the case of *Mbogo.* In the latter case, the applicant, a minor who was several months pregnant was charged alongside an adult with the offence of murder. The court considered *inter alia* that a minor cannot be sentenced to death and that the minor's mother was ready to stand surety and granted bail. Bail was however denied in *John Kahindi Karisa & 2 Others v Republic,*[36] another case of murder. Ibrahim J, considered that self-preservation is a natural reaction for any human being and the risk of flight is real when one is faced with a capital offence.

8.4.1.3 Possibility of interfering with witnesses

If there is danger of the accused interfering with or intimidating witnesses, then bail can be denied. Such allegation must however be supported by facts and should not be a mere allegation. In *Panju v R,*[37] bail was denied by the sub-ordinate court *inter alia* on the allegation that the accused would interfere with witnesses. On further application to the High Court the High Court made clear that it is not enough for the prosecution to simply allege that the accused would interfere with witnesses. The court stated that such allegations need to

---

35 *Supra,* note 26.

36 Mombasa High Court, Criminal Case No. 23 of 2010, (2010) eKLR.

37 (1973) EA 282.

be substantiated by way of affidavit otherwise it would be prejudicial for the court simply to accept the allegation from the prosecution.

In *R v Mohammed Ahmed Omar*,[38] the accused was charged alongside others with seven counts of murder. He applied for bail. Ochieng J declined to grant bail for the reasons of the gravity of the offence where he thought that there was a real possibility of the applicant being tempted to abscond from jurisdiction. He also considered that the applicant was an Administration Police Officer, who would have access to a gun and his release would cause the civilian witnesses a genuine apprehension for their safety. The possibility of interfering with witnesses is higher where the victim and the accused are related and is a consideration to be taken into account. This was precisely the situation that the court faced in the case of *R v Lucy Njeri Waweru & 3 Others*[39]. This was a case of murder in which the deceased was husband to the first accused and father to the other three accused. The prosecution successfully opposed bail *inter alia* on the grounds that the key witnesses were children and siblings to the accused persons and if released, there was a real likelihood of interference with witnesses. [40]

8.4.1.4 Detention for protection of the accused

If the public may endanger the life of the accused, this may be a consideration in denying bail. This was one of the reasons stated obiter in the Nigerian case of *Alhaji Dukubo*.[41] Ibrahim J was however not convinced that this could be a valid reason. In the *R v Karisa* case,[42] the State in objecting to the application for bail had raised the issue that for his own safety the bail application by the accused should be declined. The judge had this to say on this point,

---

38 Nairobi High Court, Criminal Case No. 14 of 2010, (2010) eKLR.

39 Nairobi High Court Criminal Case No. 6 of 2013, (2013) eKLR.

40 See also *Republic v Taiko Kitende Muinya,* Nairobi High Court Criminal Case No. 65 of 2010 (2010) eKLR.

41 *Supra,* note 30.

42 *Supra,* note 36.

"I also reject the idea that the accused should be remanded and not granted bail for their own safety... Any accused person released on bail has his Constitutional rights secured and protected. No member of the public or any other person can try him or punish him. This can only be done by a competent court with appropriate jurisdiction. The practice by sections of the Kenyan Society to kill or murder innocent persons only on mere suspicion or even upon a citizen's arrest of suspects for various perceived offences including practicing witchcraft by mob lynchings, torching etc in so called "Mob Justice" is deplorable, criminal, unlawful, illegal and unconstitutional... As a result, it would amount to a judicial aiding and abetting of this Criminal trend of public murders or so called "mob justice" for the court to purport to deny bail to the accused so as to protect them from being lynched by members of the public."

Nonetheless, despite the strong words by the learned Judge, the safety of the accused may be a consideration to take into account. This is especially so where there have been earlier attempts on the life of the accused and the possibilities of future attempts remain real. It will no doubt be futile to have an accused facing such threats released into society for at the end of the day, there may be no trial that will be held, if the threats become real.[43]

8.4.1.5 National Security

In *Republic v Muneer Harron Ismael & 2 Others,*[44] the accused had been arrested in Narok allegedly with an assortment of military equipment. The State opposed the release of the accused on bail on the basis that the accused was a threat to national security. Warsame J, in dealing with the matter stated thus:-

"The issue of national security and interest is not a casual business, its magnitude, seriousness, its gravity and implication must be brought to the attention of the court in order to make an informed and fair decision. In making allegations on matters concerning national security, the prosecution must be possessed of or have information which is definite and which clearly shows that there is a foreseeable

43 See *R v Eusobio Kobia Rugonji & 6 Others*, Meru High Court Criminal Case No. 24 of 2010, (2011) eKLR.

44 *Supra* note 32.

risk to the interest of the public or that a cognizable offence is likely to be committed if the accused person is released on bail. There must be legitimate information to support the allegations that the accused persons are likely to prejudice or jeopardize the interest of the public."

In the instant case the court was of the view that specific events and facts must be disclosed to court to enable the court to judge the genuineness and reasonableness of the allegations touching on public security. In the absence of these, the benefit of doubt must be given to the accused and bail was consequently granted.

The issue of bail and national security has become even more pronounced with the current threats of terrorism that the country is facing. In *Aboud Rogo Mohamed & Another v Republic,*[45] the accused persons were charged with the offence of engaging in an organized criminal activity by being members of an outlawed society, namely Al-Shabaab, under section 3 and 4 of the Prevention of Organized Crimes Act. Bail was denied in the first instance by the trial magistrate and the applicant filed an application for bail in the High Court. The court had to consider whether or not to grant bail. It was the considered view of the court that:-

"When it is borne in mind that a single explosion can result in multiple deaths, injuries and destruction to property, I hold the considered view that an open and democratic society would believe that any person who, if he was granted bail, may do something that would subject the said society to terror, should not be granted bail."

All the same the applicants were granted the benefit of doubt and bail was granted albeit on stringent terms.

However in the case of *Republic v Ahmad Abolafathi Mohammad & Another*[46] the High Court on an application for revision, cancelled bail that had been granted by the trial Magistrate's Court. The accused were facing charges related to terrorist activities. Twice their application to be released on bail was rejected but it was finally allowed at the third attempt. The State filed a revision seeking

45 Nairobi High Court, Criminal Case No. 793 of 2010, (2011) eKLR.

46 Nairobi Criminal Revision No. 373 of 2012, (2013) eKLR.

to reverse the release of the accused on bail. The court observed that the presumption of innocence operated in favour of the respondents, but on the other hand, the State had a duty to keep its citizens and visitors within its territory safe from threats within and from outside its borders. On that basis, bail was cancelled.

8.4.1.6 Age of the accused

Even before the promulgation of the new constitution, minors by dint of the provisions of the Children Act[47] could not be sentenced to death. They therefore could be released on bail even for charges that would otherwise carry the death sentence if the accused person were an adult. To pronounce clearly and to put into effect the spirit of the Children Act, the legislature provided for specific rules in the schedules of the Act. The relevant rules in the case of bail are found in the fifth schedule to the Children Act. Rules 9 and 10 of this schedule makes provision for bail of a child offender. First, Rule 9 (1) provides that where a child is brought before a court and charged with an offence, the court shall inquire into the case and may release the child on bail on such terms as the court may deem appropriate. Rule 9 (2) goes on to provide that where bail is not granted, the court shall record the reasons for such refusal, and shall inform the child of his right to apply for bail to the High Court. Secondly, Rule 10 (1) provides that where a child is not released on bail the court may make an order remanding the child in custody and shall order him to be detained for the period for which he is remanded to a children's remand home. This section however, has a proviso to the effect that if there is no children's remand home within a reasonable distance of the Court, the Court shall make such order as to the child's safe custody as it deems fit which shall not be a remand home or prison in which adults are detained or remanded.

It followed that though bail was not available to capital offenders, in the previous constitutional regime, bail was granted to children although it is debatable whether this was not a violation of the Constitution. Bail was thus granted in the case of *Oscar Iyaite v R*[48] where the minor was facing a charge

---

47 Chapter 141, Laws of Kenya.

48 *Supra*, note 27.

of murder. Courts are generally lenient in granting bail to children as they are supposed to take into consideration what would be in the best interest of the child. Under the Children Act, the maximum period that a child may be remanded is six months after which he shall be admitted to bail. In the *R v Mbogo & Another* case,[49] the applicant was 17 years old and bail was granted.

In *Republic v SAO (a minor),*[50] the accused was a child of about 13 years of age. She was alleged to have committed the offence of murder when she was 12 years old. The court considered that Section 4 (3) of the Children Act specifically enjoins all judicial institutions to take the interests of the child as the first and paramount consideration and to safeguard and promote the welfare of the child. The court further made reference to the fifth schedule of the Act specifically rules 9 and 10, which make provision for bail of a child offender and ruled that it had no reason before it, not to do what it was enjoined by the Act and the child offender rules, and released the accused on a free bond with two sureties.[51]

8.4.1.7 The character of the accused

In *Muiruri v R,* [52]the applicant had been granted bail by the trial court which was later cancelled. He filed an application for release to the High Court. The court declined to reinstate bond. It considered that the accused who was on trial for an offence of obtaining by false pretence had his bond canceled because he had three other convictions. On one, he had been placed under probation and on the other two he was out on bond pending appeal. In addition he had three other cases which were pending trial. In the instant case, he was facing five counts again relating to fraud. Given these circumstances the court declined to give bond.

However, the court should be cautious before denying bail on this ground, since the court ought not to be prejudiced by the alleged character of the accused.

---

49 *Supra,* note 26.

50 Nairobi High Court, Criminal Case No.236 of 2003, (2004) eKLR.

51 See also *Victor Lumbasi Muge v R*, High Court at Bungoma, Crim. Case No. 57 of 2005, (2006) eKLR and *R v Eusobio Kobia Rugonji & 6 Others* supra note 43.

52 (2005) eKLR.; See also *Mary Wambui Kinyanjui v R* (2006) eKLR

His alleged character ought not to infer guilt on the charges that he is facing, and his right to liberty ought not to be prejudiced unless his character may jeopardize the fair trial of the case or compromise the integrity of witnesses or if he may be a danger to society.

8.4.1.8 Health of the Accused

In *Lilian Kalunde Musyoki v Republic,*[53] the accused was charged with the offence of trafficking in heroine. She had earlier been denied bail but filed an application to the High Court. The court considered that she was sickly, had hypertension and diabetes, and had just delivered a baby through caesarean section and developed an infected wound. However, given the seriousness of the offence for which if found guilty she would be liable to a fine in excess of Kshs.8 million, the court put some stiff conditions for her grant of bail. It is difficult to see any other reason for the grant of bail in this case other than the consideration that the applicant was sickly. Although it may be a consideration, it would be a minor one, and only in exceptional cases would a bail application to be allowed solely on the ground of ill health

8.4.1.9 Previous Criminal Record

This can be a consideration especially in assessing the propensity of the accused in interfering with witnesses (which is a reason by itself) and also in assessing whether from his past record the accused may be said to be a danger to society. It is important to remember, that merely because one or several of these reasons exists, does not automatically mean that bail ought not to be granted. However, these are reasons which the court may consider when exercising its discretion not to grant bail. They could be considered to be compelling reasons given the circumstances surrounding the case.

---

[53] Nairobi High Court, Criminal Application No. 646 of 2004, (2004) eKLR.

8.4.2 Making Bail Applications Pending Trial

The procedure for making bail in the trial court is rather informal, probably because there is no formal procedure set out in the statutes on how such bail applications need to be made. It is common practice for the accused either by himself or through his counsel to seek bail by a simple verbal request to the trial court. The prosecutor may object to grant of bail and if so, then he should provide reasons for his objection to bail. The trial court then assesses the application for bail and the prosecutor's objection and either grants bail or rejects the same. Where there is no objection, bail would usually be granted, although the court still retains discretion to decline bail, even when the prosecutor has no objection. Bail would be granted either on the personal bond of the accused, with or without sureties, or through a cash bail. Sureties are persons who bind themselves to guarantee the attendance of the accused, and agree through their bond, to forfeit the value of the surety if the accused does not appear. This amount which the guarantee is ready to forfeit is called a recognizance. A surety does not have to remain a surety for the entire duration of the trial and can apply to withdraw, in which case, the accused in the absence of a variation of the bond terms, will either have to get another surety or be remanded in custody. A surety will be automatically discharged at the end of the trial.

When an application for bail is refused in the first instance by the trial court, it does not mean that the accused cannot make a fresh application for bail in the same court. Applications for bail are not caught by the *res judicata* rule and multiple applications for bail can be made. A renewed bail application in most instances would be more formalized with a filed application supported by an affidavit. It is important for the applicant to demonstrate that there has been a material change in circumstances otherwise such bail application would in most cases be futile.

If bail is declined by the trial court, assuming the trial court is the subordinate court, an application may still be made to the High Court. The application to the High Court would be invariably formalized into an application supported by an affidavit. The High Court has jurisdiction by virtue of Section 123 (3) of the CPC to look into a bail application afresh. This is not an exercise by the High Court of its jurisdiction on appeal or review. The High Court also has jurisdiction to vary the terms of bail granted by the subordinate court.

The issue of subsequent bail applications was made clear in the case of *Magloire v Republic,*[54] where the applicant had been denied bail by the trial court. He made a further application for bail to the High Court which was denied. Later he made a second application for bail again before the High Court. The court (Ochieng J) had this to say on the application.

"It must be stated clearly that the decision by either the trial magistrate's court or this court, to reject one application for bail pending trial is not a bar to a new application. However, it is necessary that the person making a renewed application for bail should satisfy the court that there had been material change in his circumstance."

In the instant case, the court was convinced that there was a change of circumstances and proceeded to grant bail.

8.5 Bail Pending Appeal

Appeals for trials determined by the Magistrates Courts go to the High Court whereas appeals for cases determined by the High Court go to the Court of Appeal. Bail pending appeal must therefore be seen in the light of the court which has jurisdiction to hear the appeal.

8.5.1 Bail Pending Appeal for Trials Held By the Magistrates Courts

For trials held by the Magistrates Courts, the basis for bail pending appeal is found in Sections 356 and 357 of the CPC. Section 356 (1) of the CPC provides that the High Court, or the subordinate court which has convicted or sentenced a person, may grant bail or may stay execution on a sentence or order pending the entering of an appeal. Further, subsection (2) affirms that the time during which the person has been released on bail, or during which the execution was stayed pending appeal, shall be excluded in computing the term of the appellant's sentence, unless the High Court, or the subordinate court which convicted and sentenced the person, otherwise orders. Moreover, Section 357 (1) of the CPC adumbrates that after the entering of an appeal by a person

54 Nairobi High Court, Criminal Application No. 679 of 2004, (2005) eKLR.

entitled to appeal, the High Court, or the subordinate court which convicted or sentenced that person, may order that he be released on bail with or without sureties, or, if that person is not released on bail, shall at his request order that the execution of the sentence or order appealed against shall be suspended pending the hearing of his appeal.

It will be noted therefore that one may either make the application for bail pending appeal, either in the subordinate trial court, or in the High Court. However if one makes an application for bail in the subordinate court, and that application is refused by that court, no further application for bail shall lie to the High Court. The only avenue for such person is to appeal against the refusal to the High Court. Such appeal is to be heard before one judge sitting in chambers and cannot be summarily rejected. If the application for bail pending appeal to the High Court is rejected, it is debatable whether there is a further right to apply to the Court of Appeal for bail pending such an appeal.

In *Ademba v Republic,*[55] the applicant was convicted of his own plea of guilty for the offence of personating a person employed in the public service contrary to section 105 (b) of the Penal Code. He appealed against sentence to the High Court and filed an application for bail pending appeal. The High Court felt that there were no exceptional circumstances that would warrant the court to grant bail pending appeal and rejected the application. He now appealed to the Court of Appeal. The Court of Appeal held that it had no jurisdiction to entertain an appeal from a refusal of the High Court to grant bail pending appeal to the High Court.

However bail was granted in *Shah v Republic.*[56] The applicant, who was charged with the offence of theft, applied to be released on bail pending appeal arguing that he needed a diet suitable for his diabetic condition. The Court of Appeal in determining the application, noted that the appeal appeared to have an overwhelming probability of success and granted bail.

---

55 (1983) KLR 442.

56 (1986) KLR 528.

8.5.2 Bail Pending Appeal for Appeals to the Court of Appeal

Where the appeal has been made to the Court of Appeal, the Court of Appeal can consider an application for bail pending appeal in its jurisdiction provided for under Rule 5(2) (a) of the Court of Appeal Rules.[57] That provision provides as follows:-

"5 (2) Subject to sub-rule (1), the institution of an appeal shall not operate to suspend any sentence or to stay execution, but the court may -

(a) in any criminal proceedings, where notice of appeal has been given in accordance with rule 59, order that the appellant be released on bail or that the execution of any warrant of distress be suspended pending the determination of the appeal."

In *Isaack Tulicha Guyo v Republic,*[58] it was made clear that the basis for grant of bail pending appeal to the Court of Appeal was not Section 357 of the CPC but was from Rule 5(2) (a) of the Court of Appeal Rules. The above provision applies to bail applications made where the Court of Appeal is seized with the appeal.

8.5.3 Considerations in an Application for Bail Pending Appeal

The considerations that the court would take into account when faced with an application for bail pending appeal are different from those that a court would consider in an application for bail pending trial. When a person has been tried, convicted, and sentenced to imprisonment, it is presumed, unless the contrary is demonstrated, that he has been properly tried and convicted and therefore deserves to be in jail serving sentence. The grant of bail would be antithetical to the service of the sentence. This is in contrast to bail pending trial, where the accused is entitled to the presumption of innocence, and is therefore entitled to bail as a matter of right, unless of course compelling reasons exist to deny

---

[57] Court of Appeal Rules made under the Court of Appeal Act, Chapter 9 Laws of Kenya.

[58] Court of Appeal at Nairobi, Criminal Application No. 16 of 2010, (2010) eKLR.

him his right to bail. Thus it has now been settled that the applicant must demonstrate that he has an appeal that has overwhelming chances of success or that exceptional circumstances exist that would warrant his being released on bail pending appeal. These considerations will also apply where the applicant is seeking bail pending a second appeal.

The point was put as follows in the case of *Somo v Republic*:-[59]

"...the question is whether there are exceptional or unusual circumstances. The most important ground is that the appeal has an overwhelming chance of being successful: in that case there is no justification for depriving the applicant of his freedom. The issue that; the appellant is of good character, the offence did not involve personal violence and that the appeal has been admitted to hearing, are not exceptional or unusual circumstances."

In this case, The applicant was charged before the Magistrates' Court in Nairobi with giving false information to a person employed in the public service contrary to section 129 (a) of the Penal Code and was convicted and sentenced to eighteen months imprisonment. He resolved to file an appeal against the conviction and sentence and applied, under Section 356 of the CPC, for bail pending appeal. The reasons given for the application were that, the appeal will probably succeed; that the applicant was released on appeal pending the hearing and appeared to take his trial; that he is not likely to abscond if set at liberty pending the hearing of the appeal; that he is a man of good character; that the offence with which he was charged contains no element of personal violence and hardship. Bail was denied.

In *Lamba v Republic*,[60] Spry Ag J held that the principle to be applied is that bail pending appeal should only be granted for exceptional and unusual reasons. Neither the complexity of the case nor the good character of the applicant, nor the alleged hardship to his dependents justified the grant of bail, but had the court been satisfied that there was an overwhelming probability that the appeal would succeed, the application would have been granted.

---

59 (1972) EA 476.

60 (1958) E.A 337; See also *R v Leinster (Duke), 17 Cr. App. R. 147; R v AB* (1926), I T.L.R. (R) 118 and *Habib Kara Vesta and others v Republic* (1934) 1 EACA 191.

In *Shah v Republic,*[61] the Court of Appeal in coming to its decision put the law in perspective when it held *inter alia* that:- "*The Principal consideration in an application for bail pending appeal is, the existence of exceptional or unusual circumstances upon which the Court of Appeal can fairly conclude that it is in the interests of justice to grant bail. If it appears prima facie from the totality of the circumstances that the appeal is likely to be successful on account of some substantial point of law to be urged and that the sentence or substantial part of it will have been served by the time the appeal is heard, conditions for granting bail will exist.*"

In *Dominic Karanja v R,*[62] the applicant had been charged and convicted of the offence of obtaining by false pretence and sentenced to two years imprisonment. His appeal to the High Court was summarily rejected and he filed a further appeal to the Court of Appeal. He also filed an application for bail pending the appeal. The court stated that the most important consideration would be whether the appeal has overwhelming chances of success such that there would be no justification for depriving the applicant of his liberty. The other minor relevant considerations would be whether there are exceptional or unusual circumstances. The applicant had stated that he had been of good character and his family would face hardship. The Court of Appeal was not convinced that these were exceptional circumstances, and having noted that the appeal did not have overwhelming chances of success, proceeded to dismiss the application.

Muchelule J, in the case of *Monica Kemunto Jackson v Republic,*[63] put the matter succinctly as follows:-

*"When an accused is awaiting trial he is presumed to be innocent and is therefore entitled to bail. At this stage, however, the Applicant has been convicted and sentenced. He is not entitled to bail. There is the presumption that he was properly convicted and sentenced (*Mundia v. Republic [1986] KLR 623*). For him to be released on bail pending appeal he has to demonstrate that his appeal has overwhelming chances of success (*Somo v. Republic [1972] EA 476*). The fact that the sentence is short and may be served by the time the appeal is ultimately heard may be something to consider in deciding the bail application but that, taken in*

---

61 (1986) KLR 528.

62 (1986) KLR 612.

63 *Monica Kemunto Jackson v Republic* [2009] eKLR.

isolation, does not demonstrate the circumstances herein are exceptional or unusual. It was indicated the Applicant is hypertensive and diabetic and may not survive the conditions of prison. Prisons have medical facilities for conditions like those described, and arrangements are usually made for transfer to hospitals whenever specialized treatment has become necessary or has been recommended."[64]

In *Jivraj Shah v Republic,*[65] the appellant was charged and convicted by the trial court and his appeal to the High Court was dismissed. He filed a second appeal to the Court of Appeal and filed an application for bail pending appeal vide the provisions of Rule 5 (2) (a) of the Court of Appeal Rules. In determining the application for bail pending appeal, the Court of Appeal stated that the principal consideration is whether there exist exceptional or unusual circumstances upon which the court can conclude that it would be in the interests of justice to grant bail. Further, if it appears prima facie from the totality of the circumstances that the appeal is likely to succeed on account of some substantial point of law, and that the sentence or a substantial part of it will have been served by the time the appeal is heard, conditions for granting bail pending appeal will exist. In the case, bail was granted as the court thought there was a substantial question first of the description of a "taking" in the reading of section 268 of the Penal Code, and secondly the circumstances in which the presiding judge became a complainant against the applicant. It will be seen that obtaining bail pending appeal is not an easy task. The principles now appear settled that one needs to demonstrate an overwhelming chance of success and exceptional circumstances to be entitled to bail pending appeal.[66]

* * *

64 But contrast with Shah v R (1986) KLR 528

65 *Jivraj Shah v Republic* [1986] KLR 605.

66 See for example *Wagner v R*, Nairobi Criminal Appeal No. 404 of 2009, (2010)eKLR.

CHAPTER 9

LEGAL REPRESENTATION

9.1 Introduction

Fair hearing is a cardinal facet of due process and legal representation goes to the root of a fair hearing. The parties to a criminal trial are the State and the accused. Both these parties, that is, the prosecution and the accused, have a right to be represented. There is no doubt that the State, being an abstract entity, must be represented through the agency of an individual in every trial. The accused on the other hand, being a person, may represent himself or may opt to be represented by an Advocate.

9.2 Representation of the Accused

The right of the accused to legal representation is so important that it is indeed noted by the Constitution of Kenya, 2010, as one of the ingredients of a fair trial. Article 50 (2) (g) and (h) of the Constitution provide as follows:-

50 (2) Every accused person has the right to a fair trial, which includes the right—

- *(g) to choose, and be represented by, an advocate, and to be informed of this right promptly;*
- *(h) to have an advocate assigned to the accused person by the State and at State expense, if substantial injustice would otherwise result, and to be informed of this right promptly.*

As noted from the above constitutional provisions, it is not anybody who can represent an accused; representation has to be by an advocate. There are three limbs to the question of representation of an accused. The first, noted in Article 50 (2) (g), is the issue of representation itself. The second noted in Article 50 (2) (h) is the question of the right to representation at State expense (legal aid). The third issue, is whether an accused person has the right of self-representation without counsel.

9.2.1 The Right of an Accused to be Represented by Counsel

An accused person has a right to not only be represented by an Advocate[1], but also the right to choose the advocate of his choice. The Constitution as noted above, provides that the accused needs to be "promptly" informed of this right to be represented. An accused has an option of whether to proceed with trial by himself or to be represented by an advocate of his choice. The fact that the Constitution sets out explicitly that the accused needs to be informed of this right, would infer that the court has a constitutional obligation to inform the accused, if the accused is not represented, that he has a right to be represented. The court also has a constitutional obligation to inform the accused that he has a right to be represented by an advocate of his choice. No advocate may be imposed on an accused person. These provisions may sound inconveniencing to a court, but it is clear from the reading of the same, that in every trial, the trial court needs to inform the accused of this right to be represented in the event that the accused is unrepresented. It is debatable whether a trial that proceeds, in the absence of representation for the accused and results in a conviction, may be set aside as not being a fair trial, for the sole reason that the trial court did not inform the accused of his right to representation. But it may not be too far-fetched for one to be entitled to found an appeal on the ground that he was not informed of this right. The Constitution explicitly provides that the accused needs to be informed of this right, and "promptly" too, which would probably mean at his first court appearance.

---

1 Advocate here, would mean an *Advocate* as defined by S. 2 of the Advocates Act, Chapter 16, Laws of Kenya.

9.2.2 Right to Legal Representation at State Expense

Under Article 50 (2) (h) of the Constitution, an accused has a right to have an advocate assigned to him by the State and at State expense, *if substantial injustice would result* for lack of counsel. The accused also needs to be informed promptly of this right, which again means that the trial court must inform the accused that he is entitled to representation at State expense, where in the view of the court, substantial injustice would otherwise result. What this means in practice, is that the trial court should first comply with the provisions of Article 50(2) (g), and if after informing the accused of his right to legal representation, the accused states that he wishes to engage counsel, but cannot afford one, then the court must assess the circumstances of the case, and if it feels that substantial injustice would result for lack of counsel, then advise the accused that he has a right to be represented at State expense. The accused then has a right to choose counsel, of course subject to counsel accepting, and the State must foot the bill. Alternatively, counsel may be suggested to the accused, and if the accused is agreeable to being represented by that counsel, accept his representation.

The challenge in Article 50 (2) (h) is in arriving at an objective test of what situations or circumstances can cause *substantial injustice* if the accused is not represented by counsel. This is because the Constitution does not offer any suggestions on what scenario or situation would cause "substantial injustice". The careful choice of the words "substantial injustice" rather than merely "injustice" must also be taken into consideration to mean a fairly high threshold. The practice prior to the 2010 constitution was to avail representation to accused persons facing trials before the High Court. These were invariably murder trials. There was however no law that compelled the State to provide such legal representation.[2] This was affirmed in the case of *Republic v Hassan Jama Haleys Alias Hassan Jamal & 5 Others.*[3] The six accused persons had been jointly charged with the offence of piracy. They were initially represented by counsel, who applied, and was granted permission to withdraw. The trial magistrate then ordered the State to provide counsel at State expense. The State

2 The closest being Rule 24 of the Court of Appeal Rules, which provided that the Chief Justice or Presiding Judge of the Court of Appeal could assign counsel if it appeared desirable in the interests of justice to do so.

3 Mombasa High Court, Misc. Application No. 105 of 2010, (2010) eKLR.

applied to the High Court for a review of this order. The court in accepting the application, made clear that there was no provision in the law that compelled the State to provide legal representation. The court referred to Section 77(2) (d) of the (now repealed) Constitution which provided as follows:-

Every person who is charged with a criminal offence ... Shall be permitted to defend himself before the court in person or by legal representative of his own choice.

The court interpreted the provision as only giving an accused the right to be represented by counsel of his choice but that there was no obligation on the State to provide an accused with legal representation.[4]This was indeed the correct interpretation given that Section 77 (14) of the Constitution, provided that *nothing contained in subsection (2) (d) shall be construed as entitling a person to legal representation at public expense.*

The Constitution of 2010 as framed is of course radically different from what existed in the previous regime and the issues were first tested in the case of *David Njoroge Macharia v Republic*[5] where the Court of Appeal had the occasion to review the position under the old and the new Constitution. In this case, the appellant was charged with the offence of Robbery with Violence which carries a death sentence.[6] He was not represented and he was convicted after a full trial. His appeal to the High Court was not successful and he filed a second appeal to the Court of Appeal, and for the first time, raised the issue of representation as part of his grounds of appeal. His argument was basically that he never received his constitutional right to a fair trial, as he was never represented by counsel in the subordinate court on the capital charge. The trial was held under the regime of the old constitution, but this ground of appeal was raised and decided, after the Constitution of 2010 had been promulgated. The appeal failed on the reasoning that the then prevailing provisions section 77 (14) of the repealed Constitution, categorically ruled out legal representation at state expense. However, the court in arriving at its decision made important observations on this right in the current constitution and analyzed the legal right to representation.

---

4 See also *Alloys Omondi Nanga v R, infra* note 19.

5 Court of Appeal at Nairobi, Criminal Appeal No. 497 of 2007, (2011) eKLR.

6 Penal Code, Chapter 63, Laws of Kenya, Section 296 (2).

The critical issue that the court had to decide was framed as follows: *"Is the right to free legal counsel in serious offences a fundamental right that must be availed to an accused person at state expense?"* As the court admitted, this was a novel point, being raised for the first time. It was the position of the appellant that the trial which was for a serious offence, and which was held without the appellant being represented, was a violation of his constitutional rights and also was in violation of his rights enshrined in the *International Covenant on Civil and Political Rights*[7] and the *African Charter on Peoples and Human Rights* (The Banjul Charter).[8]

The court in coming to its decision considered the rationale of the right to legal representation and quoted with approval the dictum in the English case of *Pett v. Greyhound Racing Association,*[9] where it was stated obiter that :-

"It is not every man who has the ability to defend himself on his own. He cannot bring out the points in his own favour or the weakness in the other side. He may be tongue-tied, nervous, confused or wanting in intelligence. He cannot examine or cross-examine witnesses. We see it every day. A magistrate says to a man: 'you can ask any questions you like;' whereupon the man immediately starts to make a speech. If justice is to be done, he ought to have the help of someone to speak for him; and who better than a lawyer who has been trained for the task?"

The court further in providing the rationale for legal representation especially in adversarial systems stated that :-

"The right to legal representation is almost axiomatic in an adversarial system. Under the adversarial system, court proceedings are left between the two parties to fight it out. The Bench serves as the umpire and intervenes only to enforce compliance with the rules and ensure fairness of the proceedings. Where it is applied in criminal matters, the adversarial system may result in an incalculable prejudice to the accused

---

7 *International Covenant on Civil and Political Rights* (adopted and opened for signature, ratification and accession on 16 December 1966, entered into force 23 March 1976) 99 UNTS 171 (ICCPR)

8 *African Charter on Human and Peoples Rights* ("*African Charter*"), 27 June 1981, CAB/LEG/67/3. Rev. 5, 21 I.L.M 58 (1982), Adopted in Banjul, the Gambia.

9 *Pett v. Greyhound Racing Association* (1968) 2 All E.R 545, at 549.

person whose liberty or life may be at stake. It is for this reason that accused persons are accorded the right to appoint legal representation of their own choosing. Strongly related to the adversarial system, is the principle of equality of arms which is an essential feature of a fair trial. Equality of arms is an expression of the balance that must exist between the prosecution and the defence"

The court further considered the effect of Article 2 (5)[10] and (6) of the Constitution,[11] which imports international legal texts that have been ratified into laws applicable to Kenya. The court in reviewing the jurisprudence of the international human rights under the two instruments, considered that it had been held in these international tribunals, that the right to legal representation would be available at State expense where the charge was serious or the offence complex.

The court also noted the importance that counsel plays in court proceedings and borrowed from the obiter of Trial Chamber I of the Special Court for Sierra Leone in its decision on the application of the 1st Accused, Samuel Hinga Norman in *Prosecution v. Sam Hinga Norman, Moinina Fofanah and Alieu Kondowa,*[12] which the court observed gave an insightful opinion on the role of the defence counsel. The Chamber, in determining whether to grant the said accused's application for self-representation, noted that, *"the role of a defence counsel is institutional and is meant to serve, not only his client, but also those of the Court and the overall interests of justice."* It further noted firstly, that the right to counsel was predicated upon the notion that representation by counsel was an essential and necessary component of a fair trial; secondly, that the right to counsel *"relieves trial judges of the burden to explain and enforce basic rules of courtroom protocol and to assist the accused in overcoming routine and regular legal obstacles which the accused may encounter if he represents himself, for, the Court, to our mind, is supposed, in the adversarial context, to remain the arbiter and not a pro-active participant in the proceedings".*

---

10 Article 2 (5) of the Constitution provides, *"The general rules of international law shall form part of the law of Kenya."*

11 Article 2 (6) of the Constitution provides, *"Any treaty or convention ratified by Kenya shall form part of the law of Kenya under this Constitution."*

12 *Prosecution v. Sam Hinga Norman, Moinina Fofanah and Alieu Kondowa* Case No. SCSL-04-14-T, (CDF case), for self-representation.

The court in reviewing international practice was of the view that legal representation was required where the accused faced a serious charge and also ought to be provided depending on the complexity of the case. Lack of legal representation was not frowned upon if it was for minor offences. The court cited the provisions of Article 14(3) (d) of the ICCPR[13], and the Banjul Charter,[14] and the guidelines in ACHPR, which provide that legal representation should be provided at least in cases of capital offences.

The court in reviewing the past and current law stated that:-

"Art 50 of the Constitution sets out a right to a fair hearing, which includes the right of an accused person to have an advocate if it is in the interests of ensuring justice. This varies with the repealed law by ensuring that any accused person, regardless of the gravity of their crime may receive a court appointed lawyer if the situation requires it. Such cases may be those involving complex issues of fact or law; where the accused is unable to effectively conduct his or her own defence owing to disabilities or language difficulties or simply where the public interest requires that some form of legal aid be given to the accused because of the nature of the offence...We are of the considered view that in addition to situations where "substantial injustice would otherwise result", persons accused of capital offences where the penalty is loss of life have the right to legal representation at state expense."

However in the circumstances of the case, the court pointed out that the trial of the appellant took place under the old Constitution, and he would not have been entitled to free legal representation during the first trial following the explicit provisions of Section 77 (14) of the repealed Constitution. His appeal was therefore dismissed.

---

13 Article 14 (3) (d) of the ICCPR provides, *"To be tried in his presence, and to defend himself in person or through legal assistance of his own choosing; to be informed, if he does not have legal assistance, of this right; and to have legal assistance assigned to him, in any case where the interests of justice so require, and without payment by him in any such case if he does not have sufficient means to pay for it."*

14 Article 7 (1) (d) of the Banjul Charter provides, *"Every individual shall have the right to have his cause heard. This comprises the right to defence, including the right to be defended by counsel of his choice."*

From the dictum of the Court of Appeal in the *Macharia* case, it would appear that the Court was proposing to have an accused represented, where the accused faces a charge, which if convicted would invite a capital offence. The Court of Appeal also pointed out, that apart from such cases, there could be cases where public interest will demand that legal representation be provided, and it would be in the circumstances, appropriate to provide the same. An assessment therefore needs to be made on a case to case basis, every case being dependent on its own circumstances.

The sentiments of the Court of Appeal in the *Macharia* case, came to focus in the case of *John Swaka v The Director of Public Prosecutions & 2 Others.*[15] This was a Constitutional petition which sought orders to stop the prosecution of all indigent persons in Kenya facing prosecution for offences that carried the death penalty until the State implemented the provisions of Article 50(2) (h) of the Constitution and provided defence counsel to them. The petitioner cited the *Macharia* case in support. The court in grappling with the issue held that in as much as the right is provided for in the Constitution, the Constitution itself under Article 261 and Schedule 5, provided for a time frame of 4 years, to implement the provisions of Article 50 of the Constitution. The court in its analysis noted that there would be need to make major policy and legislative changes, and to make financial resources available, in order to put into effect the constitutional requirement that accused persons be availed legal representation in the situations where 'substantial injustice' would result if the accused person was undefended, and for those charged with offences that carry the death penalty. It held further that, it could not have been the intention of the framers of the Constitution, nor of the Court of Appeal in the *Macharia* decision, to halt all criminal prosecutions of persons charged with robbery with violence until the implementation of a scheme to provide legal representation to all persons charged with the offence of robbery with violence. Accordingly, the Petition was dismissed.

It will be seen that the court appreciated the existence of the right, but, stated that the enforcement of it was premature given the provisions of Article 261 and Schedule 5 of the Constitution. These provide for a time frame of 4 years for legislature to pass legislation in respect to the rights to a fair trial, provided

---

15 Nairobi High Court, Constitutional Petition No. 318 of 2011, (2013) eKLR.

for in Article 50. It is debatable whether the same petition if presented after 4 years of the promulgation of the Constitution will be allowed and probably only time will tell. *John Swaka* was applied in the case of *Dominic Kimaru Tanui v Republic.*[16]In the matter, the appellant was charged in the Magistrate's Court with the offence of defilement of a minor aged less than 11 years old, which carries a life sentence.[17] He represented himself for a considerable duration of the trial, then briefly engaged counsel, who later withdrew. For the most part of the trial, he remained unrepresented. He was convicted of the offence and appealed. One of the grounds of appeal was that the trial was unfair, as he was not represented by counsel. It was the view of the appellate court that one facing a life sentence, faces a serious charge, and ideally ought to be represented by counsel at State expense if he is unable to afford counsel of his own. The court however, held that in the circumstances, and following the decision in the case of *John Swaka*, the State had 4 years to implement the provisions of Article 50 of the Constitution. The court (Sila J.) stated as follows:-

"In my view, a case in which one faces a life sentence is a serious case, and I would indeed place it at the same level as a case in which the penalty is loss of life, so that ideally, legal representation ought to be provided at State expense if the accused cannot afford counsel. However, the Constitution itself under Article 261 and Schedule 5, provides for a time frame of 4 years, to implement the provisions of Article 50 of the Constitution. The present Constitution was promulgated on 27 August 2010, and four years will lapse on 27 August 2014. Thus it is arguable that the provisions of Article 50, part of which relate to the right to be provided with legal representation at State expense, are yet to be fully enforceable as the State has been accorded time to put the mechanism in place."

There is of course a powerful argument that if persons facing trials in the High Court have legal representation provided by the State, because the offence carry a death sentence, then, there is no plausible reason why an accused person, facing a similar sentence, is not be provided with legal representation, simply because his trial is in the Magistrates' Court.

---

16 Eldoret High Court, Criminal Appeal No. 12 of 2012, (2014) eKLR.

17 Sexual Offences Act, CAP 62A, Section 8 (2).

The matters will probably be sorted out with time and jurisprudence on the point of when and under what circumstances the State will be obliged to provide legal representation will become settled, especially after the lapse of the 4 years provided to implement Article 50 of the Constitution. That aside, an important question may arise, as to whether the accused has a right to choose any counsel of his choice, and whether the State is bound to accept his choice and pay the legal fees asked by such counsel, or whether the accused must accept the counsel assigned to him by the State.

This issue did indeed arise, in the case of *Alloys Omondi Nanga v Republic,*[18] a matter determined before the Constitution of 2010. The appellant was convicted by the High Court of the offence of murder. He appealed to the Court of Appeal against the conviction and sentence. One of the grounds raised on appeal was that the trial was a nullity, and failed the fair trial test, as he was not represented by an advocate of his choice. It was further asserted that the trial Judge did not inquire into whether the appellant consented to the representation provided by the State; that neither did the appellant instruct nor consent to the representation by the State appointed counsel; that the counsel who conducted the appellant's defence did so without the consent, permission or other instruction from the appellant and never sought instructions or spoke to the appellant regarding the appellant's defence; and finally, that he was not permitted to defend himself before the court in person. The court was of the view that the right to a legal representation of one's choice may only arise where an accused person has the means to engage a counsel of his own choice. Where however an accused is given free legal aid he has no choice of the counsel who is to represent him. He has however a right of election – that is, he can decide to accept the counsel assigned to him or to reject him, and defend himself in person. The court found that in the instant case, there was no material to support the constitutional issue raised, as the record did not show that the appellant ever raised an objection in court, or in writing, to any of the two advocates assigned to him, nor did he inform the court that he wanted to conduct his defence in person. Instead he acquiesced to the assignment of the two advocates to conduct his defence and benefited from the legal services for which the Judiciary ultimately paid. The court therefore held that he could

---

18 Kisumu Criminal Appeal No. 7 of 2006, [2006] eKLR.

not now complain at the appellate stage. The court proceeded to recommend a practice that where free legal aid is given, an accused person should be required to indicate his acceptance of the counsel assigned to him, or otherwise in writing, or alternatively, the trial Judge should inform the accused person of his right to reject the counsel and to record his remarks before the plea is taken.

9.2.3 Is There a Right to Self -Representation?

The Constitution does not explicitly state that an accused person has a right to decline counsel. It is therefore debatable, whether a right to assert self-representation exists and if so, whether it is absolute or whether it may be qualified. If qualified what would be such qualifications? The right to represent oneself would probably become an issue where the court is of the view that there will be substantial injustice caused if the accused is not represented, yet the accused insists on representing himself. Article 50(2)(h) which we have seen above, obligates the State to provide counsel to the accused at State expense if substantial injustice would otherwise occur. It could happen that the court is not in doubt that the accused is in need of representation, and that in the circumstances, substantial injustice will occur if the accused is not represented. Can the accused, given these circumstances, insist on representing himself despite the fact that substantial injustice will be occasioned by his lack of representation?

Probably light to this important question may be found in comparing the provisions of the former Constitution with those of the Constitution of 2010. Section 77(2) (d) of the repealed Constitution provided as follows:-

77(2) (d) Every person who is charged with a criminal offence shall be permitted to defend himself before the court in person or by a legal representative of his own choice.

By the above provision, an accused person had a constitutional right in a criminal trial to defend himself before the court, in person or by a legal representative, of his own choice. The current provisions, as noted above in Articles 50(2)(g) and (h), provide an accused with the right to choose, and be represented by, an advocate, and to have an advocate assigned him at State expense if substantial injustice would otherwise result. The former Constitution had the words *"permitted to defend himself in person"* which words do not exist in the current Constitution. It is however arguable that the interpretation of the words to *"choose"* in Article 50(2)(g) would also infer the right not to choose an advocate, if the accused so wishes.

As correctly observed by the Court of Appeal in the case of *Alloys Omondi Nanga*[19] not every accused person appreciates the free legal aid given by the government.

The question of self-representation, though not too seriously argued in our jurisprudence, has vexed both national and international courts. In the USA the right of legal representation is set out in the Sixth Amendment. The same includes a compact statement of the rights necessary to a full defence and provides that:

"In all criminal prosecutions, the accused shall enjoy the right . . . to be informed of the nature and cause of the accusation; to be confronted with the witnesses against him; to have compulsory process for obtaining witnesses in his favor, and to have the Assistance of Counsel for his defence."

It will be discerned that the Sixth Amendment does not expressly mention the right of one to represent self, only acknowledging that an accused has a right to the assistance of counsel. [20] The US Supreme Court had the perfect opportunity to deal with the question whether an accused person had an absolute right to self-representation in the case of *Faretta v California.*[21] The Supreme Court held that the Sixth Amendment when naturally read, implies a right to self-representation. The Court stated that *"The language and spirit of the Sixth Amendment contemplate that counsel, like the other defense tools guaranteed by the Amendment, shall be an aid to a willing defendant - not an organ of the State interposed between an unwilling defendant and his right to defend himself*

---

19 *Ibid.*

20 However as noted in the dictum of Stewart J in the *Faretta* decision *(infra),* most US States recognize this right and the Constitutions of 36 States explicitly confer this right.

21 *Faretta v California* 422 US 806 (1975).

personally. To thrust counsel upon the accused, against his considered wish, thus violates the logic of the Amendment."

In the words of the court, *"To force a lawyer on a defendant can only lead him to believe that the law contrives against him. Moreover, it is not inconceivable that in some rare instances, the defendant might in fact present his case more effectively by conducting his own defense. Personal liberties are not rooted in the law of averages. The right to defend is personal. The defendant, and not his lawyer or the State, will bear the personal consequences of a conviction. It is the defendant, therefore, who must be free personally to decide whether in his particular case counsel is to his advantage."*

The court however pointed out that, in order to represent himself, the accused must *"knowingly and intelligently"* forgo the benefits of assistance of counsel. In order to competently and intelligently choose self-representation, the accused should be made aware of the dangers and disadvantages of self-representation, so that the record will establish that *"he knows what he is doing and his choice is made with eyes open."* In assessing the matter before it, the Supreme Court was of opinion that *Faretta* was literate, competent, and understanding, and that he was voluntarily exercising his informed free will. The Supreme Court was further of the view that the Trial Court was wrong in attempting to assess *Faretta's* grasp of the intricacies of the law and in the view of the court, *Faretta's* technical legal knowledge, was not relevant to an assessment of his knowing exercise of the right to defend himself. Finally, it concluded by adumbrating that in forcing *Faretta*, under the circumstances, to accept against his will a state-appointed public defender, the California courts deprived him of his constitutional right to conduct his own defense. Accordingly, the judgment was vacated.

However, in the case of *Sam Hinga Norman*[22] before the International Criminal Tribunal of Sierra Leone, the Court observed that the role of counsel is much wider than service to the client; he also has an important duty to the court and declined an application for self-representation. The decision in *Sam Hinga Norman*, followed in the steps of the case of the decision of the Trial Chamber of the International Criminal Tribunal for Rwanda (ICTR), in *Prosecutor v*

---

22 *Supra*, note 12.

Jean-Bosco Barayagwiza,[23] which disallowed an application for self-representation and noted that in so far as the ICTR is concerned, Counsel is assigned and not appointed by the accused. In the chambers own words:-

"In the view of the Chamber, this not only entailed obligations towards the accused but also that Counsel represents the interests of the Tribunal to ensure that the accused receives a fair trial. The Chamber noted that Barayagwiza faced serious charges and that the judiciary had to ensure the rights of the accused, taking into account what is at stake for him. In such a situation, counsel could not simply abide with the accused's instruction not to defend him. In the opinion of the Chamber, such instructions need to be seen rather as an attempt to obstruct judicial proceedings."

The Trial Chamber affirmed that Defence Counsel could be assigned over the objection of the accused and that the right to self-representation was not an absolute but qualified right.

Whether the Kenyan courts will interpret the right to self-representation as being qualified by the test of "substantial injustice" will probably be settled in future, as and when such an issue will arise.

As a final analysis, although an accused has a right to be represented by an advocate of his own choice, it is however not good practice for an advocate who is a co-accused to represent another co-accused. So too where the interests of the co-accused persons are in direct conflict, it will be improper for the same advocate to represent both accused persons. An advocate also ought to decline representation, where he has a conflict of interest, or for one reason or another, he is unable to provide proper legal service to the accused.

---

23 *The Prosecutor v Jean-Bosco Barayagwiza*, Case No. ICTR -97-19-T, Decision on Defence Counsel Motion to Withdraw (2 November 2000).

9.2.4 Children and Legal Representation

Under the Children Act,[24] Children have a legal right to representation. There are no qualifications to this right, i.e. the question of "substantial injustice" does not arise. Section 186 (b) of the Children Act provides that every child, accused of having infringed any law, shall, if he is unable to obtain legal assistance, be provided by the Government with assistance in the preparation and presentation of his defence. There is therefore no doubt that all child offenders are entitled to legal representation.

9.3 Legal Representation of the State in Criminal Prosecutions

The Director of Public Prosecutions (DPP) is now in charge of all prosecutions, a power donated by Article 157 of the Constitution. The DPP obviously cannot act in all cases, and the State inevitably must be represented by officers subordinate to the DPP. The Criminal Procedure Code (CPC)[25] in this regard provides under Section 85 that the DPP may by notice in the Gazette, appoint public prosecutors for Kenya or any specified area, and such appointment may be general or specific to a case. The DPP is also empowered to appoint an advocate of the High Court or other person employed by the public service to be a public prosecutor for a particular case. Every public prosecutor is subject to the directions of the DPP.

The Office of the DPP has counsels employed by the State who do the prosecution; they are ordinarily called "State Counsels". But we have seen that the DPP is empowered to appoint an advocate or other public servant to be a prosecutor in a case. These "Special Prosecutors" are not "State Counsels", but are contracted specifically by the State for purposes of prosecuting the particular case or class of cases. Specialized departments also have prosecutors who are not necessarily lawyers such as the National Social Security Fund. These also represent the State in prosecutions. They need to be gazetted under the instruction of the DPP for them to undertake prosecutions on behalf of the State.

---

24 Chapter 141, Laws of Kenya.

25 Chapter 75, Laws of Kenya.

It is also common to find Police Officers prosecuting on behalf of the State. These officers similarly must be gazetted to undertake prosecutions. A private person as we saw earlier can also undertake a prosecution on behalf of the State. He is not a public prosecutor but does so in his private capacity subject to permission being granted by the magistrate. If a trial is conducted by a person who has no authority from the DPP to conduct the prosecution, (the prosecution not being a private prosecution), then the proceedings are null and void. For instance, prior to 2007, the CPC provided that the AG could in writing appoint an Advocate, or a public officer, or person employed in the public service not being a police officer *below the rank of Deputy Inspector*, to be a public prosecutor for the purposes of any case. In the case of *Elirema v Republic,*[26] the trial was conducted partly by a Police inspector but also by two persons who were Corporals. The trial was held to have been a nullity and the appellant set free.

The position at the time that the *Elirema* case was decided, was that the police prosecutor had to be one of the rank of Assistant Inspector and above. However through Legal Notice No.7 of 2007, the Act was amended and now Section 85 (2*)* CPC, provides that the DPP can appoint any person in the public service to be a public prosecutor. The rank of the police prosecutor is therefore now immaterial so long as the person is duly appointed by the DPP to prosecute and is properly gazetted. Thus for a person to prosecute on behalf of the State he must be appointed by the DPP and must be an advocate or person employed in the public service. It is not therefore anyone who can prosecute on behalf of the State. As noted in the case of *Elirema* if the prosecution is conducted by a person who has no authority to prosecute, the proceedings will be a nullity.[27] Since it is the State that prosecutes, it follows that the DPP cannot represent an accused person as there would be a conflict of interest.

* * *

---

26 (2003) KLR 537.

27 See also *DPP vs Samuel Gichuru & Another*, Nairobi High Court, Criminal Revision Case No. 926 of 2011 (2012) eKLR; and *Laban Kimondo Karanja v R & 2Others*, Nyeri High Court, Criminal Appeal Nos. 310,311, 312 of 2001 (2006) eKLR.

CHAPTER 10

TRIAL

10.1 Introduction

An accused person is always presumed innocent until proven guilty and the onus of proving the guilt of the accused is on the prosecution. It therefore follows that it is the prosecution that takes the lead in providing the evidence that goes to demonstrate the guilt of the accused. After it has brought forth its evidence, the prosecution then closes its case. The court must then make a determination of whether there is sufficient evidence, which if not rebutted by the accused, will lead to his conviction. If the court is of the view that there has been ample evidence that could lead to a conviction, the accused will be put on his defence. The accused then brings forth evidence to dispel the evidence led by the prosecution. After this, the court makes a judgment.

The place in which a criminal court is held for the purpose of trying an offence is to be an open court to which the public generally may have access, so far as it can conveniently contain them. However, the presiding judge or magistrate may order at any stage of the trial of any particular case that the public generally or any particular person shall not have access to or be or remain in the room or building used by the court. [1]

10.2 The Case for the Prosecution

The manner in which trials are held in the Subordinate Courts and the High Court, are not very much at variance. For purposes of demonstrating how

1 Criminal Procedure Code (CPC), Chapter 75, Laws of Kenya, Section 77.

the trial is conducted, the trial as conducted in the subordinate courts will be utilized.

10.2.1 Appearance On the Part of the Complainant

A criminal trial contemplates that the accuser will appear in court. Under the provisions of Section 202 of the CPC,[2] if the accused person appears, but the complainant does not appear, the court shall thereupon acquit the accused unless it deems it proper to adjourn the hearing of the case. This section has been difficult to interpret as it is not clear who the term "complainant" in this instance means. Would it mean that it is the victim of the crime or does it mean the State prosecutor? Or does it mean a situation where neither the prosecutor nor any of the state witnesses are available? However, if both the accused and the complainant appear, the court is supposed to proceed and hear the case.[3]

In *Laban Kimondo Karanja & 2 Others v Republic,*[4] the High Court had this to say on the interpretation of Section 202 of the CPC:-

"The "Complainant" in this context has been interpreted to mean the Republic in whose name all criminal prosecutions are brought, and not the victim of crime who is merely the chief witness on behalf of Republic, and when a public prosecutor is present in a trial in the court, the "Complainant" is said to be present."

This appears to be the approach taken by the Sexual Offences Act[5], Section 2 (1*)* of which defines "complainant" to mean the Republic or the alleged victim of a sexual offence, and in the case of a child or a person with mental disabilities, the person who lodges a complaint on behalf of the alleged victim where the victim is unable or inhibited from lodging and following up a complaint of sexual abuse.

---

2 *Ibid.*

3 CPC Section 203.

4 High Court at Nyeri, Criminal Appeals Nos. 310-312 of 2001, (2006) eKLR.

5 Chapter 62A, Laws of Kenya.

If the complainant does not appear and the court declines to give an adjournment and no evidence is tendered by the prosecution, then the court cannot dismiss the case for non-attendance of the complainant, but can only dismiss the case under Section 210 of the CPC, for there being no evidence to place the accused on defence. This was the basis of the decision in the case of *Attorney General v Shimanyula.*[6]

10.2.2 Withdrawal of Complaint

The State does not have to proceed with every case that has been filed. Pursuant to Section 204 of the CPC, if a complainant, at any time before a final order is passed, satisfies the court that there are sufficient grounds for permitting him to withdraw his complaint, the court may permit him to withdraw it and shall thereupon acquit the accused. In *Avril Atieno Adoncia v Republic,*[7]the accused was alleged to have stolen a Kenya Airways ticket and used it to fly from London to Nairobi. The matter was resolved privately between Kenya Airways and the accused and an application to withdraw the complaint was made. The trial magistrate however rejected the same and the accused filed an application for revision. Ojwang J, in dealing with the matter stated that although the court has discretion to disallow an application to withdraw, that discretion must be in the interests of justice, must uphold the efficacy of judicial decision-making, must be objective and fair, and must be exercised according to law. The court also noted that Section 176 of the CPC gives the court mandate to promote reconciliation and settlement, and in the circumstances, faulted the trial magistrate for declining the application to withdraw.

In *Ceretta Medardo v Republic* [8]the court was of opinion that in the context of the provisions of Section 204 of the CPC, the term "complainant" refers to the person who lodges a complaint with the police, or any other lawful authority, in most instances, the victim of the crime. The respondent had been charged

---

6 (1990) KLR 157.

7 High Court at Nairobi, Miscellaneous Criminal Application No. 876 of 2007, (2008) eKLR.

8 *Ceretta Medardo v Republic* High Court at Malindi, Criminal Appeal No.73 of 2004, (2004) eKLR; See also *Republic v Mohammed* [1981] KLR 421.

with the offence of having had carnal knowledge of a person against the order of nature, contrary to Section 162A of the Penal Code. The victim of the crime was a male minor. The mother of the minor appeared in court and applied to withdraw the charges and stated that they have talked and she had agreed to withdraw the charges. The charges were then withdrawn and the respondent acquitted. The State appealed against the withdrawal and acquittal. The High Court in assessing the appeal, stated that Section 204 of the CPC, contemplates two matters. First, it is only the complainant who may withdraw the charges. Secondly, the court must be satisfied that there are sufficient reasons for the withdrawal. In this case, the withdrawal was not made by the complainant but by the mother of the complainant. Secondly, the court was of the view that the matter did not fall within Section 176 of the CPC, as the charges allegedly committed constituted a felony. The above decision though sound on its findings, makes one question who exactly is entitled to withdraw a case on behalf of a minor, and whether a minor has capacity to withdraw charges.

In Medardo, the court stated obiter that:- *However, if the child was to withdraw, the Court would have been expected to test the intelligence of the child through a voire dire examination before deciding whether or not to subject him to the oath.* It is not clear whether this statement affirms that the child, if of sufficient intelligence and understanding, can withdraw a complaint by himself. If a child is of tender years, then again, a question may arise whether the parent or guardian can withdraw the charges on behalf of the minor, even though the parent/guardian may not strictly qualify to be the complainant. It could be that the court will assess whether the desire to withdraw will be in the best interest of the child, which is a general theme running through the Children Act.

The discretion to withdraw a charge by a complainant, under Section 204 CPC, needs to be read alongside the provisions of Section 176 of the CPC. Section 176 of the CPC, provides as follows:-

*"In all cases the court may promote reconciliation and encourage and facilitate the settlement in an amicable way of proceedings for common assault, or for any other offence of a personal or private nature not amounting to felony, and not aggravated in degree, on terms of payment of compensation or other terms approved by the court, and may thereupon order the proceedings to be stayed or terminat*ed." Thus, it is not all cases that are capable of being withdrawn under the notion of reconciliation.

The offence must not be a felony and ought not to be aggravated in degree. That was indeed the rationale of the decision in the *Medardo* case. Also as noted in the case, the withdrawal must be done by the complainant himself, and not by proxy, save probably in case of minors of tender years or persons under incapacity who may have to act through the agency of another individual.

10.2.3 Evidence of the Prosecution

We saw earlier in Chapter 7[9], that an accused person has the avenue of either pleading "guilty" or "not guilty". If he pleads guilty, no trial will be held, the court's task only being to sentence the accused. If however, the accused does not admit the truth of the charge, by pleading "not guilty", a trial must be held. The court is obliged to hear the complainant and his witnesses, which totality of evidence, will now comprise the case of the prosecution.[10] The accused person or his advocate may put questions to each witness produced against him.[11] This is by way of cross examination, which is aimed to test the veracity of the witness's assertions. Where the accused is unrepresented, the court is obliged at the close of the examination of each witness for the prosecution, to ask the accused person whether he wishes to put any questions to that witness and shall record his answer.

In *Republic v Subordinate Court of the First Class Magistrate at City Hall, Nairobi & Another ex parte Yougindar Pall Sennik & Another,*[12] the applicant sought orders of *certiorari* to quash the charge sheet and all the proceedings and orders made in Criminal Case number M 867 (A) of 2004, in the 1st Class Magistrate's Court at City Hall Nairobi. The applicant also sought for an order of prohibition to issue, directed to and prohibiting the First Class Magistrate at City Hall Nairobi, from continuing with the prosecution of the said Criminal Case No M 687 (A) of 2004, in its present form at that time, or in any intended variation. The applicant was charged with various offences under the Public Health Act. Immediately after he entered a plea of 'not guilty' the magistrate

---

9 See Chapter 7 On Plea.

10 CPC, Section 208.

11 *Ibid*, Section 208 (2).

12 High Court at Nairobi, Criminal Application No. 652 of 2005, (2006) eKLR.

called and heard the evidence of five witnesses who purported to give evidence against the applicant. No opportunity was given to the applicant to cross examine the witnesses. It was the view of the applicant that there was *inter alia* a breach of the provision of Section 208 of the CPC. The court did not hesitate to hold that the trial was unfair to the applicant for violation of Section 208 of the CPC. It proceeded to issue the order of certiorari and prohibition sought.

10.2.4 Determining Whether or Not to Put the Accused on his Defence

The prosecution must tender sufficient evidence to support the charge. This is what is called a "prima facie" case. The onus to prove the guilt of the accused is always on the prosecution even in cases where statute may have put the burden of proof on the accused.[13]

If no prima facie case is made out, the accused must be acquitted.[14] In *Ramanlal Bhat v Republic,*[15] the dealt with the question of, what amounts to a prima facie case, and gave the following definition :-

"It may not be easy to define what is meant by a prima facie case but it must mean one on which a reasonable tribunal, properly directing his mind to the law and the evidence would convict if no explanation is offered by the defence."[16]

The court declined the notion that a prima facie case is made out if the case is merely one "which on full consideration might *possibly* be thought sufficient to sustain a conviction." It averred that a mere scintilla of evidence can never be enough, nor can any amount of worthless evidence.

It follows therefore that it will be pointless to put the accused on his defence, if no prima facie case has been set out. If the accused can opt to remain quite in his defence and be acquitted thereafter, then obviously no prima facie case was ever established in the first place. It is usual for the court to invite both

---

13 *Prabhulal v R* (1971) EA 52.

14 CPC, Section 210.

15 (1957) EA 332.

16 *Ibid*, p335.

prosecution and the accused to make submissions on whether or not a prima facie case has been established. The court then makes a ruling. If a prima facie case is not set out, the accused must be acquitted forthwith pursuant to the provisions of Section 210 of the CPC. [17]

10.3 The Defence Case

If a prima facie case is made out, then the court must put the accused to his defence. Section 211 requires the court to again explain the substance of the charge to the accused, and give him the various options that he has to make out his defence. It provides as follows:-

S.211 (1) At the close of the evidence in support of the charge, and after hearing such summing up, submission or argument as may be put forward, if it appears to the court that a case is made out against the accused person sufficiently to require him to make a defence, the court shall again explain the substance of the charge to the accused, and shall inform him that he has a right to give evidence on oath from the witness box, and that, if he does so, he will be liable to cross-examination, or to make a statement not on oath from the dock, and shall ask him whether he has any witnesses to examine or other evidence to adduce in his defence, and the court shall then hear the accused and his witnesses and other evidence (if any).

(2) If the accused person states that he has witnesses to call but that they are not present in court, and the court is satisfied that the absence of those witnesses is not due to any fault or neglect of the accused person, and that there is a likelihood that they could, if present, give material evidence on behalf of the accused person, the court may adjourn the trial and issue process, or take other steps, to compel the attendance of the witnesses. From the above, it will be seen that the accused has the following options in defence:-

(i) A right to give evidence on oath from the witness box, and, if he does so, he will be liable to cross-examination; or
(ii) Make a statement, not on oath, from the dock; or

[17] *Murimi v R*, (1967) EA 542.

(iii) Remain silent[18]; and

(iii) Call witnesses or bring forth other evidence (such as documentary evidence) to support his defence.

It is imperative for the court to explain to the accused the options that he has in defence as provided for in Section 211 above. A situation occurred in *Chiro Sonje Mbaga v Republic*,[19] where the appellant argued that he was never accorded a fair trial, because in his view, there was no compliance with Section 211 CPC. The appellant was charged with the offence of robbery with violence contrary to section 296 (2) of the Penal Code. He was found guilty and sentenced to death. His first appeal to the High Court was dismissed and he made a further appeal to the Court of Appeal. He argued *inter alia* that the subordinate court erred in law in failing to explain to him, his rights under Section 211 and failed to record the appellant's response thereto. On this point, the Court of Appeal held that Section 211 of the CPC is a direction to the trial court as to what steps should be taken at the close of the prosecution case if it is decided that the accused be placed on his defence. The court stated that:-

"We do not believe the subordinate courts should record the section verbatim when placing the accused person on his defence but words to the effect that: 'After perusing the prosecution evidence, I am satisfied a prima facie case has been established against the accused person which warrant he/she be placed to him/her defence and I now place him/her to his/her defence. I have also explained to the accused his/her rights to defend himself or herself.' But in order to save time in the subordinate courts Magistrates often resort to the short words: 'Section 211 complied with' to indicate they have given the requisite directions. We think this is sufficient and, we do not feel the appellant's rights in the case before the trial court were violated under that section because the appellant, nevertheless, defended himself."

---

18 This is not explicit in S. 211 of the CPC, but it is a right of every accused person granted by the Constitution to remain silent. See Article 50 (2) (i) of the Constitution.

19 Court of Appeal, Criminal Appeal No. 357 of 2008, (2010) eKLR; See also *Jane Mwikali Rumuti v Republic*, High Court at Meru, Criminal Appeal No. 185 of 2008, (2009) eKLR and *Daniel Chege Kamundia & 2 Others v Republic*, Nairobi Criminal Appeal Nos.722-724 of 2003, (2006) eKLR.

It is debatable, whether a mere record stating that "Section 211 complied with" is actually sufficient, for it is easy to record that the section has been complied with, yet in reality, it may be that there has been no compliance, or no strict compliance, with the same. To be on the safe side, it is important that there be meticulous compliance with Section 211, and the record do reflect precisely what the trial court has stated to the accused, and his response thereto.

Depending on what option the accused agrees to take, the matter proceeds for defence hearing. If the accused adduces evidence in his defence, introducing a new matter which the prosecutor could not by the exercise of reasonable diligence have foreseen, the court may allow the prosecutor to adduce evidence in reply to rebut that matter.[20]

10.4 Right to Make Submissions before Judgment

Once the defence case is closed, the parties can submit on the facts and the law. It is usual for the parties to cite authorities in their support at this stage. The accused always has a right to make submissions but this is not the case for the prosecution. The prosecution will not submit where the accused has not adduced evidence or where the evidence adduced is only that of the accused person unless the DPP has personally been appearing for the prosecution in which case he will have the right to reply. [21]

Section 213 of the CPC provides that the prosecutor or his advocate and the accused and his advocate shall be entitled to address the court in the same manner and order as in a trial under before the High Court.[22]

---

[20] CPC, Section 212.

[21] CPC, Section 161.

[22] Section 306 (3) of the CPC, which covers trials in the High Court, provides that if the accused person says that he does not intend to give evidence or make an unsworn statement, or to adduce evidence, then the advocate for the prosecution may sum up the case against the accused person.

10.4.1 Written Submissions

In *Akhuya v R,*[23] the accused had been charged and convicted of the offences of attempted robbery with violence and being in illegal possession of a firearm. At the conclusion of the hearing, the parties filed written submission apparently in compliance with Section 213 of the CPC. The trial magistrate found the accused guilty. On appeal, the Court of Appeal addressed the issue of the legality of written submissions. The court was of the view that written submissions have no place in the criminal procedure and that the CPC only recognizes oral submissions. The fact that the parties submitted by way of written submissions thus caused a mistrial. The court allowed the appeal and ordered a re-trial of the matter.

This issue was also canvassed in *Henry Odhiambo Otieno v Republic,*[24]where the appellant challenged his conviction and sentence on the charge of causing grievous bodily harm. In the court's holding it noted that, *"When section 213 and 310 of the CPC are read together with section 77 (2) of the (former) Constitution, it is clear that where written submissions are tendered without the accused's express consent, the proceedings of the court concerned are thereafter rendered null and void."*

It is difficult to see what prejudice an accused suffers, if his counsel prefers to make written rather than oral submission. What he may have said orally is probably exactly what has been put down in writing, and in any event, the trial court has to reduce the oral submissions into writing anyway. It is probably easier and it saves court the time, when submissions are made in writing. A party can then stress a point by making oral submission. Unless a party prefers to make oral rather than written submissions, the proper position is not to outlaw written submissions unless the accused has a problem with submissions being made in writing. However, given the position taken by the Court of Appeal, it is wise, for the trial court to inquire from the counsels and the accused, whether they are all comfortable with submissions being made in writing, and record their response accordingly. It is also wise for the trial court after receiving the written submissions, to inquire and place on record, whether

---

23 (2002) 2 EA 323.

24 Court of Appeal at Kisumu, Criminal Appeal No. 83 of 2005, (2006) eKLR.

any of the parties need to make any oral submissions, and if they intend to do so, give them the opportunity. After submissions, the court will then pronounce judgment on the guilt or innocence of the accused. The court will then make a judgment either convicting or acquitting the accused.[25]

10.5 Right of Accused to be Availed of the Prosecution Evidence in Advance

It will be observed from the foregoing that it is the prosecution that begins the case and presents its evidence. The accused person has a right to be informed in advance of the evidence the prosecution intends to rely on, and to have reasonable access to that evidence. This in practice entails the provision of witness statements to the accused beforehand and to have the accused know the exhibits that will be adduced by the prosecution. This right is now explicit in Article 50 (2) (c) of the Constitution. It was however not explicit in the previous Constitution, but the jurisprudence that developed, meant that it was imperative for the statements to be provided to the accused.

In the *George Ngodhe Juma & 2 Others v AG,*[26] (decided prior to the promulgation of the 2010 Constitution), the accused had applied before the trial magistrate's court to be availed of copies of the witness statements and exhibits that the prosecution intended to rely on. This request was rejected with the court reasoning that there was no equivalent in the CPC, of the provisions of discovery in the Civil Procedure Act[27], such that it was not mandatory for the prosecution to avail witness statements and copies of exhibits to the accused. The accused then filed a constitutional reference under the provisions of section 77 (1)[28] and 77 (2) (c)[29] of the repealed Constitution. The question

---

25 CPC, Section 215.

26 High Court at Nairobi, Criminal Application No. 345 of 2001, (2003) eKLR.

27 Chapter 21, Laws of Kenya.

28 Section 77 (1) of the repealed Constitution provided, *"If a person is charged with a criminal offence, then, unless the charge is withdrawn, the case shall be afforded a fair hearing within a reasonable time by an independent and impartial court established by law."*

29 Section 77 (2) (c) of the repealed Constitution provided, *"Every person who is charged with a criminal offence shall be given adequate time and facilities for the preparation of his defence."*

that the court had to address was whether the request for witness statements and exhibits was comprised in the definition of *"facilities to prepare a defence."* The court in addressing the parameters of a fair trial held that an accused is entitled to be availed of witness statements and copies of exhibits to enable him prepare his defence, only subject to, statutory limitation of disclosure and public interest immunity. The court referred to an old case, *Kariuki Kamau v R,*[30] and was categorical that a fair hearing would encompass pre-trial disclosure of material statements and exhibits and that in criminal litigation, courts should not encourage the practice under which an accused person would be ambushed. The court went further to hold that there is a general duty on the part of the State to produce all material, which is known to be material to the case, which is known or possessed, and which should be disclosed, and the evidence it intends to adduce at the trial, and especially all evidence which may assist the accused, even if the prosecution does not propose to adduce it. But the court held that the duty to disclose is not absolute and may be qualified to take into account interests such as the safety of the witnesses, in which case the trial court can allow a refusal to disclose.

However, there is no corresponding right on the accused, to present in advance, his evidence to the Prosecution. This was made clear in the case of *Cholmondeley v R.*[31] The appellant was charged with the offence of murder. The trial proceeded and the trial court held that there was a prima facie case established. The appellant was then put to his defence. Counsel for the accused then stated that the appellant would provide an unsworn statement and call seven witnesses. The DPP then applied that the appellant be ordered to supply the State with the names and statements of the intended defence witnesses and all intended documentary evidence. The trial court allowed this application which provoked an appeal. The Court of Appeal held that there was no reciprocal obligation on the part of the accused to adduce his evidence in advance to the State and allowed the appeal.

---

30 (1954) 21 EACA 203.

31 Court of Appeal at Nairobi, Criminal Appeal No. 116 of 2007, (2008) eKLR.

10.6 Right of Court to Summon Witnesses on its Own Motion

Under Section 150 of the CPC, the trial court is entitled to summon a witness who was neither called by the prosecution nor defence.

In *Murimi v R*,[32] the appellant was charged with the offence of stealing by servant. The appellant was employed as a secretary in a sisal buying post and he had custody of various sums of money. When his accounts were checked, the books showed a balance of Shs. 2,827/- but which he explained he had handed over to the Assistant Manager, one Premini. The manager told the police that the appellant was lying and he was duly arrested. At the trial, Premini was not called by the prosecution as a witness and despite there not being any evidence adduced to prove the theft, the appellant was placed on his defence. He gave sworn evidence and stated that he would call four witnesses, one of whom was Premini. When Premini came to testify, the appellant made it clear to the court that he no longer wished to call him as Premini's evidence would not assist his case. The magistrate however decided that the court would itself call Premini under powers similar to our Section 150 of the CPC. As expected, Premini denied having received any money from the appellant, and this provided the missing link in the prosecution's case. The appellant was convicted. One of the issues on appeal was whether the court was justified to call a witness for the prosecution at the defence stage. The court held that Section 150 was not designed to empower the trial court immediately after the prosecution has closed its case, to call a witness in order to establish the case against the accused, except possibly, where the evidence is purely of a formal nature.[33]

The interpretation of Section 150 can be difficult for neither party wants to be put into a situation where it thinks that the court has called a witness to assist the other. Probably the court only ought to call a witness to clarify an issue, or summon a witness whom the accused intends to call but the accused is unable to avail to court, or summon a witness, who can clearly shed light on the matter, but whom the prosecution inexplicably refuses to summon, so long as the evidence of such witness will be "essential to the just decision of the

---

32 *Supra*, note 17.

33 Contrast with the decision in *Bonface s/o Muhindi v R* (1957) EA 566. See also *Manyaki s/o Nyaganya v R* (1958) EA 495; and *R v Otim* (1963) EA 253.

case." However, as held in the case of *Murimi v R*, such witness, if it is a witness for the prosecution, needs to be called before the accused has been put on his defence, unless the witness is only called to clarify an issue.

The trial court can ask questions in unsworn statement. In *Maina Ngotho v R,*[34] the appellants were convicted of murder and were sentenced to death. At the trial, the appellants chose to make unsworn statements and questions were put to two of them by the judge. Having all been convicted they appealed against conviction and contended that the trial judge had erred in law *inter alia* by posing questions to the second and fourth appellants when they were making unsworn statements from the dock. The court held that even if, but without deciding that, the questions asked by the trial judge went beyond explaining or clarifying something obscure or ambiguous in the appellants statements, the complaint amounted at the most to no more than an irregularity curable under the now Section 382 of the CPC as no failure of justice had been occasioned.

The power to ask questions in an unsworn statement again ought to be sparingly used, to clarify a point, and ought not to be seen as a cross-examination of the accused on his unsworn statement. The matter did arise in the case of *R v Pirmin bin Kunjanga*[35] where the appellant had been charged with murder. He gave an unsworn statement in defence and the trial court questioned him regarding a discrepancy between his statement and his statement at the preliminary inquiry. He was convicted and he appealed. On this point the court stated that :- *"No questions should be asked of an accused person who has not given evidence on oath unless for the purpose of explaining or clarifying something obscure or ambiguous in his unsworn statement."*[36]

10.7 Adjournments

The law recognizes the fact that, due to unforeseen eventualities the court may be compelled to adjourn the hearing of a case. Section 205 (1) of the CPC provides that the court may, before or during the hearing of a case, adjourn

34 (1960) EA 453.

35 (1935) 2 EACA 64.

36 *Ibid*, at p 65.

the hearing to a certain time and place to be then appointed and stated in the presence and hearing of the party or parties or their respective advocates then present.

In *Republic v Misheck Muyuri,*[37] the State had appealed against the decision of the lower court dismissing the case against the respondent under Section 202 of the CPC for the non-attendance of the complainant. The respondent had been charged with assault. The case had been adjourned a number of times for various reasons; twice on account of the absence of the respondent's counsel and once when the case could not be reached. On 28th October, 2005 according to the record, the respondent was in court but witnesses were not present. The court proceeded to dismiss the case. The court noted that the appellant's main complaint was that the court failed to adjourn or ascertain whether or not the witnesses were in attendance. Pursuant to Section 205 of the CPC the court affirmed that there is a legal basis for adjournment of criminal trials. However in granting an adjournment the court noted that courts must not do so as a matter of course and that there must be sound justification for granting an adjournment in a criminal case as the suspect is entitled to a fair and speedy trial. Courts therefore must strive to avoid lengthy and unnecessary adjournments the court concluded.

In *Ngui v R,*[38] the Court of Appeal stated that, *"We feel strongly, however that in all such cases lengthy adjournments should be avoided and that the trial should continue from day to day until completed. Undue consideration should not be given to the convenience of advocates when the accused is facing a possible death penalty."*[39] In *Wycliffe Kisanya Lusigi v Republic,*[40] the Court of Appeal frowned upon a trial that had been conducted over a period of 5 years where only 5 prosecution witnesses testified. The court stated obiter that it was scandalous for adjournments to be granted routinely.[41]

---

37 High Court at Meru, Criminal Case No. 204 of 2005, (2007) eKLR.

38 (1985) KLR 268.

39 *Ibid*, at p272.

40 Court of Appeal at Eldoret, Criminal Appeal No. 64 of 2005, (2008) eKLR.

41 See also *Patrick Kibanda Onzere v R*, Kakamega Criminal Application No. 49 of 2007, (2008) eKLR.

10.8 Trial of persons who are of Unsound Mind

Where in the course of a trial the court has reason to believe that the accused is of unsound mind, the court must stop the proceedings and first inquire into the fact of unsoundness.[42] If the court is of the opinion that the accused is of unsound mind and consequently incapable of making his defence, it shall postpone further proceedings in the case. If the case is one in which bail may be taken, the court may release the accused person on sufficient security being given that he will be properly taken care of and prevented from doing injury to himself or to any other person, and for his appearance before the court, or such officer as the court may appoint in that behalf.[43]

If the case is one in which bail may not be taken, or if sufficient security is not given, the court shall order that the accused be detained in safe custody in such place and manner as it may think fit, and shall transmit the court record or a certified copy thereof to the Minister for consideration by the President.[44] Upon consideration of the record, the President may by order under his hand addressed to the court, direct that the accused be detained in a mental hospital or other suitable place of custody, and the court shall issue a warrant in accordance with that order. The warrant shall be sufficient authority for the detention of the accused until the President makes a further order in the matter, or until the court which found him incapable of making his defence, orders him to be brought before it again in the manner provided by Sections 163 and 164 of the CPC. Sections 163 and 164 in effect, provide that if the person is upon certification by a medical officer later found to be capable of making his defence, he may stand trial, unless the DPP opts to withdraw the charges.

It will be seen that a person who is of unsound mind, cannot be allowed to stand trial unless and until his state of mind changes. The court has discretion, to either release the person on bail or have him detained at the President's direction. The law is not clear on how long, a person may be detained. The danger here is that such person may be detained indefinitely, if he does not recover from his unsoundness of mind.

---

42 CPC, Section 162.

43 *Ibid*, Section 162 (3).

44 *Ibid*, Section 162 (4).

In *Republic V J W K,*[45] the accused was a minor aged 17 years old and was suffering from moderate mental retardation, a condition which psychiatrists described as a congenital medical condition which is a developmental disorder without any prospects whatsoever of getting better. The unsoundness of mind of the juvenile offender made him unfit to plead, understand the proceedings, or make his defence. The juvenile offender had pleaded not guilty but the mental fitness of the juvenile offender to plead was not brought to the attention of the court. Fortunately, before the case could proceed to hearing, the prosecution informed the court that on perusal of their file, they noted that the doctor had given an opinion that the juvenile offender was not fit to plead. The court faced with the dilemma that the accused may not recover, opted to terminate the proceedings, instead of having the accused held indefinitely. The court (Gikonyo J) had this to say:-

"I pointed out earlier and I repeat, that I am of the opinion that the circumstances of this case require the court to give effect to the right to fair trial under Article 50, rights of children under Article 53, the provisions of the Children Act and the requirements of International instruments on rights of a child. A combination of all these, gives an initial feeling that the trial should be suspended, and perhaps indefinitely under section 162(2) of the CPC, and commit the juvenile offender to the care of a person who will be able to prevent him from harming himself or somebody else and for his attendance in court as per section 162 (3) of the CPC. But objectively, on second thought, even with the advanced modern medical and scientific knowledge, the doctors opine that his condition is not likely to improve and he may not have the benefit of medicine or admission. I am also aware that the scientific and medical knowledge of today is far in advance of that of the past years, and that of the years to come will even be far in advance than the current one, but none offers evidence of any prospects that the condition the juvenile offender is suffering will be reversed or become better. Thus, in the absence of any such evidence, I do not think it would be appropriate to give any hope that the trial may resume in the future. Also, to place a person suffering from such a condition, and more so a juvenile, under a cloud of criminal proceedings ad infinitum will be a great prejudice to all known human qualities, the right to fair trial and rights of a child, and largely, will be a disparage of the Constitution. In the absence of any

---

45 High Court at Bungoma, Criminal Application No. 57 of 2009, (2013) eKLR.

such medical and scientific hope of the condition becoming better, I am convinced that suspending the trial is not the appropriate path."

This appears to be the fairest approach. Where the accused cannot recover, then it may be unfair to hold him *ad infinitum* at the pleasure of the President. It is therefore wise for the court to periodically mention a case where an accused has been placed under care, and where it is clear that there are no prospects of recovery, or that his recovery will take a long time, release the accused so that his rights to liberty are not curtailed. [46]

An acute situation arose in the case of *Grace Nyoroka v Republic.*[47] The appellant had been charged with murder. After entering a plea of not guilty, the High Court ordered for the accused to be examined to ascertain her mental status. A report came back with the conclusion that the appellant suffered from a mental disorder and needed treatment. The court then proceeded to order that the case against the accused be postponed, and the accused be referred to a psychiatric hospital for treatment. It gave a date to assess the progress of the accused. The Court of Appeal noted that the provisions of Section 162, which required a report to be made to the President, had not been complied with and observed that the court had shortened the process by cutting out the report to the Minister and then to the President, and directly ordered the appellant's treatment at the psychiatric hospital. The court noted that the "short-circuiting" of the whole process had become the practice, which is probably based on the sound reason that if the whole process is followed to the letter, the matter might take a very long time to conclude. After a while, a report was adduced before the court that the appellant was fit to plead to the charge. When the charge was read over, the appellant pleaded as follows: - *"I killed the deceased but I did not kill her. She had wronged me."* The Judge entered a plea of not guilty for the appellant, but then, the appellant's counsel told the Judge that he had instructions from the accused person to offer a plea on the lesser charge of manslaughter. The next time trial resumed, the lesser charge of manslaughter was substituted, read out to the appellant by the Judge, and the appellant's answer as recorded by the Judge, was that it was true. The facts showed that the appellant had attacked and killed her mother over some land measuring

46 See also *Muraya v R* (2001) KLR 50.

47 Court of Appeal at Meru, Criminal Appeal No.246 of 2006, [2007] eKLR.

½ an acre and the appellant admitted the facts as being correct and the Judge convicted her to life imprisonment. She appealed. On appeal the Court of Appeal was not convinced that the plea was unequivocal and was of the view that the court ought to have made an inquiry as to whether the appellant was sane when she allegedly committed the offence. The appeal was allowed and an order for retrial made.[48]

In *Francis Saisi Omae v Republic,*[49] the appellant in this case was charged with murder. He pleaded not guilty. The trial commenced, and at the end of it, the court found him guilty and convicted him. Aggrieved by that decision, he appealed, with insanity being the principal ground of appeal. The Court of Appeal noted that there was sufficient evidence on record to suggest the possibility that the appellant was of unsound mind, and the learned Judge ought to have ordered an inquiry under section 162 of the CPC. The court agreed with the learned counsel for the appellant, that the evidence adduced, demonstrated strange behavior on the part of the appellant (carrying a lit torch in broad daylight, asking PW 7 if he had seen a "thug", the brutal and bizarre manner in which he killed the deceased, his obsession with a wayward chicken) together with an earlier report that he was not fit to plead, were indicative of the need to inquire further into the soundness of the appellant's mind. The court held that it was the duty of the trial Judge, to direct himself or herself and the assessors on the issue, and if necessary, to invoke the provisions of section 162 (1) of the CPC.

The court cited the case of *Muraya v Republic,*[50] where a similar situation was considered. The court held that immediately an issue arises as to the unsoundness of mid of the accused, an inquiry needs to be held. If upon inquiry, there is evidence of unsoundness of mind, further proceedings must be adjourned and further consequences follow to ensure the accused is medically treated and becomes mentally fit to understand, follow and participate in the

---

48 Interestingly the appellant was then acquitted of the offence of murder in the retrial being Meru High Court Criminal Case No. 74 of 2011, *R v Grace Nyoroka* (2011) eKLR. See also *Festus Mbuthia Mwangi v R,* Court of Appeal at Nyeri, Criminal Appeal No. 250 of 2004, (2006) eKLR.

49 Court of Appeal at Eldoret, Criminal Appeal No. 1 of 2007, (2009) eKLR.

50 *Supra*, note 42.

trial. This is because it is a fundamental requirement in criminal trials that an accused person should understand, follow and fully participate in his trial.

If the court is of the opinion that a person may be insane, he is to be remanded in a mental hospital for treatment until he is capable of making his defence.[51] The doctor attending to him is supposed to send a medical certificate to the DPP certifying that the accused is fit to plead or stand his trial. Upon receipt of the certificate, the DPP is obliged to inform the court which remanded the accused whether the proceedings against him shall continue or not. The decision to prosecute or not, will be the discretion of the DPP, who will consider the factors outlined in the constitution.[52]

If the trial proceeds, without evidence indicating that the accused is fit for trial, the resulting conviction may be quashed.[53] Where an accused person develops some mental disturbance in the course of trial, which makes him/her unable to proceed with his trial, the court has an obligation to postpone further proceedings until he is lucid. The magistrate is not to make the order of guilty but insane. In *R v Undule,*[54] the accused complained of feeling unwell and began to cry at the close of the prosecution case. The trial magistrate was of the view that the accused was mentally disturbed and made a finding of guilty but insane. In revision, the High Court held the magistrate confused section 164 with section 168 of the CPC. The magistrate having found the accused was unfit to make his defence, after pleading, due to mental disturbance, should have made an order under section 164 of the CPC postponing other proceedings in the case. The proceedings disclosed no evidence of the accused's unsoundness of mind at the time the offence was committed although he had first pleaded that he was then of unsound mind. Until this issue was resolved, section 168 of the CPC did not arise. The order made under section 168 of the CPC quashed except for the finding that the accused was unable to make

51 CPC Section 163.

52 See Chapter 5 on discretion of the DPP to prosecute.

53 *Kaplotwa s/o Tarino v R* (1957) EA 553.

54 (1965) EA 451.

his defence by reason of unsoundness of mind. The proceedings ordered to be postponed in accordance with Section 164 of the CPC.[55]

10.9 Trial of Children

Article 53 (2) of the Constitution provides that a child's best interests are of paramount importance in every matter concerning the child. Section 2 of the Children Act[56] defines a child to mean any human being under the age of eighteen years. The Act,[57] provides for specialized courts to be known as Children's Courts constituted to hear cases against children.[58] "The words "conviction" and "sentence" are not to be used in relation to a child dealt with by the Children's Court. Only a finding of guilty is entered.[59] The court has power to compel the attendance of the parents of the child facing trial.[60]

Cases involving children are supposed to be handled expeditiously and without unnecessary delay.[61]Rule 12 (2) provides that where the case of a child appearing before a Children's Court is not completed within 3 months after his plea has been taken the case shall be dismissed and the child shall not be liable to any further proceedings for the same offence and where the case involves a serious offence to be heard by a superior court, the case needs to be completed within 12 months.[62]

---

55 See also *Sonah Singh v R* (1958) EA 28; *Mandi s/o Ngoda v R* (1963) EA 153 (T) and *Mose v R* (2002) 1 EA 163.

56 Chapter 141, Laws of Kenya.

57 *Ibid*, Section 73 (b).

58 For a more elaborate discussion, See Chapter 2 on jurisdiction of the Children Court.

59 Children Act, Section 189.

60 *Ibid*, Rule 8 of the 5th Schedule.

61 *Ibid*, Rule 12.

62 *Ibid*, Rule 12 (3) and (4); and see *Oscar Iyaite v R*, High Court at Bungoma, Crim. Appl. No. 34 of 2006 (2006) eKLR

10.10 Place of Trial

Section 71 of the CPC provides that every offence shall ordinarily be tried by a court within the local limits of whose jurisdiction it was committed, or within the local limits of whose jurisdiction the accused was apprehended, or is in custody on a charge for the offence, or has appeared in answer to a summons lawfully issued charging the offence.[63]

Section 74 of the CPC comes in to deal with uncertainties that may arise as to the place of commission of an offence. When it is uncertain in which of several local areas an offence was committed, or an offence is committed partly in one local area and partly in another, or an offence is a continuing one, and continues to be committed in more than one local areas, or an offence consists of several acts done in different local areas, it may be tried by a court having jurisdiction over any of those local areas.

An offence committed whilst the offender is in the course of performing a journey or voyage may be tried by a court through or into the local limits of whose jurisdiction the offender or the person against whom or the thing in respect of which the offence was committed passed in the course of that journey or voyage.[64]

However, whenever a doubt arises as to the court by which an offence should be tried, the court entertaining the doubt may report the circumstances to the High Court, and the High Court shall decide by which court the offence shall be inquired into or tried and this decision shall be final except in the case where it is shown that no court in Kenya has jurisdiction in the case.[65]

Pursuant to the provisions of Section 78 (1) of the CPC if upon the hearing of a complaint it appears that the cause of complaint arose outside the limits of the jurisdiction of the court before which the complaint has been brought, the

63 However, this is subject to the provisions of Section 69, and to the powers of transfer conferred by Sections 79 and Section 81 of the CPC.

64 CPC, Section 75.

65 *Ibid*, Section 76.

court may, on being satisfied that it has no jurisdiction, direct the case to be transferred to the court having jurisdiction where the cause of complaint arose.

10.10.1 The Power to Transfer Cases

The power to transfer cases is vested in both sub-ordinate and the High Court. Transfer of a case between magistrates is under Section 78 and 79 and 80 of the CPC. The High Court always has residual and supervisory powers and thus is empowered to order the transfer of a case pending before a magistrate to another magistrate. The High Court can make an order transferring a case if either party applies under Section 81 under the grounds set out in that section. Also under Section 76 a magistrate can apply to the High Court if there is doubt on jurisdiction.

Under Section 81 of the CPC, the entities that can apply for transfer are the court itself, or the accused or the prosecution. If it is the court, this is done by way of a report. If it is the accused, he makes an application (a notice of motion) with the grounds set out and supported by an affidavit and 24 hours must lapse between the giving of notice and the hearing of the application. The High Court may direct the applicant to execute a bond. If the applicant is the DPP, no affidavit is necessary.

In *Mushao v R*,[66] the accused had been charged with stock theft before the resident magistrate. He made an application to the High Court for an order transferring a criminal trial to another court on the ground that the advocate instructed to appear for the accused could not be present on the date fixed for hearing. This was due to the fact that his advocate was due to appear in the High Court on the day of the trial in a civil matter. In effect, the application amounted to an appeal against the order of the resident magistrate on the fixing of the hearing date. His advocate had submitted that if he was not present in the court at the time of the trial, a fair trial could not be had and that the order sought was expedient for the ends of justice. The court held that an order of transfer can only be made where a fair trial could not be had. A fair trial could be had in the absence of legal representation and the discretion of the trial court

66 *Mushao v R* (1971) EA 201.

in fixing a hearing date would not be interfered with. This was an order made in exercise of the court's discretion. A higher court is always loath to interfere with such an order, unless it was unjudicial or an error in principle had been made and that there was no ground for holding that he had acted unjudicially or erred in principle.

In *R v Hashimu,*[67] the accused while being charged on a charge of stealing a bicycle, became dissatisfied with the order in which the prosecution witnesses gave evidence and applied for the case to be transferred to another magistrate. The trial magistrate forwarded the file to the High Court for directions. The court held that before the transfer of a trial is granted on the application of an accused person, a clear case must be made out that the accused person has a reasonable apprehension in his mind that he will not have a fair and impartial trial before the magistrate from whom he wants the trial transferred.[68] There was nothing arising from the facts of the case or the attitude of the magistrate that could be taken to indicate that the accused would not have a fair and impartial trial. The application for transfer was rejected and the magistrate directed to continue with the trial.

In *Kinyatti v R,*[69] the appellant was charged with the offence of sedition. When he appeared before the trial magistrate's court, his counsel made an application that the case be transferred to another magistrate for hearing, as the same court had heard similar cases before and in which some of the witnesses had been heard and commented upon by the court. The Chief Magistrate dismissed this application on the ground that it could set a dangerous precedent that could land the administration of courts in chaos and further that he had heard only one similar case and being an experienced judicial officer who had heard the same witnesses give evidence in similar cases he was able to decide dispassionately and on its merits the facts and circumstances of the case. This ruling formed a ground of appeal to the High Court which considered and dismissed it. A further appeal was made to the Court of Appeal. The Court of Appeal in considering the issue held that *"the true test for making an order for*

---

67 *R v Hashimu* (1968) EA 656 (T).

68 *Herman Milde v Republic* (1937) 1 TLR (R) 129; and *Bhag Singh v Republic* (1941) 1 TLR (R) 133.

69 (1976-85) EA 234.

transfer was not whether or not the magistrate was biased but whether a reasonable apprehension existed in the mind of the accused from incidents which had occurred that he may not have a fair and impartial trial".[70] The Court of Appeal held that the trial magistrate applied the wrong test. Similarly the High Court ought to have looked at the incidents before the Chief Magistrate and then asked whether in the light of those incidents the apprehension was reasonable. It was essential for the trial court to make a full inquiry into the issue before dismissing it. In the instant however, the Court of Appeal held that there was no miscarriage of justice and the conviction was upheld.

10.11 Death or Transfer of Trial Magistrate/Judge

It is of course best if the judicial officer who started the trial, proceeds to hear it to its conclusion. This is because he has the benefit of seeing all witnesses and of taking down the evidence himself. He also has the benefit of having in mind the entire evidence of both prosecution and defence. However, instances may, and do arise, where the case cannot be heard and concluded by one judicial officer. It could happen that the judicial officer who had commenced the hearing of a criminal case dies, or is transferred, or leaves service. In such an instance it is not mandatory that the trial must commence *de novo*. The law allows for a succeeding judicial officer to continue with the case. The relevant provision is found in Section 200 (3) of the CPC which provides as follows:-

"Where a succeeding magistrate commences the hearing of proceedings and part of the evidence has been recorded by his predecessor, the accused person may demand that any witness be re-summoned and reheard and the succeeding magistrate shall inform the accused person of that right."

The consequences of failing to abide by the above provision may result in a conviction being set aside, if the appellate court is of opinion that the accused person was materially prejudiced and a new trial may be ordered. [71]

---

70 Following the decision in *Re MS Patel* (1913/14) KLR 66.

71 CPC, S. 200(4).

In the case of *Ndegwa v R*[72] Court of Appeal averred that the provisions of S. 200 CPC, which allow a succeeding magistrate to continue with a case, should be used sparingly and should not be invoked where the trial can conveniently be started *de novo*. It will be seen from Section 200 (3) that the accused in such instance, may demand any witness to be re-summoned and reheard, and the succeeding judicial officer, has a duty to inform the accused of this right. If the accused is not informed of this right, then the judgment may be set aside.[73] It is not enough for the trial court to state that *"Section 200 complied with"*. It must be clear from the record that the accused has been advised of his rights to recall witnesses and his answer thereto. In the case of *Bob Ayub v R*[74], the appellant faced a charge of murder. The first trial judge died, and the matter was taken up by the succeeding judge. There was no record of compliance with S. 200 (3). On appeal, the Court of Appeal, did not hesitate to hold that compliance with that section was mandatory and set aside the conviction. [75]

Mbogholi Msagha J, in the case of *Rebecca Mwikali Nabutola v R*[76] put the matter as follows:-

The requirement to comply with the provision thereof (of S. 200) *is mandatory. The record of the trial court must of necessity contain the fact that the trial court, in this case the succeeding magistrate, has informed the accused person of the right to recall or rehear any witness. The reply by the accused person must also be placed on the record and the order relating thereto should be signed by the succeeding magistrate. It is not enough for counsel to state that they have taken instructions because, as the Court of Appeal has said, the duty of the court is to the accused person and not the advocate.*

---

72 Court of Appeal at Nakuru, Criminal Appeal No. 125 of 1984, (1985) eKLR.

73 High Court at Embu, Criminal Appeal No.90 of 2009, (2011) eKLR.

74 Court of Appeal at Kisumu, Criminal Appeal No. 106 of 2009, (2010) eKLR.

75 See also *Charles Kuria Macharia v R*, Muranga High Court, Criminal Appeal No. 418 of 2013, (2013) eKLR; *Willis Ochieng Odero v R*, Court of Appeal at Kisumu, Criminal Appeal No.80 of 2004, (2006) eKLR; and *Richard Charo Mole v R,* High Court at Nairobi, Criminal Appeal No. 135 of 2004, (2010) eKLR.

76 High Court at Nairobi, Misc. Crim. Applications No.445, 448,452 of 2012, (2012) eKLR.

The question arises whether the court in all instances, must start the matter *de novo*, or must continue with the case, where it has reached, if demanded by the accused. Such a demand may at times cause considerable difficulty to the prosecution for some witnesses may have died in the interim, or relocated, or may not be found. Again owing to effluxion of time, memories will inevitably fade.

The CPC is not clear on whether the court must defer to the demands of the accused, and it is probable that the court has discretion, depending on the surrounding circumstances of the case, so long as the reasons thereof are clearly given, and justice is done to all parties. However, if the matter can conveniently begin *de novo*, then the succeeding judicial officer would have no reason to deny the request, and the matter ought to be heard *de novo*.[77]

It is also important to note that there is no bar to the number of judicial officers who can continue the matter. Each magistrate or judge who takes over the case, is considered to be a succeeding judicial officer for the purposes of Section 200 (3). This was the holding in the case of *R v Wesley Chepchieng alias "Chain Giant."*[78] In this case, two judges had heard the case, and the matter was taken over by the third judge. The State, argued that the matter must start *de novo*, and contended that a matter cannot be heard by more than two judicial officers. The State relied on the Tanzanian decision in the case of *Eustace v R.* [79] This argument was dispelled by the court which declined to be persuaded by the Tanzanian decision, and held that there is no bar to the number of succeeding judicial officers in so far as the Kenyan law is concerned.

* * *

77 *Ndegwa v R*, supra note 66.

78 High Court at Eldoret, Eldoret Crim. Case No. 4 of 2007.

79 (1970) EA 393.

CHAPTER 11
JUDGMENT

11.1 Introduction

The judgment is the opinion of the court that finally determines the issue in dispute. This should be differentiated from a ruling which is a preliminary or interlocutory determination on a matter that arises in the course of trial but is not the final opinion of the court after a full hearing. Thus for example, a court may make a ruling on whether or not an accused person should be provided with legal representation at state expense, or rule whether the accused should be granted bail. In a criminal trial, the issue in dispute is whether the accused is guilty or not guilty. If the accused is guilty, the court will convict and pass sentence. If not guilty, the court will acquit him. In between the two, there may be a special finding in cases of insanity through the verdict known as "guilty but insane".

11.2 Formalities and Content of a Judgment

Judgment pursuant to the provisions of Section 168 (1) of the Criminal Procedure Code[1] is supposed to be read in open court. If judgment is not read immediately after the termination of trial the court must give notice of the time when the judgment will be delivered. The court has the option of reading or explaining the whole judgment or the substance of it. However, the judge or magistrate must read the full judgment if either the prosecution or the defence so requests.[2] The personal attendance of the accused at the time

1 Criminal Procedure Code, Chapter 75, Laws of Kenya.

2 *Ibid*, Section 168 (1).

of pronouncing judgment is required unless his attendance was dispensed with, although a judgment would not be declared invalid only by reason of the absence of a party or his advocate.[3]

Every judgment is supposed to be written by the magistrate or judge or under his direction.[4] There is therefore the requirement that the judgment be in writing. There is no bar to the trial court preparing a draft judgment as the proceedings commence. The same cannot be considered a judgment until it is read. In *Misango v R*,[5] the appellant was charged with 24 counts; 12 of forgery and 12 of stealing by servant. The trial commenced on 28th September 1968 and there were numerous adjournments. Between November 15 and 25, 1968, defence counsel requested and was granted permission to peruse the case file. Defence counsel saw in a sheaf of paper which was headed "Judgment" and accordingly on November 25th 1968, submitted that, as the magistrate had already started writing his judgment, the defence was prejudiced and no more witnesses could be called. The magistrate ruled against this submission. The case then proceeded with the prosecution calling two more witnesses who were not cross examined by the defence. The appellant was convicted on all the 24 counts. On appeal it was contended that it was irregular for the magistrate to write a substantial part of the judgment before the close of the prosecution's case thus the magistrate had prejudiced the issues; that the further prosecution evidence was admitted to bolster and fill the gaps in the prosecution case to the prejudice of the appellant; and that because of the irregularities the conviction should be quashed.

It was held that a judgment is not a "judgment" until it has been reduced into writing and delivered in an open court. Further that, the magistrate did not prejudge the case before the close of prosecution case, and the sheaf of papers on which he had written constituted his rough notes or summary of the evidence and to this extent he had committed no irregularity. However, the appellate court ordered a retrial, as in its view, the trial magistrate did not treat the evidence tendered with the degree of consideration required by law.

---

3 *Ibid*, Section 168 (3).

4 *Ibid*, Section 169.

5 (1969) EA 538.

The judgment is required to be in the language of the court.[6] The language of the court in the subordinate courts is English and Kiswahili whereas the language of the court in the High Court is English. The judgment is also required to contain the points for determination, the decision and the reasons for the decision.[7] In *Republic v Ezekiel Muriuki Mungania,*[8] the respondent was charged with creating disturbance in a manner likely to cause a breach of the peace contrary to Section 95 (1) (b) of the Penal Code. The trial court dismissed the charge against the respondent under section 215 of the CPC. The State appealed on two grounds *inter alia* that the trial magistrate grossly misdirected himself in law by failing to analyze the evidence before him as envisaged in section 169 of the CPC. On this ground the High Court acknowledged that the provisions thereof require that every judgment shall contain the point or points for determination the decision thereon and the reasons for the decision. The court noted that paragraph 2 of the judgment by the learned trial magistrate contained the point or points for determination and that unfortunately though, the judgment did not contain a summary of both the prosecution's case and defence case. The judgment also lacked an analysis of the evidence on record. Nonetheless, the High Court found that on the evidence, there was no good reason to interfere with the judgment of the trial court.

The court must particularly set out its findings on the ingredients of the offence. In *Livingstone v Uganda*,[9] the appellant was charged with unlawfully doing grievous harm to the complainant which arose from a quarrel in a bar. The trial magistrate substituted a charge of doing an illegal act with intent to cause grievous harm. In the judgment there was no finding of intent. On second appeal, the Court of Appeal held that a judgment must set out the points for determination which must cover the essential ingredients of the offence. Intent was an essential ingredient of the offence charged, and in the absence of a finding, no irresistible inference of intent could be found.

---

6 CPC, Section 169.

7 *Kigotho v R* (1967) EA 445.

8 High Court at Meru, Criminal Appeal No. 210 of 2003(2006) eKLR; See also *Emmanuel Mushina Mwalili v Republic*, High Court at Nairobi, Criminal Appeal No.25 of 2004, (2006) eKLR; and *Republic v Shadrack Musembi Kaloki*, High Court at Mombasa, Criminal Appeal No. 186 of 2004, (2006) eKLR.

9 (1972) EA 196.

Similarly, in *Macharia v R,*[10] the appellant was driving a motor car which was four feet over the center of the road when it collided with a motor scooter travelling in the opposite direction. He was charged with dangerous driving, and after a submission that there was no case to answer, the magistrate put him on his defence on a charge of careless driving and thereafter convicted him. On appeal it was contended that the magistrate had merely found that the appellant's car was over the center of the road, that the magistrate had not given reasons for his judgment nor shown how the appellant was careless, and that there should not have been a conviction of careless driving. It was held *inter alia* that the judgment did not show how the appellant was careless. In arriving at this conclusion the High Court noted that although one does not expect an elaborate judgment in a simple traffic offence case, the magistrate failed to spell out valid reasons for the decision as required by Section 169 (1) of the CPC.[11]

In *R v Mallo,*[12] the AG appealed against the acquittal of the respondent, who had been prosecuted on seven charges of theft by servant. The respondent was a clerk in the service of administration from consignees of goods, which he had converted to his own use without accounting for it. The consignees gave evidence of the payment, but the accused in evidence blamed his superior officer, a pier clerk, for ordering him to release consignments of goods without making proper entries or receiving the cash for the transport charges. He also alleged that the pier clerk himself dealt with some of the consignments. The magistrate, whilst recognizing that the evidence against the accused was strong, found that there was a reasonable doubt whether the accused committed the offence alleged. On appeal, it was contended that the magistrate did not consider the evidence tendered by the prosecution relative to the payments mentioned in the seven counts and whether the money alleged to have been stolen had in fact come into possession of the accused. The High Court held that whilst Section 169 of the CPC requires every judgment to contain the points for determination, the decision thereon and the reasons for the decision, a magistrate is not required in the case of an acquittal to deal with every point which would have to be decided in the case of a conviction, but when a judgment acquitting the accused fails to deal at all with one of the main ingredients constituting the offence, that is

10 (1975) EA 193.

11 See also *Ratilal Shal v R* (1959) EA 3.

12 (1958) EA 11.

a substantial error of the law. In this case the judgment did not deal with the question whether the accused received the money as alleged by the prosecution. The matter was remitted for retrial.

A defective judgment will not necessarily invalidate a conviction. If there is sufficient material on record to enable the appellate court to consider the appeal on its merits, the appellate court will proceed to do so, and may uphold a conviction, despite the defect in the judgment. [13] Unless a miscarriage of justice has occurred, a mere defect in the judgment does not mean that the appellant must succeed in his appeal.[14]It is important that the judgment do follow the evidence and not externalities or hypothesis by the trial court. In *Okethi Okale v R*,[15] the four appellants were convicted of murder. One of the core issues in the trial was of identification and the prosecution case consisted of evidence from the widow of the deceased and the evidence of a dying declaration. The judge after discounting the evidence of the widow, proceeded to put forward a theory of his own and he accepted the deceased's brother's evidence as to the dying declaration without giving any reasons. It was held that in every criminal trial a conviction can only be based on the weight of the actual evidence adduced and it is dangerous and inadvisable for a trial judge to put forward a theory not canvassed in evidence or counsel's speeches, but arising out of fanciful theories or attractive reasoning.

The judgment must be dated and must be signed by the judge or magistrate in open court at the time of pronouncing it. Accordingly, these are the formalities that a judgment must have regard to. They may be reduced into the following points. The judgment must:-

(i) Be written by or under the direction of the presiding officer;
(ii) Be in the language of the court;
(iii) Contain the point/s of determination;
(iv) Contain the decision;
(v) Contain the reasons for the decision;

---

13 *Kisongo v R* (1960) EA 780.

14 CPC, Section 382. See also *Willy John v R* (1953) 23 EACA, 509, *Desiderio Kuwanya v R* (20 EACA) 281, and *Kagoye s/o Bandala v R* (1959) EA 900.

15 *Okethi Okale v R* (1965) EA 555.

(vi) Be dated;
(vii) Be signed by the presiding officer in open court at the time of pronouncing it.

Note however, that a failure to abide by these formalities will only invalidate the judgment if a miscarriage of justice has occurred. This is clear from the provisions of Section 168 (4) of the CPC,[16] which refer to the provisions of section 382 of the CPC.[17] The judgment will therefore stand irrespective of a failure to abide by the required formalities unless a failure of justice occurs.

In the case of a conviction, the judgment shall specify the offence and the section of Penal Code or other law under which the accused person is convicted, and the punishment to which he is sentenced.[18] On the other hand, in the case of an acquittal, the judgment shall state the offence of which the accused person is acquitted, and shall direct that he be set at liberty.[19]

An interesting scenario occurred in the case of *Baland Singh v R* and the case is worthy of mention given the brevity of the judgment. [20] The appellant was charged with murder and after a hearing the judge pronounced the following judgment:-

"On the first count the Court finds that on the 6th day of May, 1953, Baland Singh did kill Mahmud Abubaker by shooting him. That shot was fired without

---

16 Section 168 (4) of the CPC provides, *"Nothing in this section shall limit in any way the provisions of section 382."*

17 Section 382 of the CPC provides, *"Subject to the provisions hereinbefore contained, no finding, sentence or order passed by a court of competent jurisdiction shall be reversed or altered on appeal or revision on account of an error, omission or irregularity in the complaint, summons, warrant, charge, proclamation, order, judgment or other proceedings before or during the trial or in any inquiry or other proceedings under this Code, unless the error, omission or irregularity has occasioned a failure of justice: Provided that in determining whether an error, omission or irregularity has occasioned a failure of justice the court shall have regard to the question whether the objection could and should have been raised at an earlier stage in the proceedings."*

18 CPC, Section 169 (2).

19 *Ibid*, Section 169 (3).

20 *Baland Singh v R* (1954) 21 EACA 209.

malice aforethought. The Court therefore finds Baland Singh not guilty of murder, but guilty of manslaughter. On the third count the Court finds Nirmal Singh not guilty. Nirmal Singh can leave the dock. Baland Singh, have you anything to say why sentence should not be passed upon you."

The judgment was attacked for not containing the points for determination, nor the reasons for the decision. The Court of Appeal was of the view that the failure to set out the point/s in detail could not in the circumstances have had any practical effect, since the issues were never in doubt. On the submission that no reasons were given, the Court of Appeal was not impressed, reasoning that if justice is done, then there is no real failure of justice, although the correctness of the decision may not be clearly apparent to the parties or the public. The Court of Appeal was of the view that any failure to abide by the formalities in Section 169, is an irregularity. The appeal was accordingly dismissed. [21]

Vide the provisions of Section 170 of the CPC, the accused person is entitled to have a copy of the judgment if he requests for the same. He is also entitled to a translation, if he so desires, and if it is practicable.

11.3 The Holding of Guilty but insane

In the celebrated *M'Naghten's Case*[22] it was held that in order to establish an insanity defence, it must be clearly proven that at the time of the act, the accused was under such a defect of reason from disease of the mind that he did not know the nature and quality of the act he was committing; or if he did know, he did not know that what he was doing was wrong. This position seems to have been adopted in Kenya. The legal position is spelt out in Section 12 of the Penal Code and Section 166 of the Criminal Procedure Code. These two provisions are worded as follows:-

21 See also *Wahome v R* (1969) EA 580; *Samwiri Senyange v Republic* (1953), 20 EACA 277; and *Kalihose v R* (1960) EA 760.

22 *M'Naghten's Case* (1843-1860) All E.R 229. His real name is said to be McNaughton, but has come to be spelt ordinarily as M'Naghten.

Section 12 Penal Code :- *A person is not criminally responsible for an act or omission if at the time of doing the act or making the omission he is through any disease affecting his mind incapable of understanding what he is doing, or of knowing that he ought not to do the act or make the omission; but a person may be criminally responsible for an act or omission, although his mind is affected by disease, if such disease does not in fact produce upon his mind one or other of the effects above mentioned in reference to that act or omission*

Section 166 (1) CPC :- *Where an act or omission is charged against a person as an offence, and it is given in evidence on the trial of that person for that offence that he was insane so as not to be responsible for his acts or omissions at the time when the act was done or the omission made, then if it appears to the court before which the person is tried that he did the act or made the omission charged but was insane at the time he did or made it, the court shall make a special finding to the effect that the accused was guilty of the act or omission charged but was insane when he did the act or made the omiss*ion.

Section 166 of the CPC continues to elaborate that once a holding of "guilty but insane" is made, the court is to report the matter for the order of the President. The President may then order the person to be detained in a mental hospital, prison, or other suitable place of safe custody. At the expiration of three years, and thereafter at the expiration of every two years, the officer in whose custody the person is, ought to make a report of the circumstances of the detained person. The President has discretion to order the transfer of such person to prison from mental hospital, or to mental hospital from prison.[23]

In *Jeremano M'Ngai v R,*[24] it was argued that the accused should be acquitted on account of insanity. This was rejected by the court which held that section 12 of the Penal Code does not give an accused person a complete defence to the charge against him. The court also held that there was no conflict between the provisions of Section 12 of the Penal Code and Section 166 (1) of the CPC. Thus what the accused would get is a qualified acquittal of guilty but insane. But in *Uganda v Matte,*[25] the prosecution called a psychiatric doctor

23 CPC, Section 166 (2) - (7).

24 *Jeremano M'Ngai v R* (1980) KLR 18.

25 (1974) EA 575.

as a witness and it was indicated that the accused was insane at the time the offence was committed. The court then proceeded to hold that by accepting the defence of insanity, the prosecution had abandoned its case, and since the offence was not proved, the accused was acquitted. The decision in the *Matte* case was considered and disapproved by the judge in the case of *M'Ngai* and it is seems as if the *Matte* case was wrongly decided. In *Mbeluke v R,*[26] the trial court convicted the appellant for murder and sentenced him to death. On appeal, the finding of guilty but insane was substituted.

It is upon the accused to prove insanity, if it is raised as a defence, since the law presumes every individual to be of sound mind.[27] The standard of proof is on a balance of probabilities. This was asserted by the Court of Appeal in the case of *Nyinge Suwato v R*[28]where the court stated as follows[29] :-

"An accused must not merely raise a reasonable doubt; his burden, as in a civil case, is to prove insanity upon a balance of probability; that is to say he must show, on all the evidence, that insanity is more likely than sanity, though it may be ever so little more likely. Merely to raise a reasonable doubt might still leave the balance tilted on the side of sanity."

If the defence wishes to raise insanity as a defence, it is bound to call medical evidence to prove this. The prosecution can however do this in the discharge of its duty to lay all evidence irrespective of whether it is favourable or not.[30] In order to establish this, the accused needs to prove that at the time of committing the offence, he was suffering from a disease of the mind, and thus incapable of understanding what he was doing and unable to know that he ought not to have committed the offence.[31]

---

26 (1971) EA 479.

27 Penal Code, Section 11.

28 (1959) EA 974.

29 *Ibid*, page 980.

30 As indeed happened in *Nyinge Suwato v R, ibid.*

31 See *Philip Muswi v R* (1956) 23 EACA 622.

In *Tadeo Oyee s/o Duru v R,*[32] the appellant was convicted of murder by the High Court of Uganda. At the trial, evidence was given that the appellant was a high grade mental defective, but a medical witness, was unable to suggest any disease of the mind from which the appellant was suffering. The trial judge rejected the defence of insanity holding that this defence was not open to the accused, because section 12 of the Penal Code, used the *words "he is through any disease affecting his mind incapable of understanding what he is doing..."* On appeal it was argued that the appellant was at the time of the incident a high grade mental defective, and for this reason, and also because he had had some drinks when he attacked the deceased, he was incapable of knowing that what he was doing was wrong. The court held that a high grade mental deficiency may be a "disease affecting the mind" within section 12 of the Penal Code. The trial judge took the restricted view of the meaning of disease in section 12 and was not correct in ruling that the defence of insanity was not open to the appellant; there was evidence of insanity which should have been considered and upon which, if believed, a special finding under section 166 of the CPC might have been recorded. The appeal was allowed and a new trial ordered.

In *Muiruri v R,*[33] the evidence against the appellant was that he had been asleep with his wife on the material day in the master bedroom. The daughter then heard screams coming from the bedroom. The appellant walked out of the bedroom and returned carrying a panga. Afterwards he left the house and the daughter found her mother lying in a pool of blood. The cause of death was found to have been head injuries causing severe brain damage leading to cardio vascular collapse. The appellant made a statement of inquiry which he neither repudiated nor retracted. He also gave an unsworn statement at the trial in which he stated that he discovered on waking up in the middle of the night that his wife had changed into a leopard. He wrestled with the animal and then hit 'it' (her) with his panga. The medical report produced in evidence showed that the appellant had suffered from a psychiatric illness some years back, and since then occasionally relapsed. He suffered from bipolar (mood) disorder, which would have periods of remission and relapse. The trial judge entered a verdict of "guilty but insane" and ordered that the appellant be kept

---

32 (1959) EA 407 (U) (CoA); See also *R v Kemp* (1957) 1 QB 399 and *R v Retief* (1941) 8 EACA 71.

33 (2005)1 EA 293; See also *Mwangi v Republic* (1982) KLR 120.

in custody subject to the president's pleasure. The appellant appealed against entry of the verdict on the basis of circumstantial evidence. The court held that in this case, the appellant had not been convicted of the offence of murder nor sentenced to death nor imprisonment. Rather the court made a special finding that the accused was guilty of the act charged but was insane when he did it. Such a finding is neither a conviction nor an acquittal. The court ceases to have jurisdiction over the accused person after such a finding, and the detention at the president's pleasure is not punitive but preventive.

11.4 Convicting on Lesser Offence

Let us first recall that it is upon the prosecution to decide what charges to prefer against a suspect. It is also upon the prosecution to draw up the charges and to present evidence in proof of the charges. Strictly speaking, if the evidence adduced does not support the charges, then the accused should be acquitted. The law however recognizes instances where the accused may be convicted of an offence of which he has not been charged with. Most of these instances give leeway to the court to convict for a lesser offence that is covered by the evidence and of which its particulars are closely similar to the offence that the accused was originally charged with. The CPC sets out these instances which are considered below.

11.4.1 When Offence Proved is Included in Offence Charged

Pursuant to Section 179 (1) of the CPC when a person is charged with an offence consisting of several particulars, a combination of some only of which constitutes a complete minor offence, and the combination is proved, but the remaining particulars are not proved, he may be convicted of the minor offence although he was not charged with it. Further, sub-section (2) provides that when a person is charged with an offence and facts are proved which reduce it to a minor offence, he may be convicted of the minor offence although he was not charged with it. Here, the particulars of the offence as set out in the charge are not all proved such that the accused cannot now be convicted of the primary offence. However, part of the particulars that have been proved, in themselves point to an offence which is lesser to the primary offence. The court in this instance may proceed to convict for the lesser offence.

In *Peter Odhiambo Owino v Republic*,[34] the appellant was convicted in the subordinate court of the offence of attempted robbery with violence contrary to section 297 (2) of the Penal Code. The High Court dismissed his first appeal and he appealed to the Court of Appeal. PW-1 was a security guard to the premises of PW-2. In the middle of the night of 22nd /23rd September, 2002, a group of six men invaded the place, caught hold of him and tied him up before they broke the door into a store in which some items were stored. As they were breaking the door, PW1 managed to untie himself and raised an alarm. A guard to a neighboring premises (PW-4) was one of the persons who responded to the alarm. As he approached, he saw someone running away with a panga in his hand. When the person realized the people following him were close he threw away the panga but was caught. That person was the appellant. The Court of Appeal stated that it was not satisfied that the evidence disclosed the offence of attempted robbery with violence. Accordingly it quashed the appellant's conviction for that offence and set aside the sentence of death passed against him. The issue that followed was whether as a result, the appellant should have been set at liberty. The Court referred to Section 179 of the CPC and observed that the facts disclosed two minor offences, one of store breaking contrary to section 306 of the Penal Code, and the second, assault causing actual bodily harm contrary to section 251 of the Penal Code. The court then proceeded to convict and sentence the appellant for the two offences.[35]

11.4.2 Persons Charged With Any Offence May Be Convicted of Attempt

Pursuant to Section 180 of the CPC when a person is charged with an offence, he may be convicted of having attempted to commit that offence although he was not charged with the attempt. In this situation, the accused has been

---

[34] Nairobi Court of Appeal, Criminal Appeal No. 291 of 2007 (2010) eKLR; See also *Evaline Wangari Njeri & another v Republic* (2008) eKLR and *Peter Kamonjo Njoroge v Republic* (2006) eKLR.

[35] See also *Thomas Oecha Anunda v R*, Kisii High Court, Criminal Appeal No. 295 of 2006, (2009) eKLR.

charged with committing an offence say robbery. However, the evidence adduced is not enough to convict the accused for the complete offence but proves an attempt. In this case, the accused may be convicted of the attempt, although he was never charged with the offence of attempt, but was charged with the complete offence.

11.4.3 Charges of Certain Offences Respecting Infant and Unborn Children, and Abortion

These offences are canvassed in Section 181 (1) of the CPC which provides that when a woman is charged with the murder of her child, being a child under the age of twelve months, and the court is of the opinion that she by a willful act or omission caused its death, but at the time of the act or omission she had not fully recovered from the effect of giving birth to that child, and that by reason thereof, or by reason of the effect of lactation consequent upon the birth of the child, the balance of her mind was then disturbed, she may, notwithstanding that the circumstances were such that she might be convicted of murder, be convicted of the offence of infanticide although she was not charged with it. [36]

This is a situation where the woman is charged with murder of her child who is aged below 12 months. The Penal Code under section 210 recognizes that such a woman may be imbalanced owing to the effects of child birth or lactation. In such a case, although the charge of murder may be have been proved, the court is free to instead convict for the offence of infanticide, although the accused was not charged with it. Infanticide is a lesser offence to murder and is equated to the offence of manslaughter.

---

[36] Section 210 of the Penal Code provides, *"Where a woman by any willful act or omission causes the death of her child being a child under the age of twelve months, but at the time of the act or omission the balance of her mind was disturbed by reason of her not having fully recovered from the effect of giving birth to the child or by reason of the effect of lactation consequent on the birth of the child, then, notwithstanding that the circumstances were such that but for the provisions of this section the offence would have amounted to murder, she shall be guilty of a felony, to wit, infanticide, and may for that offence be dealt with and punished as if she had been guilty of manslaughter of the child."*

Further sub-section (2) provides that when a person is charged with the murder or manslaughter of a child or with infanticide, or with an offence under section 158 or section 159 of the Penal Code, and the court is of the opinion that he is not guilty of murder, manslaughter or infanticide or an offence under section 158 or section 159 of the Penal Code, but that he is guilty of the offence of killing an unborn child, he may be convicted of that offence although he was not charged with it. Sections 158 and 159 deal with procuring abortion.

At, Section 181 (3) of the CPC, when a person is charged with killing an unborn child and the court is of the opinion that he is not guilty of that offence but that he is guilty of an offence under one of the sections 158 and 159 of the Penal Code, he may be convicted of that offence although he was not charged with it. (I.e. attempts to procure abortion). If the charge of killing an unborn child is not proved, the court is free to convict for the offence of attempt to procure abortion if the evidence is sufficient to support the charge. When a person is charged with the murder or infanticide of a child or with killing an unborn child and the court is of the opinion that he is not guilty of any of those offences, and if it appears in evidence that the child had recently been born and that the person did, by some secret disposition of the dead body of the child, endeavour to conceal the birth of that child, he may be convicted of the offence of endeavouring to conceal the birth of that child although he was not charged with it.[37]

11.4.4 Charge of Manslaughter in Connexion With Driving of Motor Vehicle

Pursuant to Section 182 of the CPC, **w**hen a person is charged with manslaughter in connexion with the driving of a motor vehicle by him and the court is of the opinion that he is not guilty of that offence, but that he is guilty of an offence under section 46 of the Traffic Act,[38] he may be convicted of that offence although he was not charged with it. The aforementioned section is with regard to the offence of Causing Death by Dangerous Driving or obstruction.

---

37 CPC, Section 181 (4).

38 Chapter 403, Laws of Kenya.

11.4.5 Charge of Administering Oaths

Section 183 of the CPC expressly manifests that where a person is charged with an offence under paragraph (a) of section 61 of the Penal Code, and the court is of the opinion that he is not guilty of that offence but is guilty of another offence under the same paragraph, he may be convicted of that other offence although he was not charged with it. This deals with administering or taking of an oath. There are various instances covered by Section 61 (a) and the court is free to convict of any.

11.4.6 Charge of Rape

As regards the charge of rape, Section 184 of the CPC is categorical that if the court is of the opinion that the accused person is not guilty of that offence but that he is guilty of an offence under one of the sections of the Sexual Offences Act[39], he may be convicted of that offence although he was not charged with it. These may include offences such as sexual assault, attempted rape, or sexual harassment.

11.4.7 Charge of Defilement of a Girl Under 14 years of age

Pursuant to Section 186 of the CPC when a person is charged with the defilement of a girl under the age of fourteen years and the court is of the opinion that he is not guilty of that offence but that he is guilty of an offence under the Sexual Offences Act, he may be convicted of that offence although he was not charged with it.[40]

11.4.8 Charge of Burglary, etc.

Section 187 of the CPC provides that when a person is charged with an offence mentioned in Chapter XXIX of the Penal Code and the court is of the opinion

---

39 Chapter 62A, Laws of Kenya.

40 As noted above in considering section 184 of the CPC.

that he is not guilty of that offence but that he is guilty of another offence mentioned in that Chapter, he may be convicted of that other offence although he was not charged with it. Chapter XXIX deals with offences such as Burglary, Housebreaking, breaking into a vehicle, and related charges.

11.4.9 Charge of Stealing

Section 188 of the CPC explicitly directs that when a person is charged with stealing anything and -

(a) The facts proved amount to an offence under section 322 or section 323 of the Penal Code, he may be convicted of that offence although he was not charged with it;[41]
(b) it is proved that he obtained the thing in a manner as would amount, under the provisions of the Penal Code or of any other law for the time being in force, to obtaining it by false pretences with intent to defraud, he may be convicted of the offence of obtaining it by false pretences although he was not charged with it.

11.4.10 Charge of Obtaining by False Pretences

Pursuant to section 189 of the CPC, when a person is charged with obtaining anything capable of being stolen by false pretences with intent to defraud and it is proved that he stole the thing, he may be convicted of the offence of stealing although he was not charged with it.

11.4.11 Charge of Stock Theft

Section 190 of the CPC provides that when a person is charged with the offence of stock theft under the Penal Code and the court is of the opinion that he is not guilty of that offence but that he is guilty of an offence under section 9 of the

---

41 Section 322 and 323 of the Penal Code deal with the offences of Handling Stolen Property and Conveying Stolen Property respectively.

Stock and Produce Theft Act[42], he may be convicted of that offence although he was not charged with it. Section 9 of the Stock and Produce Theft Act, deals with the offence of being in illegal possession of stock.

11.4.12 Misdemeanours and Felonies

Section 192 of the CPC provides that if on a trial for a misdemeanour the facts proved in evidence amount to a felony, the accused shall not be acquitted of the misdemeanour; and no person tried for the misdemeanour shall be liable afterwards to be prosecuted for a felony on the same facts, unless the court thinks fit to direct that person to be prosecuted for felony, whereupon he may be dealt with as if not previously put on trial for misdemeanour. What this means is that if you have been charged with a lesser offence, which is a misdemeanor, you cannot be convicted of the more serious offence, a felony, despite the facts showing otherwise. Neither can you be tried in a subsequent trial for the felony. However, the accused ought not to be acquitted of the misdemeanour.

* * *

42 Chapter 355, Laws of Kenya.

CHAPTER 12

SENTENCE

12.1 Introduction

Sentence is passed when the accused has been convicted of an offence. The Penal Code[1] in Chapter VI deals with punishments upon conviction. It is good practice first to pass judgment on the conviction and then later make a decision on sentence. This gives the court opportunity to take submissions and consider the appropriate sentence to be meted out to the offender. There are various punishments that are prescribed some of which are mandatory and some discretionary.

12.2 Mitigation before sentence

Before passing sentence, the Court must invite the accused to mitigate. Mitigation is an opportunity given to a convicted person to give reasons to the court why he deserves a light punishment. If opportunity is not given to mitigate, this may invalidate the sentence.

In *John Muoki Mbatha v Republic,*[2] this principle was stated in these words:-

"As we have stated over and over again when considering sentences in respect of murder cases, the sentences should be reserved and pronounced only after mitigating factors are known. This is important because in mitigation, matters such as age, and

1 Chapter 63, Laws of Kenya.

2 *John Muoki Mbatha v Republic* Machakos Criminal Appeal No. 72 of 2007 (unreported).

pregnancy in cases of women convicts, may affect the sentence even in cases where death sentence is mandatory. In our view, no sentence should be made part of the main judgment. Sentence should be reserved and be pronounced only after the court receives mitigating circumstances if any are offered."

Mitigation is therefore a critical component before sentencing even in cases where the court is of the view that it must pass a mandatory sentence.

12.3 Punishments

Section 24 of the Penal Code provides for the punishments that may be inflicted by a court. These are sentences of death, imprisonment, community service, fine, forfeiture, payment of compensation, finding security to keep the peace and be of good behavior, and any other punishment provided by the Penal Code or by any other Act. The sentence is the punishment that is meted out to an accused person who has been found guilty and convicted. Probably the word punishment may be misplaced because it is not in all instances that the offender will be "punished" in the ordinary sense of the word as there are sentences that are not necessarily punitive, such as a discharge.[3] Nonetheless, that definition conjures up the essence of a sentence, which is to prescribe a punishment as the consequence of a conviction.

The court may, before passing sentence receive such evidence as it thinks fit in order to inform itself as to the sentence or order properly to be passed or made.[4] What this means is that the court may seek evidence which was not available at trial to enable it consider the sentence suited for the circumstances of the case and of the offender. This may include his past criminal record.

Where a person of not less than eighteen years of age is convicted by a subordinate court of the second class of an offence which is punishable by either that court or a subordinate court of the first class, and the court convicting him, after obtaining information as to his character and antecedents, is of the opinion that they are such that greater punishment should be inflicted than it has power

3 Section 35 Penal Code.

4 Criminal Procedure Code (CPC) CAP 75, Section 216.

to inflict, that court may, instead of dealing with him itself, commit him in custody to the Resident Magistrate's Court for sentence.[5] Thus a subordinate court of the second class can refer the accused to the magistrate's court of the first class to be sentenced by that court if it is of opinion that the accused deserves a more severe penalty than it can mete out. [6]

Where a person who is not less than eighteen years of age is convicted by a subordinate court of the first class of an offence which is punishable by either that court or the High Court, and the court convicting him, after obtaining information as to his character and antecedents, is of the opinion that they are such that greater punishment should be inflicted than it has power to inflict, that court may, instead of dealing with him itself, commit him in custody to the High Court for sentence.[7] This is a situation where the magistrate's court refers the matter to the High Court for sentencing. But this is extremely rare and in reality this provision serves little or no purpose.

The court to which the matter has been referred to for sentencing must pass a sentence which the court convicting him had power to pass; if not, the offender may appeal against the sentence to the High Court (if sentenced by a subordinate court of the first class), or to the Court of Appeal (if sentenced by the High Court), but otherwise he shall have the same right of appeal in all respects as if he had been sentenced by the court which convicted him.

For trials in the High Court, sentence is provided for under Section 322 (2) of the CPC, which provides that if the accused is convicted, the judge shall pass sentence on him according to law.

12.4 Nature and Types of Sentence

The nature and type of sentence that is to be meted is guided by the law which specifically sets out the types of sentences that may be prescribed in the event of

5 *Ibid*, Section 221 (1).

6 See Chapter 2 which provides for jurisdiction of Magistrates.

7 CPC, Section 221 (2).

a conviction. Let us look at some of these sentences starting with the sentence with the most severe consequences.

12.4.1 Death Sentence

Section 25 (1) of the Penal Code provides that where any person is sentenced to death, the form of the sentence shall be to the effect only that he is to suffer death in the manner authorized by law. In other words, the court is not to specify how the accused person is going to suffer death. All it is supposed to state is that he should suffer death in the manner authorised by law. However, the sentence of death is prohibited if the person convicted committed the offence when he was under the age of 18 years; in lieu thereof the court is supposed to sentence such person to be detained during the President's pleasure.[8] If so sentenced, he shall be liable to be detained in such place and under such conditions as the President may direct, and whilst so detained shall be deemed to be in legal custody.[9] It is important to note that when a person has been sentenced to be detained during the President's pleasure under the provisions of section 25 (2) of the Penal Code, the presiding judge is mandated to forward to the President a copy of the notes of evidence taken on the trial, with a report in writing signed by him containing any recommendation or observations on the case he may think fit to make.

Pursuant to section 330 of the CPC when an accused person is sentenced to death, the court must inform him of the time within which, if he wishes to appeal, his appeal should be preferred.

As regards the authority for detention, a certificate under the hand of the Registrar or other officer of the court that the sentence of death has been passed, and naming the person condemned, shall be sufficient authority for the detention of that person.[10] Thereafter the record and the report is sent to the President pursuant to Section 332 (1) of the CPC which provides that as soon

8 See *Turon v R* (1967) EA 788.

9 Penal Code, S.25 (2); See also section 190 (2) of the Children Act (CAP 141) Laws of Kenya.

10 CPC, S.331.

as the sentence of death has been pronounced, if no appeal from the sentence is confirmed, then as soon as conveniently may be after confirmation, the presiding judge shall forward to the President a copy of the notes of evidence taken on the trial, with a report in writing signed, by him containing any recommendation or observations on the case he may think fit to make. Subsection (2) provides that the President, after considering the report, shall communicate to the judge, or his successor in office, the terms of any decision to which he may come thereon, and the judge shall cause the tenor and substance thereof to be entered in the records of the court.

Subsection (3) is categorical that the President shall issue a death warrant, or an order for the sentence of death to be commuted, or a pardon, under his hand and the Public Seal of Kenya to give effect to the decision, and -

(a) if the sentence of death is to be carried out, the warrant shall state the place where and the time when execution is to be had, and shall give directions as to the place of burial or cremation of the body of the person executed;
(b) if the sentence is commuted for any other punishment, the order shall specify that punishment;
(c) if the person sentenced is pardoned, the pardon shall state whether it is free, or to what conditions (if any) it is subject.

The death sentence is the most severe penalty and is prescribed for the most serious of offences such as murder, treason, robbery with violence and attempted robbery with violence. Indeed for these offences, the death penalty is the only prescribed sentence, the statute providing that the person convicted of these offences *"shall be sentenced to death."*[11] The question that arises, is whether the court has discretion to prescribe a lesser sentence so that the sentence of death in such instance remains the heaviest penalty.

In *Geoffrey Ngotho Mutiso v R,*[12] the appellant had been convicted of the offence of murder in the High Court and sentenced to death. He appealed on sentence and raised the issue that the imposition of a mandatory death sentence upon

11 See for example section 202 Penal Code for the prescribed sentence for the conviction of murder.

12 Court of Appeal at Mombasa, Criminal Appeal No. 17 of 2008, (2010) eKLR.

him was arbitrary and unconstitutional and the execution of the same in the instant case would amount to:-

a) An inhuman and degrading punishment in breach of section 74 (1) of the (repealed) Constitution.[13]
b) An arbitrary deprivation of life in breach of section 71 (1)[14] and 70 (a) of the (repealed) Constitution.[15]
c) A denial of the appellant's rights to fair trial in breach of section 77 of the (repealed) Constitution.

The appellant argued against the notion, that the death penalty is mandatory. He also argued that even if the death penalty may not itself be inhuman and degrading, not everyone convicted of murder deserves to die, and therefore, a sentencing regime that imposes a mandatory sentence of death on all proven murder cases, or all murders within specified categories, is inhuman and degrading because it requires the sentence of death to be passed without any opportunity for the accused to show why such sentence should be mitigated and without consideration of the detailed facts of the particular case, or the personal history and circumstances of the offender, and in cases where such sentence might be wholly disproportionate to the accused's criminal culpability.

---

13 Section 74 (1) of the repealed Constitution provided, *"No person shall be subject to torture or to inhuman or degrading punishment or other treatment."* The equivalent of the provision in the *Constitution of Kenya*, 2010 can be said to be found in Art 29 (f) which provides, *"Every person has the right to freedom and security of the person, which includes the right not to be treated or punished in a cruel, inhuman or degrading manner."*

14 Section 71 (1) of the repealed Constitution provided, *"No person shall be deprived of his life intentionally save in execution of the sentence of a court in respect of a criminal offence under the law of Kenya of which he has been convicted."* The equivalent of this provision in the Constitution of Kenya 2010 is found in Art 26 (3) which provides that, *"A person shall not be deprived of life intentionally, except to the extent authorised by this Constitution or other written law."*

15 Section 70 (a) of the repealed Constitution provided, *"Whereas every person in Kenya is entitled to the fundamental rights and freedoms of the individual, that is to say, the right, whatever his race, tribe, place of origin or residence or other local connexion, political opinions, colour, creed or sex, but subject to respect for the rights and freedoms of others and for the public interest, to each and all of the following, namely life, liberty, security of the person and the protection of the law."*

The court held in the appellant's favour and had this to say,

"On our own assessment of the issue at hand and the material placed before us, we are persuaded, and now so hold, that section 204 *of the Penal Code which provides for a mandatory death sentence is antithetical to the Constitutional provisions on protection against inhuman or degrading punishment or treatment and fair trial. We note that while the Constitution itself recognizes the death penalty as being lawful, it does not say anywhere that when a conviction for murder is recorded, only the death sentence shall be imposed. We declare that* section 204 *shall, to the extent that it provides that the death penalty is the only sentence in respect of the crime of murder is inconsistent with the letter and spirit of the constitution, which as we have said, makes no such mandatory provision."*

After the decision in the *Mutiso* case, courts proceeded to apply that holding in their judgments, and several persons convicted of offences that otherwise would have been construed as carrying the death penalty, were not sentenced to death.[16]

However, the decision in *Mutiso* came under heavy criticism by the High Court (Warsame J), in the case of *Republic v Munene & Another.*[17] The judge insisted that the sentence of death is the only prescribed penalty for the offence of murder and proceeded to sentence the two accused persons to death. The judge stated that:-

"...My understanding of criminal law is that, when it comes to sentencing, the section either uses the words "shall or is liable". Where the word "shall" is used or employed, the discretion of the court has been deliberately and intentionally restricted by Parliament. If Parliament in its wisdom has restricted the liberty of the court, it is not the duty of the court to put words or meaning which are non-existent in the statute or particular section. That is a basic and elementary rule of interpretation..."

---

16 See for example *R v John Kimita Mwaniki,* Nakuru High Court Criminal Case No. 116 of 2007 (2011)eKLR where the accused was convicted of murder and sentenced to 30 years imprisonment without the option of a parole for the first 20 years.

17 High Court at Nairobi, Criminal Case No. 11 of 2009, (2011) eKLR.

The court noted that the law currently in existence provides for the death penalty, notwithstanding the noble position taken in the case of *Mutiso,* and that the only available sentence for a person convicted for murder is death. The court observed that the mandatory use of the word 'shall' gave no other option or route other than to impose the death penalty.

The position as to whether the death penalty is discretionary or mandatory where prescribed by the words "shall", resurfaced in the Court of Appeal in the case of *Joseph Njuguna Mwaura & 3 Others v Republic.*[18] The appellants were tried and convicted of the offence of robbery with violence and sentenced to death. Their first appeal to the High Court was dismissed and they preferred a second appeal to the Court of Appeal. *Inter alia*, it was contended that the death sentence was outlawed and therefore improper to have been imposed on the appellants. The case of *Mutiso* was cited as authority. The five judge bench[19] held that the only sentence provided for the offence of robbery with violence was the death sentence[20] and affirmed that the death sentence is provided for by both the constitution and statute. On the arguments that the death sentence amounts to cruel and inhuman treatment, the court was of the view that the deprivation of life as a consequence of unlawful behavior is not disproportionate in relation to the offences in which it is prescribed in Kenya. The court declined to follow the decision in *Godfrey Ngotho Mutiso,* and held the view that the decision in *Mutiso* that it was *per incuriam,* as the words "shall" must be construed to be mandatory and left no discretion to the courts.

Given the decision in the *Joseph Njuguna Mwaura* case, it appears as if the current position is that where the death sentence is prescribed as the only sentence, then the court has no discretion and must impose it upon the accused,

---

18 Court of Appeal at Nairobi, Criminal Appeal No.5 of 2008, (2013) eKLR.

19 Significantly, one of whom was Warsame J, who had then been elevated to the Court of Appeal.

20 Penal Code Section 296 (2) which provides that upon conviction *"... he shall be sentenced to death."*

if convicted.[21] It is however left to be seen whether this question will be carried forward to the Supreme Court for it to consider the position.

If the accused is convicted of several counts which carry the death sentence, the proper cause is to sentence him to death on one count and hold the other sentences in abeyance. This was held in the case of *George Otieno Dida & Another v Republic*[22] because a person cannot die more than once. In this case, the appellants were charged with four counts of robbery with violence. They were found guilty in all the four counts and thereafter sentenced to death on each count. The appellate court stated that *"It should, however, be noted that a person cannot die more than once. That being the case, the trial court should have sentenced the appellant to death in one count but order any other sentence against them to be in abeyance."*

Similarly in *John Kinyua Miriti v R*,[23] the Court of Appeal stated:-

"On sentence, this Court has said time without number that it is improper to sentence an accused person to death on more than one count. For the foregoing reasons, we dismiss the appeal with an order that the sentence of death in the second count relating to robbing, (SNL) shall remain in abeyance."

Where the accused is convicted of various counts, some of which carry the death sentence and some of which do not, and the accused is sentenced to death, the proper procedure is for the court to suspend the other sentences. In *Gachuru v R*[24] the appellant was convicted and charged with four counts of robbery with violence and one count of illegal firearm possession. He was sentenced to death for the four capital counts of robbery with violence and to a five year term for the count of illegal firearm possession. On appeal, the court held that where an accused person is convicted on more than one capital charge, the sensible

---

21 But see the contrary interpretation given in the old Ugandan case of *Opoya v Uganda* (1967)EA 752, where the Court of Appeal, interpreted the words "shall be liable on conviction to suffer death" as only prescribing the maximum penalty and that the courts had discretion to impose a sentence of death or imprisonment.

22 Court of Appeal at Kisumu, Criminal Appeal No. 404 of 2009, (2011) eKLR.

23 Court of Appeal at Nairobi, Crim. App. No. 325 of 2007, (2011) eKLR.

24 (2005) 1 EA 56; See also *Boye v R* Criminal Appeal No. 19 of 2001 (UR), *Kaimoi v R* (2005) 1 EA and *Muiruri v R* (1980) KLR 70.

thing to do is to sentence him to death on only one count and leave the rest in abeyance, including any sentence of imprisonment. If there is subsequently a successful appeal on the imposed capital penalty, the appellate court could then consider the other counts and if necessary impose the appropriate sentence on the count on which the appeal is not allowed.

In *Gachunga & Another v R,*[25]the appellants were convicted of the offence of robbery with violence and one was also convicted of Rape. They were sentenced to death on account of the offence of robbery with violence but the trial court, probably faced with the dilemma of what to do with the appellant convicted of rape, proceeded to discharge him of this offence. The Court of Appeal frowned upon this practice and stated as follows:-

"This Court has consistently held that where a person is sentenced to death upon conviction for an offence which provides for a death penalty and at the same trial he is convicted of any other offence carrying a lesser sentence, such lesser sentence should be ordered suspended." It is common knowledge that the death penalty has not been executed in the Kenya since 1987. Further, in 2009, President Kibaki commuted 4,000 death sentences and called for a study to determine whether Kenya's mandatory death sentence for murder or armed robbery actually deters crime. This can be said to be evidence of a *de facto* moratorium on the death penalty. However, Kenya has still not signed the Second Optional Protocol to the International Covenant on Civil and Political Rights (ICCPR) aiming at abolition of the death penalty.[26] Thus it can be said that Kenya has not *de jure* abolished capital punishment, but de *facto* the death penalty is not effected.

The ICCPR itself provides that in countries which have not abolished the death penalty, sentence of death may be imposed only for the most serious crimes in accordance with the law in force at the time of the commission of the crime.[27] This penalty can only be carried out pursuant to a final judgment

25 Nairobi Court of Appeal, Criminal Appeal No. 11 of 2006, (2007) eKLR.

26 2nd Optional Protocol to the International Covenant on Civil and Political Rights (ICCPR), aiming at the abolition of the death penalty. Adopted and proclaimed by the UN General Assembly resolution 44/128 of 15 December 1989 and came into force on 11 July 1991.

27 ICCPR, Article 6 (2).

rendered by a competent court. Generally, international courts and tribunals do not provide for the death penalty. This is indeed so for the Statute of the International Criminal Court (ICC), statutes of the International Criminal Tribunal for Rwanda (ICTR) and the International Criminal Tribunal for the former Yugoslavia (ICTY) and the Sierra Leone Special Court, which prosecute the most serious crimes against humanity.

12.4.2 Imprisonment

Section 26 of the Penal Code provides that a sentence of imprisonment for any offence shall be to imprisonment, or to imprisonment with hard labour, as may be required or permitted by the law under which the offence is punishable. Sub-section (2) is categorical that, save as may be expressly provided by the law under which the offence concerned is punishable, a person liable to imprisonment for life or any other period may be sentenced to any shorter term. Further, sub-section (3) makes provisions to the effect that a person liable to imprisonment for an offence may be sentenced to pay a fine, in addition to, or in substitution of imprisonment. However, where the law provides for a minimum sentence of imprisonment, a fine shall not be substituted for imprisonment. Imprisonment can range from a day to life.

Where a term of imprisonment is prescribed, unless that term is stated to be the minimum sentence, then the same must be construed as the maximum sentence to be imposed. In *Daniel Kyalo Muema v R,*[28] the appellant had been charged with the offence of being in possession of cannabis sativa contrary to section 3(1) as read with section 3 (2) of the Narcotics and Psychotropic Substances (Control) Act[29]of 1994. The same provides as follows:-

3. Penalty for possession of narcotic drugs, etc.

(1) Subject to subsection (3), any person who has in his possession any narcotic drug or psychotropic substance shall be guilty of an offence.
(2) A person guilty of an offence under subsection (1) shall be liable—

[28] Court of Appeal at Nairobi, Criminal Appeal No. 479 of 2007, (2009) eKLR.
[29] Chapter 245, Laws of Kenya.

(a) *in respect of cannabis, where the person satisfies the court that the cannabis was intended solely for his own consumption, to imprisonment for ten years and in every other case to imprisonment for twenty years; and*

(b) *in respect of a narcotic drug or psychotropic substance, other than cannabis, where the person satisfies the court that the narcotic drug or psychotropic substance was intended solely for his own consumption, to imprisonment for twenty years and in every other case to a fine of not less than one million shillings or three times the market value of the narcotic drug or psychotropic substance, whichever is the greater, or to imprisonment for life or to both such fine and imprisonment.* He was sentenced to 6 years by the trial magistrate and he appealed on sentence. The High Court, on appeal, enhanced the sentence to 20 years, apparently on the belief that the Act prescribed a minimum sentence of 20 years for the offence. The appellant appealed to the Court of Appeal which clarified that where a sentence is prescribed, then that is the maximum sentence, and the court has discretion to sentence the accused to any period not exceeding the prescribed one.

This principle is contained in section 66 (1) of the Interpretation and General Provisions Act[30] which provides that, *"Where in a written law a penalty is prescribed for an offence under that written law, that provision shall, unless a contrary intention appears, mean that the offence shall be punishable by a penalty not exceeding the penalty prescribed."* This principle is entrenched in section 26 of the Penal Code which expressly authorizes a court to sentence the offender to a shorter term than the maximum provided by any written law and further authorizes the court to pass a sentence of a fine in addition to, or in substitution of imprisonment, except where the law provides for a minimum sentence of imprisonment.[31] There is a proviso to section 26 (3) of the Penal Code, that a fine cannot be substituted for imprisonment, where the law concerned provides for a minimum sentence of imprisonment.

It is open for the law to prescribe minimum sentences for imprisonment, in which event, the trial court has no choice but to sentence the accused, at the very least, to the prescribed minimum. Examples of minimum sentences can

---

30 Chapter 2, Laws of Kenya.

31 Penal Code, Sections 26 (2) and (3).

be found in the Sexual offences Act,[32] and the Firearms Act.[33] The law may also provide for a mandatory sentence in which case the court's hands are tied in its discretion and must mete out the mandatory sentence.

Where the court has discretion, it is upon the court to weigh the circumstances of the case in order to come up with the most appropriate term of imprisonment. In *Khalif v R*,[34] the appellant was convicted of dangerous driving, failing to stop after an accident, and using an unlicensed vehicle. He was sentenced to 15 months imprisonment. On appeal it was argued *inter alia*, that a non-custodial sentence should have been imposed. On this point, the High Court held that a prison sentence is appropriate where there is an element of deliberative risk taking; the court noted that the appellant's actions were as a result of a deliberate and calculated judgment, and that no prudent driver would have done as he did.

12.4.3 Fines

A fine is the payment of a sum of money as punishment for committing an offence. A fine may be given alone or in addition to other penalty. In most cases, a fine would be imposed with a proviso, that if the same is not paid, then the offender will serve a prison sentence. Section 28 (1) (a) of the Penal Code provides that where the Court imposes a fine under any law, but the law does not expressly provide for the amount of the fine that can be imposed, then, the amount of fine that may be imposed is unlimited but shall not be excessive. A fine may be imposed irrespective of the status of the accused. It does not

---

32 For example Section 8 (3) of the Sexual Offences Act, (CAP 62A) Laws of Kenya, provides:- *"A person who commits an offence of defilement with a child between the age of twelve and fifteen years is liable upon conviction to imprisonment for a term of not less than twenty years."*

33 For example Section 4 (3) (a) of the Fire Arms Act (CAP 114) Laws of Kenya, provides :- *"Any person who is convicted of an offence under subsection (2) shall if the firearm concerned is a prohibited weapon of a type specified in paragraph (b) of the definition of that term contained in section 2 or the ammunition is ammunition for use in any such firearm be liable to imprisonment for a term of not less than seven years and not more than fifteen years."*

34 (1973) EA 364; See also *Wanjema v Republic* (1971) EA 493 and *R v Tyre* (1972) Crimm. L.R. 55.

matter that the offender is well off and payment of a fine would mean no more than a mere inconvenience. In *Mita v R*,[35] the appellant, an air hostess, bit the complainant on the chin. She pleaded guilty to causing actual bodily harm. The magistrate sentenced her to two months imprisonment, although she was a first offender and was contrite. In doing so he commented that he did not think a fine would serve any purpose as the appellant appeared to be earning a lot of money. On appeal against the sentence, the High Court held that irrespective of an accused person's earning capacity, it is not wrong to impose a fine, unless the circumstances of the case irresistibly preclude the mode of punishment, and that in the circumstances the sentence was excessive. The sentence was set aside and a fine of sh. 400 or two months in default substituted.

Fines are ordinarily applied to first offenders and to unaggravated offences or misdemeanors. It is prudent for the court to determine whether the offender can pay the fine, otherwise it would be futile to fine a person who is unable to pay, as in essence this would mean a prison sentence where the same is not necessary. The imprisonment or detention which is imposed in default of payment of a fine, shall terminate whenever the fine is paid. Where the accused is convicted of various counts, he must be sentenced for each count, and if a fine is imposed, there must be a default sentence, again separately for each count.

In *Wakitata v R*,[36] the appellant had been convicted and sentenced on two counts of being in possession of game trophies without a certificate of ownership, contrary to section 42 (1) (b) of the Wildlife (Conservation and management) Act; on the first count, to a fine of Shs. 6,000/= for the first Colobus monkey skin, and Shs 3,000/= for each of the other five (a total of Shs. 21,000/=) or to six months' imprisonment in default; and on the second count to a total fine of Shs 30,000/= or to nine months' imprisonment in default for the 12 skins found. Both terms were to run concurrently and the animal skins were forfeited to the government. On appeal it was held that where a court imposes separate fines for individual offences, it cannot impose an omnibus default sentence of imprisonment, but must indicate a separate default sentence for each fine in the event of non- payment. Therefore, the High Court set aside the sentences

---

35 (1969) EA 598.

36 (1976-80) KLR 168.

passed by the magistrate, including the order of forfeiture, and substituted the following sentences;

Count 1: Fine Shs 10,000/=, or default four and a half months imprisonment.

Count 2: Fine of Shs 10,000/= or in default four and a half months imprisonment

Total: Fine of Shs, 20,000/=, or in default nine months imprisonment.

Some statutes provide for fairly steep fines which may be graduated depending on the gravity of the offence, as in the Traffic Act[37] or the Narcotics Act[38]. For example, in the latter statute, Section 4 (a) provides as follows:-

"Any person who traffics in any narcotic drug or psychotropic substance or any substance represented or held out by him to be a narcotic drug or psychotropic substance shall be guilty of an offence and liable in respect of any narcotic drug or psychotropic substance to a fine of one million shillings or three times the market value of the narcotic drug or psychotropic substance, whichever is the greater, and, in addition, to imprisonment for life."

The above provision came up for interpretation in the case of *Kingsley Chukwu v R.*[39] The appellant was charged with trafficking heroin which was valued at Kshs. 9,605,000/=. After a full trial, the trial court found him guilty of the offence, convicted him and sentenced him to imprisonment for 15 years. He appealed to the High Court. The High Court, upheld the conviction but varied the sentence. In place of the sentence of 15 years, the High Court imposed upon the appellant a sentence of a fine of Kshs. 28,800,000/= and in default, the appellant to serve 12 years imprisonment. In addition to this, the judge sentenced the appellant to a further independent sentence of 3 1/2 years. Still dissatisfied, the appellant filed a second appeal to the Court of Appeal. The conviction was again upheld. With regard to sentence, the Court of Appeal was of the view that the sentences imposed by both the courts below it contravened Section 4 of the statute, as the provision as drawn indicated for

37 Chapter 403, Laws of Kenya.

38 *Supra* note 29.

39 Nairobi Court of Appeal, Criminal Appeal No. 257 of 2007, (2010) eKLR.

a convict to be fined a sum of Kshs. 1,000,000/= or three times the value of the drugs, whichever was greater and in addition to imprisonment for life. The court was of the view that the statute did not permit either of the sentences imposed by the trial court and the first appellate court. In its place, the Court of Appeal passed a sentence of a fine of Kshs. 28,800,000/= and in addition to imprisonment for life.[40]

The essence of fines is probably to decongest prisons and to impose a punishment for persons who really do not need to be kept away from society and therefore it is not necessary to jail them. It is expected to be more of a deterrent sentence so that the accused would not repeat the offence. If he repeats he may be sent to jail.

12.5 Non-Custodial Sentences

12.5.1 Expulsion from the Country

This provision applies to a person who is a non-citizen of Kenya, and who is convicted of an offence punishable with imprisonment for a term not exceeding 12 months. The court may direct that such person, be removed from Kenya and remain outside Kenya either immediately or on completion of any sentence or imprisonment imposed.[41] However, if the person is convicted for an offence punishable with imprisonment for a term exceeding 12 months, the court, if it is of the view that such person needs to be expelled, has no power to make a direct order of expulsion, but can only recommend to the Minister responsible for immigration that an order for removal from Kenya be made in accordance with section 8 of the Immigration Act.

---

40 It is of course open to conjecture whether one will pay such a steep fine, if he is going to be imprisoned for life, anyway.

41 Penal Code, Section 26A.

12.5.2 Forfeiture

Forfeiture refers to a penalty where the offender is obliged to surrender the property which was the subject of the offence to the State or other authority. Various statutes provide for forfeiture as a punishment. For offences under the Penal Code, section 29 (1) of the Penal Code, provides for forfeiture as a mode of punishment where a person is convicted for the offences of compounding a felony or compounding penal actions.[42] If the property to be forfeited cannot be found or is incapable of being forfeited, the court is at liberty to assess the value of the property or sum of money to be forfeited and payment of such money may be enforced in the same manner and subject to the same incidents as in the case of payment of a fine.[43]

Under the Forest Act[44], if one is convicted of an offence of damaging, injuring or removing forest produce from any forest, the court may in addition to any other ruling, *inter alia*, order the forfeiture to the Kenya Forest Service, of any vessel, vehicle or tool used in the commission of the offence.[45]

It is possible for an order of forfeiture to affect a person who was not an accused in the case. In the case of *Muya v R*[46] two persons were accused of the offence of cutting and removing forest produce. They were convicted and the lorry that was being used to transport the timber ordered to be forfeited. The owner, of the vehicle, applied to revise the order. This was declined.

To avoid an adverse order being made on an innocent party, it is prudent for such party to appear in the proceedings and make a case for non-forfeiture.

---

42 These offences are provided for under Sections 118 and 119 of the Penal Code.

43 Penal Code, Section 29 (1).

44 Chapter 385 Laws of Kenya.

45 See *Muya v R* (2004) 1 KLR 515 and *Lochab Brothers Ltd v Republic*, Kericho High Court, Miscellaneous Criminal Application No. 12 of 2008, (2008) eKLR.

46 *Ibid.*

12.5.3 Suspension or Forfeiture to Carry on Business

This is a sentence in which a person is barred from carrying on his usual or other business for a specified duration of time as a punishment for the offence committed. This sentence is noted in Section 30 of the Penal Code. The sentence is prescribed for offences mentioned in Chapter XXXI of the Penal Code.[47] For example, a trader may be a conduit for stolen property. If so the court, in addition to any other penalty may make an order suspending or forfeiting the business of the offender. A failure to comply with an order of suspension or forfeiture of business is itself an offence punishable by payment of a fine of Shs. 2,000/= or imprisonment for a term of 6 months or to both.[48]

12.5.4 Compensation

The court has discretion to order an offender to pay compensation to any person injured by the offence. Such compensation may be in addition to or in substitution of any other punishment.[49] It will be seen that this remedy is almost akin to the civil remedy of damages for injury caused through a wrongful action. If granted, it may save one the expense and necessity of filing a suit for damages in a civil action.

Indeed the court has discretion, if the facts proven in the case, also demonstrate a civil liability, order the convicted person to pay such damages as could be recovered in civil proceedings. But the court in making such order, cannot impose an award which is higher than it has jurisdiction to award in a civil action, or where such award could not be made in a civil action, say, owing to a question of limitation of time, or want of evidence.[50] Section 175(6) of the CPC provides that such order of compensation is enforceable in the same manner as a judgment in civil proceedings.[51]If subsequent civil proceedings are filed, the fact that an award was made may be used as a defense, to the extent of the

---

47 These involve offences of handling stolen property or property unlawfully obtained.

48 Penal Code, Section 30 (2).

49 *Ibid*, Section 31.

50 CPC, Section 175.

51 *Ibid,* Section 175 (6).

amount awarded. This prevents the offender from suffering double jeopardy.[52] For inexplicable reasons, this punishment is rarely meted out by courts and there are only a few decisions reported on this mode of punishment.[53]

12.5.5 Costs

A court may order a person convicted of an offence to pay the costs of the prosecution or any part thereof.[54] In a private prosecution, the court may direct the private prosecutor to pay costs to the accused but no such order should be made if the trial court is of the view that the private prosecutor had reasonable grounds to make his complaint.[55] However, the costs payable cannot exceed Shs. 20,000/= for a trial held in the High Court, and Shs. 10,000/= for a trial held in the Magistrate's Court.[56]

12.5.6 Security for Keeping the Peace

For an offence not punishable by death, the court may, instead of or in addition to any other punishment, order the offender to enter into his own recognizance, with or without sureties, to keep peace and be of good behavior for a certain duration to be fixed by the court. The court may order such offender to be imprisoned until such recognizance and sureties execute the bond. Such term of imprisonment cannot however exceed one year and ought not, together with the fixed term, extend for a term longer than the longest term for which he might be sentenced to be imprisoned without fine.[57] This provision cannot however be used, where the court is obliged to mete out a minimum sentence for a particular offence.

---

52 *Ibid*, Section 175(7).

53 See for example *Terrah Mukindia v R* (1966) EA 425.

54 Penal Code, Section 32.

55 CPC, Section 171.

56 *Ibid.*

57 Penal Code, Sections 33 and 34. See also *Menezes v R* (1975) EA 209.

12.5.7 Cancellation of Certificate of Competency (Driving Licence) in Traffic Offences

The Penal Code under section 39 canvasses the issue of cancellation or suspension of certificate of competency or what is popularly called a "Driving Licence". Under subsection (1) where any person has been convicted under the Penal Code of an offence connected with the driving of any vehicle in respect of which a certificate of competency is required, the court in addition to, or in substitution for any other punishment on one hand, if the person convicted holds a certificate of competency, suspend the certificate for such time as the court thinks fit, or cancel the certificate and declare the person convicted disqualified for obtaining another certificate either permanently or for a stated period, and shall cause particulars of the conviction and of any other order made endorsed upon the certificate, which should be produced within a reasonable time and shall also cause a copy of these particulars and of the order to be sent to the Commissioner of Police, who shall endorse them on the duplicate certificate in his custody. On the other hand, if the person convicted does not hold a certificate of competency, the court can declare him disqualified from obtaining such a certificate for such time as the court thinks fit.

An appeal concerning this decision may be filed within fourteen days of the making of the order.[58] Applying or obtaining a certificate of competency while disqualified by an order of a court or, applying for or obtaining another such certificate without disclosing the particulars of the endorsement of an earlier certificate, is an offence and make one liable to a fine not exceeding two thousand shillings or to imprisonment for a term not exceeding six months, or to both.[59]

12.5.8 Community Based Orders (CBOs)

This punishment is canvassed under the Community Services Orders (CSO) Act.[60]The CSO Act provides for instances where instead of the court sentencing

58 Penal Code, Section 39(4).

59 *Ibid,* Section 39(5).

60 Act No. 10 of 1998, Chapter 93, Laws of Kenya.

the offender to imprisonment, it sentences him to undertake community service. This form of sentence may be applied where the person is convicted of an offence punishable with imprisonment not exceeding three years, with or without the option of a fine, or imprisonment for a term exceeding 3 years but for which the court has passed a sentence for three years or less.[61]

Community service comprises of unpaid public work within a community, for the benefit of that community, for a period not exceeding the term of imprisonment for which the court would have sentenced the offender. For the purposes of the CSO Act, public work includes but is not be limited to -

(i) construction or maintenance of public roads or roads of access;
(ii) afforestation works;
(iii) environmental conservation and enhancement works;
(iv) projects for water conservation, management or distribution and supply;
(v) maintenance work in public schools, hospitals and other public social service amenities;
(vi) work of any nature in a foster home or orphanage;
(vii) rendering specialist or professional services in the community and for the benefit of the community.[62]

The nature or type of public work, in any particular case, is determined by the court after consultation with the community service orders committee. Ordinarily before a court determines whether or not to make a CSO order, it directs a community service officer, usually a probation officer, to conduct an inquiry into the circumstances of the case and of the offender and report the findings to the court. This report assists the court in coming to a decision on whether or not to commit the offender to CSO.

If an offender is committed to CSO, and breaches the same or fails to comply with any of the conditions or requirements of a community service order, the court may, on the application of the area community service officer or supervising officer, issue summons to the offender to appear before the court at the time specified in the summons or issue a warrant of arrest for the offender

---

[61] *Ibid*, Section 3 (1).

[62] *Ibid*, Section 3 (2).

to be arrested and brought before the court, as the case may be, and the court may, after hearing the offender, do any of the following -

(a) caution the offender and require the offender to comply with the order; or
(b) amend the order in such manner as may suit the circumstances of the case; or
(c) revoke the order and impose any other sentence under the law as the court deems appropriate.[63]

An offender may seek a review of a community service order in any material point by informing the community service officer or supervising officer in writing of the material particulars upon which such review is sought. The CSO Officer then applies to the court and the court if it deems fit may review or vary the order. The offender also has avenue to make the application directly to court if special circumstances exist.[64]

12.5.9 Probation

This form of punishment is canvassed in the Probation of Offenders Act.[65] This is a type of sentence in which the convicted person is assessed in his capacity to reform and is not sentenced to a prison term. Section 4 (1) and (2) of the Act make provisions to this effect with subsection (1) making provision for the subordinate courts and subsection (2) making provision for the High Court. In essence where a person is charged and the court thinks that the charge is proved, but is of the opinion that, having regard to youth, character, antecedents, home surroundings, health or mental condition of the offender, or to the nature of the offence, or to any extenuating circumstances in which the offence was committed, it is expedient to release the offender on probation, the court may convict the offender and make a probation order; or without proceeding to conviction, make a probation order, and in either case may require the offender

---

63 *Ibid*, Section 5.

64 *Ibid*, Section 6.

65 Chapter 64 Laws of Kenya.

to enter into a recognizance, with or without sureties, in such sum as the court may deem fit.[66]

It is important to note willingness by the offender to comply with the probation order. If the offender fails in any respect to comply with the order or commits another offence, he will be liable to be sentenced for the original offence. Commission of a subsequent offence or defaulting on any of the terms of the probation order could occasion a forfeiture of any of the recognizance entered into by or on behalf of the offender.[67]

12.5.10 Detention at the President's Pleasure

This is the prescribed sentence for persons who have been found guilty but insane and also for child offenders who cannot be sentenced to death.[68]

12.5. 11 Restitution of Property

This is canvassed under Section 177 of the CPC to the effect that any property taken from an arrested person shall be restored to the person entitled to them. If this person happens to be the accused person, the property shall be restored to him or to any other person as he may direct. This property or a part thereof may be applied to the payment of any fine or any costs or compensation directed to be paid by the person charged.

12.5.12 Corporal Punishment

This sentence although previously provided for under section 27 of the Penal Code is now not available pursuant to amendments made to the Penal Code in 2003. Further Article 29 (e) of the Constitution outlaws corporal punishment by providing that every person has the right to freedom and security of the person, which includes the right not to be subjected to corporal punishment.

---

66 *Ibid*, Section 4 (3)

67 *Ibid*, Section 4 (4).

68 For a more elaborate discussion, see Chapter 11 on Judgment.

12.5.13 Discharge

A discharge is a form of sentence where the accused person is convicted but the court feels that there is no need to punish him and instead allows him to go unpunished. Though unpunished, the offender remains convicted of the offence. The court has discretion to discharge, where having regard to the circumstances, including the nature of the offence and the character of the offender, it is inexpedient to inflict punishment and that a probation order[69] is not appropriate.[70]

A discharge can either be absolute or conditional. If conditional, the condition of the discharge is that the accused ought not to commit an offence during a period not exceeding 12 months and the court needs to explain this to the offender.[71] If he proceeds to commit an offence within the duration provided, the court may sentence him for the original offence. The court still retains the discretion to order the offender to pay costs or compensation.[72]

12.5.14 Reconciliation

Reconciliation refers to the situation where the party injured by the offence and the accused, agree to have the matter settled amicably without the necessity of having the accused go through the criminal trial. The Constitution obliges courts to promote reconciliation.[73] Reconciliation is permitted for common assault, or for any other offence of a personal or private nature, not amounting to a felony, and not aggravated in degree.[74] The parties are free to enter into an agreement for compensation or other terms subject to approval by the court. If the parties reconcile, the proceedings are terminated and there is no point of proceeding with the trial.

---

69 Under the Probation of Offenders Act, Chapter 64, Laws of Kenya.

70 Penal Code, Section 35(1).

71 *Ibid*, Section 35 (2).

72 *Ibid*, Section 35 (3).

73 Constitution, Article 159 (2).

74 CPC, Section 176.

12.6 General Punishment for Misdemeanours

Where under the Penal Code no punishment is specially provided for any misdemeanor, it shall be punishable with imprisonment for a term not exceeding two years or with a fine, or with both.[75]

12.7 Concurrent and Cumulative Sentences

A sentence may be concurrent or cumulative. This applies in instances where the offender has been convicted of an earlier offence and before he has been sentenced on it or before the term of the first sentence has expired. The default position is that the sentence on the second or subsequent conviction should be served after expiration of the first sentence, that is, that sentences remain cumulative. However, the court has discretion to direct that the subsequent sentence be served concurrently (at the same time) with the first or earlier sentence.[76] Such direction cannot however be made where a prison term is being served in default of payment of a fine. Neither can it be made where the sentence is one of death.[77]

Where an accused has been convicted of several counts in the same trial, it is wise for the trial court to make clear whether the sentences are going to be served concurrently or cumulatively so as to avoid any ambiguity.

12.8 Factors Influencing Sentencing

Regrettably, there are no set guidelines on sentencing. Sentencing is wholly in the discretion of the court and one may therefore find wide disparities in sentences for fairly similar offences. Before sentencing, the court invites both the prosecutor and the accused to submit. The prosecutor's role will be advise the court on whether the accused has had previous convictions (as it will be seen later, the question of whether or not the accused has previous convictions

---

[75] *Ibid*, Section 36.

[76] Penal Code, Section 37.

[77] *Ibid*.

is material in determining sentence). The accused person who has now been convicted will be invited to mitigate, i.e. give reasons why the court should be lenient in its punishment.

If the accused is a first offender it is the practice not to impose the maximum sentence. Indeed a court should seriously consider a non-custodial sentence for a first offender. However, in some instances if the offence is very serious or aggravated a custodial sentence may be imposed.

In passing sentence, the trial court needs to balance the expectations of society, which demands to see that justice has been done, and the situation of the offender. If the offence is serious, it may look unjust for the court to pass a non-custodial sentence and imprisonment is a sentence to consider. If the offence is light or not aggravated, and the accused is a first offender, it will be harsh on the accused to imprison him in as much as society may demand some form of punishment.

In sentencing, the court ought to endeavour to mete out the least of punishment necessary to attain the desired result, but which punishment at the same time, must balance both the circumstances of the offender, the expectations of society, and public policy. The purpose of sentencing is varied, and one is aimed at reforming the offender. If this can be attained by the least of sentences, then that is the sentence to give. Long prison sentences are indeed probably not necessary, unless given the situation of the offender, it is necessary to keep him away from the society, as there is reason to believe that he may be a danger to society. This may especially be so in sexual offences or aggravated assaults. The remorsefulness shown by the accused should be considered, for example, if he has restored property that has been stolen or has demonstrated some genuine remorse in one way or another.

12.9 Sentencing of Minors

Pursuant to Section 189 of the Children Act, the words "conviction" and "sentence" are not be used in relation to a child dealt with by the Children's Court. What the court does is to simply make a finding of guilty and make an order upon such finding. There are sentences which the Children Act outlaws with regard to children. To wit; no child is to be imprisoned or be placed in a detention camp; no child should be sentenced to death; no child under the age of ten years is to be ordered by a Children's Court to be sent to a rehabilitation school; and no child offender is to be subjected to corporal punishment.[78]

The sentences which may be passed against a child are to be found in section 191 of the Children Act and they are as follows; discharge under section 35 (1) of the Penal Code; Probation under the provisions of the Probation of Offenders Act; committing the child to the care of a fit person, whether a relative or not, or a charitable children's institution willing to undertake his care. If the offender is above ten years and under fifteen years of age, by ordering him to be sent to a rehabilitation school suitable to his needs and attainments; an order to pay a fine, compensation or costs, or any or all of them. For a child who is above 16 years, committing him to a borstal institution.

A court can also pass a sentence against a child by placing the child offender under the care of a qualified counselor; by ordering the child offender to be placed in an educational institution or a vocational training program; by ordering the child to be placed in a probation hostel under provisions of the Probation of Offenders Act; or by making a community service order.[79]

If it appears to the court on the evidence of a medical practitioner that a child, requires or may benefit from mental treatment, the court when making a probation order against him, may require him to undergo mental treatment at the hand or under the direction of a medical practitioner for a period not exceeding twelve months, subject to review by the court, as a condition of the probation order.[80]Where a child is charged with an offence for which a fine, compensation or costs may be imposed, if the court is of the opinion that the case would best be met by imposition of a fine, compensation or costs, whether with or without any other punishment, the court may in any case order that the fine, compensation or costs imposed or awarded be paid by the child's parent or guardian instead of by the offender, unless the court is satisfied that the parent or guardian cannot be found or that he or she has not induced the commission

---

78 Children Act (CAP 141), Sections 190 and 191.

79 *Ibid.*

80 *Ibid,* Section 192.

of the offence, by neglecting to exercise due care of the offender. Any sums imposed and ordered to be paid by a parent or guardian may be recovered from him or her in a like manner as if the order had been made on the conviction of the parent or guardian of the offender.[81] A parent or guardian may appeal to the High Court against an order made under this section by a Children's Court. Where a child is charged with an offence, the court may order his parent or guardian to give security for his good behaviour. [82]

In *Kaisa v R,*[83] the appellant who was 12 years old was convicted of handling stolen property and was sentenced to seven years imprisonment. On appeal the High Court held that no one under the age of 14 years old could be imprisoned. The appeal was allowed and the minor was instead committed to an approved school. In arriving at this conclusion the court noted that a boy, so young as the accused who had committed the offence of assault when only ten years old, was clearly in need, not only of discipline but also of care, guidance and encouragement given and provided by persons equipped with sustainable training and qualifications, and possessed of enough time and the requisite facilities to attempt rehabilitation. The court averred that rehabilitation is the most important factor to be borne in mind when considering what to do with someone who is about to enter, or has only just entered, upon his formative years.[84]

12.10 Traffic Offenders

Traffic offenders are not the classical criminals as their acts are generally presumed to be unintended. It is therefore the practice to avoid as much as practicable having a mandatory prison sentence for such offenders. In most instances, a fine would do, unless the accused is a habitual offender in which instance a prison sentence may be appropriate to act as deterrence.[85]

---

81 *Ibid,* Section 193 (1)

82 *Ibid,* Section 193 (2).

83 (1975) EA 260.

84 See also *Maina v R* (1970) EA 370.

85 *Misiani v R* (1979) KLR 285. See also *Atito v R* (1975) EA 278.

12.11 Post Sentence

The criminal process does not end with the judgment and sentence. The criminal justice system still continues. There are certain matters which arise after the sentence. These include remission, and the power of mercy.

12.11.1 Remission

Remission refers to the partial reduction of a prison sentence. The offender does not have to serve the whole of the sentence if he is of good conduct while in prison. His term of imprisonment may be subjected to a reduction. Remission of part of the sentence of prisoners is provided for under section 46 of the Prisons Act.[86] This section provides that convicted criminal prisoners sentenced to imprisonment, whether by one sentence or consecutive sentences, for a period exceeding one month, may, by industry and good conduct, earn a remission of one-third of their sentence or sentences. However, remission will not be granted if it will result to a prison term of less than one calendar month.[87] There is also no remission for a person sentenced to life. Neither is remission available to those who have been convicted of the offences of robbery and attempted robbery[88] or those detained at the President's pleasure.

Remission of a prisoner's sentence can be lost if one commits an offence against prison discipline. Remission cannot also be earned for any period spent in hospital through the prisoner's own fault or malingering or where the prisoner is undergoing solitary confinement as a punishment.[89]

A prisoner can be deprived of his right to remission in the following circumstances:- [90]

86 Prisons Act, Chapter 90, Laws of Kenya.

87 *Ibid*, Section 46(1) (i).

88 *Ibid*, Section 46(1) (ii). These offences are provided for in Section 296(1) and 297(1) of the Penal Code.

89 *Section 46 (3)* of the *Prisons Act.*

90 *Ibid.*

(a) where the Commissioner considers that it is in the interests of the reformation and rehabilitation of the prisoner; and
(b) where the Minister for the time being responsible for internal security considers that it is in the interests of public security or public order.

The decision to deprive of a prisoner remission has been subject to judicial challenge in a number of cases.[91] In the case of *Oloo v R*[92] the prisoner had been convicted and sentenced to five years and was entitled to a full amount of remission. About a year into his sentence the Commissioner of Prisons deprived him of remission on the ground of being in the interest of reformation and rehabilitation. Aggrieved by this decision, he challenged it on the ground that it was arbitrary, in breach of the rules of natural justice and *ultra vires*. This called forth the question of how the power of the Commissioner of Prisons to deprive a prisoner of the right of remission under the Prisons Act section 46(3A) (a) should be exercised. The Court of Appeal ruled that the Commissioner's act in depriving him of remission was *ultra vires*, illegal, null and void, and quashed it.

12.11.2 Presidential Pardon

Presidential pardon in its simplest conceptualization is the pardon granted to prisoners by the President that enables them to be released before they serve their full sentence. This pardon power is anchored in Article 133 of the Constitution. A person may petition the President for a pardon. The President may grant a free or conditional pardon, postpone the carrying out of a punishment for either a specified or indefinite period, or substitute a less severe form of punishment; or remit all or part of a punishment. The Constitution establishes a Committee termed as the Advisory Committee to advise the President on the exercise of his pardon power. This Advisory Committee comprises of the Attorney-General, the Cabinet Secretary responsible for correctional services and at least five other members as prescribed by an Act of Parliament, none of whom may be a State officer or in public service.[93]

---

91 See for example *Kinyatti v R,* (1976-85) EA 234; and *David Onyago Oloo v R* (1986) KLR 711.

92 *Ibid.*

93 Article 133 (2) of the Constitution.

To actualize the provisions of Article 133 of the Constitution, the Power of Mercy Act[94] was enacted in the year 2011. The Act governs all matters relating to a petition for the exercise of the power of mercy by the President. A person petitions the President through the Committee.[95] For a petition to be admissible, the petitioner needs to have served at least one-third of this sentence, or to have served at least five years if he was convicted and sentenced to imprisonment for life or to death.[96] To assist it in arriving at a decision, the committee has power to call for evidence, conduct interviews, conduct investigations, and receive reports from appropriate government agencies.[97]

In making a recommendation to the President, the Committee is to consider factors such as the age of the convicted criminal prisoner at the time of the commission of the offence; the circumstances surrounding the commission of the offence; whether the person, for whose benefit the petition is made, is a first offender; the nature and seriousness of the offence; the length of period so far served by the convicted criminal prisoner; the length of period served by the convicted criminal prisoner in remand; the personal circumstances of the offender at the time of making the petition, including mental and physical health and any disabilities; the interest of the State and community; the post-conviction conduct, character and reputation of the convicted criminal prisoner; the official recommendations and reports from the State organ or department responsible for correctional services; where the petitioner has opted to pursue other available remedies, the outcome of such avenue and the representation of the victim where applicable. Further, the Committee may consider a report of fellow inmates or reports from probation services as the circumstance of each case demands.[98]

It is important to keep in mind that the opinion of the committee is entirely advisory and not binding.[99] The President can reject or accept the recommendations. He must either approve or reject the recommendations

---

94 Power of Mercy Act, Chapter 94, Laws of Kenya.

95 *Ibid*, Section 19 (1).

96 *Ibid,* Section 21(1) (a).

97 *Ibid*, Section 21(1) (b).

98 *Ibid*, Section 22.

99 *Ibid*, Section 23.

within 30 days of its receipt. The committee is to notify the petitioner of the President's decision within 7 days. Approved petitions are to be published in the Kenya Gazette within 21 days of receipt of the President's decision.[100] The decision of the President is final and not subject to appeal. A person however has leeway to re-petition, but only once more, and the second petition must be on new grounds.[101]A pardon, once granted, shall operate as conclusive proof that the Committee and the President are satisfied that the petitioner pardoned is deserving of the relief. The pardon however, is not to be construed as an acquittal.[102]

The need for the enactment of all these provisions was to streamline this process which until the enactment of the Constitution of 2010 had been shrouded in mystery and controversy. It is in the public domain that a number of high-profile, and without doubt, controversial pardons had been granted, such as the pardon of the former National Aids Control Council boss after serving only a few months of her sentence on corruption charges and who was among 6,949 petty offenders released by presidential amnesty countrywide in December 2004. Further, in 2010 it was recorded in the Kenya National Assembly Official (Hansard),[103] that hard core criminals had been released through the presidential pardon.

* * *

100 *Ibid*, Section 23(3).

101 *Ibid*, Section 24(1).

102 *Ibid*, Section 25.

103 26 August 2010 (stated by Hon C. Kilonzo MP for Yatta constituency in a question to the Ministry of Home Affairs).

CHAPTER 13

APPEALS

13.1 Introduction

At the outset, it is important to remember that trials are held in both sub-ordinate courts and the High Court. A party aggrieved by a decision of the trial court may appeal to a court of higher jurisdiction. Thus an appeal from the sub-ordinate court will be preferred to the High Court, whereas an appeal from the High Court will be preferred to the Court of Appeal. Further, in cases involving the interpretation and application of the Constitution, and in cases where the Supreme Court or the Court of Appeal certifies that a matter of general public importance is involved, an appeal can be preferred from the Court of Appeal to the Supreme Court.[1] There may be instances where what one can appeal against is restricted and instances where a second appeal is not allowed. The provisions on appeal are set out in the Criminal Procedure Code[2] (CPC) at Part XI.

13.2 Appeals to the High Court

Sections 347 to 361 of the CPC cover appeals from the subordinate courts to the High Court. Section 347 provides that a convicted person tried by a subordinate court of the first or second class may appeal to the High Court. Such person may appeal on determination of both fact and law. Note that, a person who pleaded guilty cannot appeal against conviction, but, can only appeal against

1 For a more elaborate discussion, see Chapter 2.

2 Chapter 75, Laws of Kenya.

the sentence.[3] This however does not prevent one from appealing where it is alleged that a plea is not unequivocal. In this instance the challenge strictly is on the entry of the plea as being unequivocal. If the court hearing the appeal is convinced that the plea of guilty was unequivocal, then the appellant will only be restricted to appealing against the sentence only.

Pursuant to the provisions of Section 348 A of the CPC, the DPP can appeal on a matter of law only when an accused person has been acquitted on a trial held by a subordinate court, or where an order refusing to admit a complaint or formal charge, or an order dismissing a charge, has been made by a subordinate court. As may be noted, this right of appeal is on a matter of law only. The DPP has no right to appeal on matters of fact. Sentence is deemed to be a question of fact and therefore the State has no right to make an appeal either to enhance or vary a sentence passed by the trial court.

The prescribed period for appealing is 14 days from the day of passing the order intended to be appealed from.[4] The appellate court however has discretion to admit an appeal out of time if there are good reasons to explain the delay. The court is obligated to admit the appeal if it is satisfied that the failure to enter the appeal within time is because copies of the judgment or order appealed from and the record could not be obtained within reasonable time. The appeal is made in the form of a petition. The document in which the grounds of appeal are set out is therefore called, "The Petition of Appeal." The petition must comply with the following set down provisions.

(a) It must be signed by the appellant himself if he is acting in person, or if represented by an advocate, must be signed by the advocate.
(b) It must contain the particulars of the matters of law or fact in regard to which the subordinate court appealed from is alleged to have erred.
(c) It must specify an address of service.

The petition of appeal needs to be drawn carefully and it is advisable to have the grounds specified in as wide a language as possible. This is because the appellate court will not entertain or hear arguments on grounds of appeal which have

3 *Ibid*, Section 348.

4 *Ibid*, Section 349.

not been set out in the petition.[5] However, there appears to be great leeway given in amending the petition of appeal only subject to leave. The courts have been fairly liberal in the grant of leave so that justice is done and the appellant is not shut out on a technicality.

13.3 The Record of Appeal

The appeal is usually contained in a record of appeal which contains the proceedings of the trial court. The question that arises is what ought to happen if there are no proceedings upon which to prepare the record of appeal. In *Mulewa v R*,[6] The appellants were convicted of robbery with violence. Their appeal to the High Court was dismissed prompting their second appeal to the Court of Appeal. On 23rd July, 2001 the Court of Appeal adjourned the appeal to the next session in January so that the trial court file which had gone missing could be traced. When the appeals came up for hearing in January 2002, the missing court file had still not been found and the court was informed that the police file had also disappeared. Consequently, the appellant applied for an acquittal on the ground that ordering a retrial would serve no useful purpose. The Court of Appeal noted that where a court file had disappeared, the court had to try an act in the interest of justice. To this end, the court had to consider all the circumstances under which the loss occurred and noted that the suggestion that where a file had disappeared and it was not reasonable possible to order a retrial an acquittal had to follow, had to be rejected, as it would inevitably lead to more disappearances with justice being the loser. In the particular circumstances of this case, there were typed proceedings which had been prepared and made available to the appellants before the court file had disappeared and taking into consideration all the circumstances, the Court of Appeal was satisfied that there was sufficient material before it to enable the appeal to be tried on merit. It is however open for conjecture on what avenue the court ought to take if there were absolutely no proceedings.

---

5 *Ibid,* Section 350 (2).

6 (2002) 2 EA 487; See also *Zaver v Rex* (1952) 19 EHCH 244 and *Wainaina v R* (2004) 2 EA 349.

13.4 Summary Rejection or Allowance of an Appeal

The High Court has liberty to summarily reject or allow an appeal without the necessity of going through a hearing.[7] Where the appeal alleges that the conviction is against the weight of evidence or that the sentence is excessive, and the judge is of opinion that the evidence is sufficient to support the conviction and there is no reason to vary the sentence, the appeal may be summarily rejected. In any other case, the appellant must be given a hearing before summarily rejecting the appeal.[8] The court may also summarily allow an appeal against conviction if it is satisfied that the conviction cannot be supported and the DPP has informed the court in writing that he does not support the conviction.[9]

If the appeal is not summarily rejected, then it must be heard on merits.[10] Summary rejection of an appeal is a power that ought to be exercised with caution so that a deserving person is not denied a hearing. The court indeed ought to incline towards hearing the appeal on merits rather than proceeding to summarily reject the same. The court has affirmed that the summary procedure is only meant to dispense of appeals for trivial cases, where the appeal is based on evidence and evidence alone, and no issues of law are raised.[11] In *Ndungu v R*,[12] the appellant was charged, tried and convicted of two counts of robbery with violence which carries the death sentence. The Court of Appeal was of the view that although there was nothing to bar the court from summarily rejecting an appeal arising from a capital offence, it noted that as a rule of practice, a person facing such a serious charge and grave penalty should be given an opportunity to be heard.

So too in *Okang v R*[13] where the appellant appealed to the High Court *inter alia* on the grounds that his plea was equivocal. His appeal was summarily rejected.

---

7 CPC, Section 352 and 352A.

8 *Ibid*, Section 352 (2).

9 *Ibid*, Section 352 A.

10 *Ibid,* Section 353.

11 See *Mahan v R* (1954) 21 EACA 383; *Kuyate v R* (1967) EA 815; *Raphael v R* (1973) EA 473; *John Mwangi v R* (1983) KLR 652; and *Muthara v R* (1999) LLR 937.

12 (2003) 1 EA 19.

13 (1982-88) 1 KAR 276.

On further appeal to the Court of Appeal, the Court of Appeal noted that the grounds raised were not restricted to grounds that the conviction was against the weight of evidence or that the sentence was excessive. The High Court was therefore in error in summarily rejecting the appeal. In *Ombena v R,*[14] the appellants were convicted of selling goods over the maximum price and for failing to display a price list contrary to the Price Control Act.[15] He appealed to the High Court on the ground that only one plea was recorded, yet there were six counts, and that the plea entered was unequivocal and the magistrate convicted them without hearing and recording the facts of the case. This appeal was summarily rejected by the High Court. Aggrieved by this decision they appealed to the Court of Appeal challenging the High Court's summarily rejection of their appeal. The Court of Appeal noted that the appeal to the High Court raised points of law and should not have been summarily rejected.

The High Court will however be justified to hold that an appeal fell within section 352 (2) CPC, and summarily reject it, if the ground of appeal is too vague to exclude the appeal from the provisions of the sub-section.[16]

13.5 Hearing of an Appeal

If an appeal is not summarily rejected, then it must be listed for hearing. The appellant starts by arguing his appeal and then the respondent argues his part. The appellant may then reply on the matters of law or fact raised by the respondent. If the appeal is against a conviction the appellate court may reverse the finding and sentence, and acquit or discharge the accused, or order him to be tried by a court of competent jurisdiction; or alter the finding, maintaining the sentence, or, with or without altering the finding, reduce or increase the sentence; or with or without a reduction or increase and with or without altering the finding, alter the nature of the sentence. If the appeal is against sentence, the appellate court may increase or reduce the sentence or alter the nature of the sentence.[17]

---

14 (1981) KLR 450.

15 Cap 504.

16 *John Mwangi v R* (1983) KLR 652

17 CPC, Section 354.

If the appeal is from an acquittal, the High Court will proceed to hear and determine the matter of law which has been raised by the prosecution and may reverse, affirm or vary the determination of the subordinate court, or remit the matter with the opinion of the High Court thereon to the subordinate court for determination, whether by way of re-hearing or otherwise, with such directions as the High Court may think necessary, and make such other order in relation to the matter, including an order. The appellate court may not however impose a sentence which is greater than what the trial court could impose.[18]

The High Court is empowered to take additional evidence on appeal if it feels that the same is necessary. It can take the evidence by itself or direct a subordinate court to take the evidence. Appeals from subordinate courts are supposed to be heard by two judges except where the Chief Justice or a Judge empowered by the Chief Justice orders that the appeal be heard by a single judge.[19] The practice in Kenya is for all appeals save for capital appeals to be heard by one judge. This has emanated from a practice where the Chief Justice writes an authority to a judge allowing him to hear appeals as a single judge. This practice is however questionable given the provisions of Section 359 of the CPC. The default position in the statute is indeed to have all appeals heard by two judges, and the section insinuates that the hearing of an appeal by one judge, ought not to be of general application to a particular judge, but actually a specific application to a particular case. This practice has so far however not been the subject of an appeal to the Court of Appeal. If on a two bench court the Court is equally divided, the appeal is to be heard by three judges.

13.6 Duty of A First Appellate Court

In *Kipng'etich v R*,[20] the appellant had been convicted by a subordinate court of the offence of robbery contrary to section 296 (1) of the Penal Code. He unsuccessfully appealed to the High Court prompting a second appeal to the Court of Appeal. The appellant contended that the learned judge erred in confirming the conviction of the subordinate court and further erred in

18 *Ibid*, Section 354 (6).

19 Ibid, Section 359.

20 *Kipng'etich v R* (1985) KLR 392. See also *Pandya v R* (1957) EA 336.

evaluating the prosecution case in isolation with the appellant defence. He further contended that the conviction was based on circumstantial evidence without the trial court holding that the inculpatory facts were incompatible with the appellant's innocence.

The Court of Appeal held that, the task of the first appellate court from a conviction is;

a) To consider its own views of the evidence as a whole and reach its own decisions thereon.
b) To rehear the case and reconsider the materials before the judge or magistrate and any other materials it may have decided to admit.
c) To take into account the judgment appealed from carefully weighing and reconsidering it.
d) In considering the question of whether a witness is to be believed rather than another, the appellate court must be guided by the impression made on the judge who witnessed, as this touches on the question of manner and demeanour.

In *Galgalo and another v R*,[21] the two appellants were tried, charged and convicted on two counts of robbery with violence and sentenced to suffer death. Aggrieved by this decision they unsuccessfully appealed to the High Court. This prompted their second appeal to the Court of Appeal. It was clear that the trial court and the first appellate court totally ignored their defence and did not even refer to it. The Court of Appeal held that the total failure by the trial court and the superior court on first appeal to consider the appellant's defence was a grave omission thus was contrary to justice and unsettled the judgment.[22]

13.7 Additional Evidence in Appeals

Section 358 of the CPC canvasses the issue of power to take further evidence. It provides that the High Court, when dealing with an appeal from a subordinate court if it is of the considered opinion that additional evidence is necessary, shall record the reasons informing such opinion and proceed to take the evidence

---

21 (2005) 1 EA 63; See also *Okethi Okale v Republic* (1965) EA 555.

22 See also *Omusa v R* (2003) 1 EA 230.

itself, or direct the subordinate court to do so. In the latter case, the subordinate court is obligated to certify the evidence to the High Court. Presence of the accused or his advocate is required in the process of taking additional evidence and this evidence shall be regarded as if it were taken at trial.

13.8 Appeals to the Court of Appeal

This is covered in Section 379 of the CPC. The Court of Appeal only hears appeals in which the person convicted has either been sentenced to death or imprisoned for a term exceeding 12 months or to a fine exceeding Shs. 2,000/=[23] except where the Court of Appeal grants leave, which leave can only be granted, where a question of law of great public importance is involved.[24] One can appeal against conviction on both grounds of law and fact or mixed law and fact.[25] There can be no appeal to the Court of Appeal against sentence, without the leave of the Court of Appeal, unless the sentence is one fixed by law.[26]

Where the trial was held by the High Court, and the appellant pleaded guilty, he cannot appeal against the conviction, but only against sentence.[27] There is however no bar to one contesting that his plea of guilty was not unequivocal. If the trial was held by the High Court and the accused was acquitted, the State cannot appeal against that acquittal, but can only ask for a determination on the point of law if the issue therein raises a point of law of exceptional public importance and it is desirable in the public interest that the point be determined by the Court of Appeal. The Court of Appeal can then hear the point and deliver a declaratory judgment, which will henceforth be binding upon all courts subordinate to the Court of Appeal but such determination cannot reverse the order of acquittal.[28]

---

23 CPC, Section 379 (1).

24 *Ibid*, Section 379 (2).

25 *Ibid*, Section 379 (1) (a).

26 *Ibid*, Section 379 (1) (b).

27 *Ibid*, Section 379 (3).

28 *Ibid*, Section 379 (5) and 379 (6).

In hearing second appeals, that is, a further appeal from the High Court's appellate jurisdiction, the appeal must be restricted to points of law and the Court of Appeal cannot hear points of fact. Severity of a sentence is considered to be a point of fact and therefore cannot be entertained on a second appeal. The Court of Appeal is further barred from hearing second appeals against sentence unless the sentence was enhanced by the High Court on first appeal, or unless the subordinate court that tried the matter in the first instance, had no power to pass that sentence. This is precisely what the Court of Appeal held in *Ngure v R.*[29] The appellant had been charged with the offence of Causing Death by Dangerous Driving and was sentenced to 10 years in jail. His first appeal to the High Court was dismissed and he preferred a second appeal to the Court of Appeal. The Court of Appeal appreciated that the sentence of 10 years was undoubtedly high and severe in the circumstances, but held that S. 361 of the CPC denied the court jurisdiction to deal with severity of sentence as long as the sentence is lawful and within the law.

In deciding the appeal, the Court of Appeal can determine the matter or remit the same for determination by either the High Court or the trial court. [30] It can also allow or dismiss the appeal. It can also substitute the conviction for another, if the facts prove another offence and proceed to convict and sentence on the substituted charge. [31] The appellant may succeed on a point, but it does not mean that he must be acquitted. Unless a failure of justice occurred, the Court of Appeal, may, despite resolving the point of law in favour of the appellant, dismiss the appeal.[32]

In *Kipng'etich v R,*[33] the Court of Appeal further noted that on second appeal, it becomes a question of law as to whether the first appellate court in approaching its tasks applied or failed to apply the correct principles. In the instant case the Court of Appeal noted that the first appellate court failed to do so. In arriving at this conclusion, the court adumbrated that in a conviction based

---

29 (2003) 1 EA 202.

30 *Ibid*, Section 361 (2).

31 *Ibid*, Section 361 (4).

32 *Ibid*, Section 361 (5) and see cases of *Omusa v R* (2003) 1 EA 230 and *John Onyango Obala v R*, Kisumu, Court of Appeal, Criminal Appeal No. 4 of 2010, (2011) eKLR.

33 *Supra*, note 20.

purely on circumstantial evidence, the inculpatory facts must be incompatible with the innocence of the appellant and not capable of explanation on any other hypothesis, than that of the appellant's guilt. In this case the appellant put forward a defence in his unsworn statement and the judge should have considered it. In the instant, the Court of Appeal ordered a re-trial.

13.9 Right of Appeal on Applications for Revision

As we shall see in the next chapter, there is a right of revision. A decision made pursuant to a revision is subject to appeal to the Court of Appeal.[34]

13.10 Appeals Against Interlocutory Orders

In between the trial, the court may make several interlocutory rulings. Some, such as orders for bail, are subject to review by the High Court in trials held in the subordinate court. There is also the inherent supervisory power granted to the High Court, to supervise proceedings before the subordinate courts and make such orders that the court may deem just. Such orders may form part of applications for judicial review or petitions alleging violations of the constitution, or applications for revision. Apart from these instances, or those that statute may provide, on a general note, interim orders made by the trial court are not appealable, with the position being that the accused or State is advised to await the end of the full trial and thereafter make a full appeal if need be. One therefore has no right of appeal if he is contesting a decision of the magistrate that he has a case to answer under Section 210 of the CPC. This was affirmed in the case of *Twagira v Uganda*[35]. The applicant had been charged with the offence of embezzlement and stealing by agent. Upon conclusion of the prosecution's case, the trial magistrate found the accused had a case to answer and put him on his defence. The accused chose to appeal the magistrate's ruling. His appeal was denied in both the High Court and Court of Appeal.

---

34 See Section 361 (7) of the CPC and the case of *Muya v R* (2004) 1 EA 180.

35 (2003) 2 EA 689; See also *Jethwa and Another v Republic* (1969) EA 459; *Republic v Wachira* (1975) EA 262; *Republic v Kidasa* (1973) EA 368 and *Merali v Uganda* (1963) EA 647.

It was held that a right of appeal in respect of interlocutory orders made by a trial magistrate, such as on finding a case to answer, does not exist. The practise in such an instance is to appeal at the conclusion of the trial and include any complaints about the finding that there was not a case to answer.[36]

In *Cholmondeley v Republic,*[37] the trial judge, where the accused was charged with murder, made an order directing the accused, who had been placed on his defence, to avail to the prosecution the evidence that he intended to table. He appealed against this order on the ground that the same was a violation of his constitutional rights. The Court of Appeal, though affirming his right to appeal, stated as follows in respect to appeals on interlocutory orders :-

> *"... We would, nevertheless, sound a caution against the exercise of the undoubted right of appeal under section 84 (7) of the Constitution. First the fact that a trial Judge has made an adverse ruling against an accused person in a criminal trial does not and cannot mean that the Judge will inevitably convict. The Judge might well acquit in the end and the adverse ruling, even if it amounted to a breach of fundamental right, falls by the wayside and causes no harm to such an accused. The advantage of that course is that the long delay in the hearing of the charge is avoided and in the event of a conviction the matter can be raised on appeal once and for all. In the present appeal the delay has spanned the period from 25th July, 2007 to date, nearly one year. The trial before the learned Judge will, however, resume and go on to its logical conclusion. We think it is against public policy that criminal trials should be held up in this fashion and it is our hope that lawyers practising at the criminal bar will appropriately advise their clients so as to avoid such unnecessary delays. We would add that in future if such appeals are brought the Court may well order that the hearing of the appeal be stayed pending the conclusion of the trial in the High Court."*[38]

---

36 See also *Kinoti v R* (2005) 1 EA 209.

37 Court of Appeal at Nairobi, Criminal Appeal No. 116 of 2007, (2008) eKLR.

38 Note that the provisions of the constitution cited in this excerpt are provisions from the repealed Constitution as this case was tried and decided in the previous Constitutional regime.

13.11 Appeals against Sentence and Enhancement of Sentence on Appeal

While determining an appeal, the High Court is empowered to either, enhance, reduce, or vary the sentence, whether or not the appeal is against conviction and/or sentence.[39] However, the court ought not to enhance sentence unless the appellant has first been warned, either through a cross-appeal by the State, or by the court itself, that if the conviction is upheld, the sentence meted by the trial court may be enhanced. In *JWW v R*[40] the appellant and his co-accused were tried and convicted by the Magistrate's court of the offence of manslaughter. They were sentenced to 7 years in jail.[41] They preferred an appeal to the High Court against both conviction and sentence. The State opposed the appeal but did not file a cross-appeal, and neither did they seek an enhancement of the sentence at the hearing of the appeal. The court did not also warn the appellants that they stood the risk of suffering an enhanced sentence. The judge dismissed the appeal and enhanced the sentence to 10 years. The appellant filed a second appeal to the Court of Appeal. In considering the appeal, the Court of Appeal held that the High Court erred in enhancing the sentence of the appellant as the State never urged an enhanced sentence, and neither did the court warn the appellant, that he stood the risk of having his sentence enhanced, if he pursued his appeal. The Court of Appeal stated that the need for prior information to be given to the appellant is to enable him to prepare and argue his side of the case as regards such intended enhancement. The court held that the enhanced sentence was in the circumstances unlawful and the original sentence of 7 years was reinstated. It should also be recalled that the High Court if minded to enhance sentence, cannot sentence the person to a sentence in excess of that which the trial court had jurisdiction to give.[42]

* * *

---

39 CPC, Section 354 (2) and (3).

40 Court of Appeal at Kisumu, Criminal Appeal No. 11 of 2011, (2013) eKLR.

41 The heaviest sentence for manslaughter is life imprisonment.

42 CPC, Section 354 (6)

CHAPTER 14

REVISION

14.1 Introduction

Revision is an avenue that is available to either an accused or the State to contest a decision, ruling or judgment of the trial court. Only the High Court has powers of revision and only the orders of the subordinate courts are subject to revision. Revision is a useful tool especially in instances where one has no right of appeal. It is premised upon the inherent powers given to the High Court to supervise the subordinate courts. This power emanates from the provisions of Article 165 (6) and (7) of the Constitution which provide as follows:-

(6) *The High Court has supervisory jurisdiction over the subordinate courts and over any person, body or authority exercising a judicial or quasi-judicial function, but not over a superior court.*
(7) *For the purposes of clause (6), the High Court may call for the record of any proceedings before any subordinate court or person, body or authority referred to in clause (6), and may make any order or give any direction it considers appropriate to ensure the fair administration of justice.*

Within statute, revision is provided for in Section 362 of the Criminal Procedure Code (CPC)[1] which provides as follows:-

The High Court may call for and examine the record of any criminal proceedings before any subordinate court for the purpose of satisfying itself as to the correctness,

1 Chapter 75, Laws of Kenya.

legality or propriety of any finding, sentence or order recorded or passed, and as to the regularity of any proceedings of any such subordinate court.

It is debatable whether the powers granted in Articles 164(6) and (7) of the Constitution go beyond the established regime of revision as provided for under Section 362 of the Criminal Procedure Code or whether the statute merely puts into application the provisions of the Constitution.[2] Revision should not be equated to the power of the High Court in Judicial Review. In the latter instance the High Court has jurisdiction to supervise not only judicial but also administrative bodies in which it can issue orders of prohibition, mandamus and certiorari.

14.2 Extent of Revision

The purpose of revision as provided under Section 362 of the CPC is for the High Court to satisfy itself as to thee correctness, legality, or propriety of any finding, sentence or order recorded or passed, and as to regularity of any proceedings in the subordinate courts. There is therefore not going to be any interference if the proceedings were conducted according to law.[3] An immediate question is whether an order made vide revision is an order in exercise of the High Court's original or appellate jurisdiction. In the case of *Muya v R*[4] it was held that an order made by the High Court in the exercise of its revisionary jurisdiction is deemed to be a decision of the High Court in its appellate jurisdiction. [5]

A revision is heard by one judge[6] unlike an appeal, where the default position is that an appeal ought to be heard by two judges although some appeals may

2 See *Royal Media Services vs Attorney General & 2 Others*, Nairobi High Court Petition No. 59 of 2013 (2013) eKLR and *Royal Media Services v Attorney General*, Nairobi High Court Miscellaneous Application No. 43 of 2013 (2013) eKLR.

3 See *Esther Wambui Ngure v R* (2008) eKLR.

4 (2004) 1 KLR 515.

5 See also *Malde & 2 Others v Republic*, Court of Appeal at Nairobi, Criminal Application No.14 of 2010, (2011) eKLR and *Kanji v Halai* (1976-80) 1 KLR 938.

6 CPC, Section 366.

be heard by a single judge.[7]The powers of the High Court on revision are set out in Section 364 of the CPC. In the case of a conviction, the High Court in revision, may exercise any of the powers conferred on it as an appellate court. [8] In case of any other order, other than an order of acquittal, the court may alter or reverse the order.[9]It is not necessary for a court to hear the parties in a revision.[10] The court has discretion to either hear or not hear the parties. However, it is not permissible for the court to make any order in revision, which is to the prejudice of an accused person, before he has been given an opportunity to be heard, unless the circumstances of the matter are that the subordinate court failed to pass a sentence which it was required to pass under the law that created the offence.[11] The High Court in revision is also barred from passing a sentence greater than that which might have been inflicted by the court which passed the sentence. [12]

In a revision, the High Court cannot convert a finding of an acquittal into one of a conviction.[13] A revision is also precluded where the party has a right of appeal.[14]It will be seen that in a revision, the High Court can make orders that are similar to the orders that the High Court can make in an appeal. A revision however in several aspects is different from an appeal. For example:-

- An order of acquittal can be reversed on appeal but not on a revision.[15]
- One cannot substitute an appeal for a revision. Thus if you have avenue to appeal you cannot apply for revision.[16]
- In an appeal the prosecution cannot appeal on sentence, only on an acquittal, but can seek to have the sentence varied in a revision.
- On a general scale, revisions are heard by a single judge whereas appeals are heard by two judges.

---

7 See Chapter 13 on Appeals for a discussion.

8 CPC, Section 364 (1).

9 *Ibid*, Section 364 (2).

10 *Ibid*, Section 365.

11 *Ibid*, Section 364(2).

12 *Ibid*, Section 364(3).

13 *Ibid*, Section 364(4).

14 *Ibid*, Section 364 (5).

15 *Ibid*, Section 364 (4). See also *Uganda v Polasi* (1970) EA 638.

16 *Section 364 (5)* of the *CPC*.

- Revisions strictly should not be in the nature of a hearing as contrasted with appeals, unless in the revision, the court is going to make orders adverse to the accused.

A revision thus is not a complete substitute for an appeal. It is however a good remedy in situations where the party has no avenue for appeal or where the error sought to be the subject of revision is glaring on the face of the record. There is however potential conflict between revision and appeal especially in instances where the review is undertaken before the lapse of the period of appeal. It could be that a party may wish to appeal and the High Court, before the right of appeal is exercised, proceeds to revise the order of the subordinate court but in a way that the aggrieved party is not satisfied with. An order made in respect of a revision is appealable to the Court of Appeal[17] and generally the High Court frowns on applications for revision made in respect of an interlocutory order.[18]

In *R v Ajit Singh S/o Vir Singh*[19] the accused person was tried for theft of timber and at the end of the prosecution's case, the magistrate held that there was no case to answer. The accused was acquitted and awarded Shs. 500 as compensation as the magistrate regarded *"it frivolous in the extreme for him to have been re-charged."* About a month earlier, the accused had been charged with an exactly similar charge but which was withdrawn under section 87 (a) of the CPC. The AG filed a revision to review the finding that the charge was frivolous and the consequent order for compensation. At the hearing, the accused took the preliminary point that the court was precluded from exercising revisional jurisdiction because the matter was brought to the notice of the court by a party who had a right of appeal against the magistrate's decision. It was held that the court is not precluded from considering the correctness of a finding, sentence or order merely because the facts of the matter have been brought to its notice by a party who has or had a right of appeal.

17 See *Malde & 2 Others v R*, supra note 5.

18 *Uganda v Dalal*, (1970) EA 355.

19 *R v Ajit Singh S/o Vir Singh* (1957) EA 822; Contrast with *Chhagan Raja v Gordhan Gopal* (1936) 17 KLR 69.

In *Obiero v R*,[20] the appellant was convicted of forging and uttering and was given an absolute discharge under Section 35 of the Penal Code. The court called for the proceedings under its revisionary jurisdiction and listed the case for arguments whether the sentence or final order should be altered. It was submitted for the appellant that an order for absolute discharge under section 35 of the Penal code is not a sentence and that there is no power in revision to set aside such an order. The crown submitted that an order of absolute discharge is technically a sentence in as much as it is a definite judgment pronounced by the court. The court held that an order of absolute discharge under section 35 of the penal Code is technically a sentence and may be enhanced in revision and altered the finding of absolute discharge to a conditional discharge.

In *Keshallilla (Juma Shabani) v R*,[21] the appellant was convicted of stealing, by a magistrate who made a probation order, to the effect that the appellant be released upon entering a bond to appear and receive sentence at any time within three years if called upon and meantime to be of good behaviour. In revision the High Court set aside the order of the magistrate and substituted it with a sentence of one year imprisonment. The appellant thereafter appealed on the ground that the High Court had no power to substitute a sentence of imprisonment for an order made by the magistrate. The Court of Appeal held that the order by the magistrate did not amount to a sentence. Further that the word 'alter' under the revision powers of the High Court should be construed as embracing the substitution of another order, in the same way as the power to alter a finding gives power to substitute a different conviction; a sentence is an order by the court and is one of the nature of which may be altered by the revising court. It was further held that in revision, the High Court has power to substitute a sentence of imprisonment for a probation order to come up for sentencing if called upon.

In *R v Telenga*,[22] the accused had pleaded not guilty to an offence under the corruption ordinance. Evidence for the prosecution and for the defence was taken but then the court realized that the consent in writing of the AG had not be taken as required under the Corruption ordinance. Consequently, the

---

20 *Obiero v R* (1962) EA 650.

21 *Keshallilla (Juma Shabani) v R* (1963) EA 184 (T) (CoA).

22 *R v Telenga* (1967) EA 407.

prosecution applied to withdraw the charge under a section which entitled an accused to an acquittal as the defence had already been entered into. The court in granting the application acquitted the accused. The DPP applied for a revision by the High Court to set aside the whole proceedings including the acquittal. The High Court held that it did not have jurisdiction to entertain revisional proceedings against an acquittal.

14.3 Procedure for Initiating a Revision

There is no prescribed method or procedure to initiate a revision. The judge, so long as he has received information from any source, or has come across the proceedings by itself, may initiate a revision. In the case of *Lochab Brothers v R,*[23] the High Court attempted to set out a procedure for a revision. This however is not provided in statute and a party cannot be faulted for not following this procedure though the same can serve as a guideline to any party wishing to make an application for a revision. First, a letter should be written to the Registrar or Deputy Registrar of the High Court. The said Registrar would immediately open a file, call for the lower Court proceedings and place the file before the Judge. Thereafter, the Judge would read the lower Court file to examine whether there is any unlawful order and/or procedure undertaken by the trial Court. If there is any unprocedural conduct of the lower Court proceedings, the High Court will administratively conduct a revision.

It is very important to note that at this stage there is no necessity of appearance in Court by any party, including the advocate for the applicant. The Judge though, has a discretion to allow such appearance to be made only if the Court is of a view that the matter requires further clarification. Basically, then, the procedure under a revision in criminal matters is done more or less administratively.

* * *

[23] High Court at Kericho, Misc. Crim. Application No. 12 of 2008, (2008) eKLR.

CHAPTER 15

WITNESS PROTECTION

15.1 Understanding Witness Protection[1]

A "witness protection programme" is a security apparatus provided for threatened witnesses and their families or other related persons or any person involved in the justice system whose lives are endangered due to testimonies they are willing to divulge to shed light to a crime in order to propel the rule of law. The idea behind this programme is to protect vital informants and to guarantee fair and successful prosecutions. This is driven by the recognition that the person who committed the crime may be prone to take retribution against the party who is willing to provide evidence or may be inclined to stifle the presentation of such evidence.[2]

It is not uncommon to find witnesses being predisposed not to give evidence for fear of physical harm, loss of social standing, threats to their families or their economic wellbeing. There are also instances where witnesses have been coaxed into retracting or declining to give evidence in exchange for favours, such as cash payments, promotions at work or other inducements. Such cases deeply weigh down the prosecution of crimes and lead to a miscarriage of justice. It is against this backdrop, that independent witness protection programmes have been established to secure the protection of witnesses from intimidation, threats or inducements, with the aim of ensuring credible criminal trials.

---

1 For a more elaborate discussion on Witness Protection, see Munyao Sila and Edwin Saluny Kimatu, *An Appraisal of the Witness Protection Regime in Kenya*, Journal of the Law Society of Kenya (2014).

2 S Lopez, *Witness Protection Program Beginnings* (2008).Available at <http://socyberty.com/crime/witness-protection-program-beginnings/> (last accessed 2 February, 2012)

15.2 Development of Witness Protection

Historically in most criminal jurisdictions, the rights of an accused person have been momentously recognized while the witnesses' and victims' rights have been greatly disregarded. However, in modern times there has been a renaissance in the appreciation that victims and witnesses need protection, and there has been an emergence of witness protection programmes in many countries.

Contemporary witness protection regimes are believed to have their roots in the United States of America (USA) which initially developed witness protection programmes for purposes of safeguarding witnesses willing to testify against suspects of organised crime.[3] These developments in the USA were replicated in other jurisdictions such as Australia which promulgated a Witness Protection Act in 1994, Colombia in 1997, Germany in 1998, and Italy in 2001.[4] International Tribunals such as the International Criminal Tribunal for Rwanda (ICTR), The International Criminal Tribunal for Yugoslavia (ICTY) and the International Criminal Court (ICC) were created with elaborate witness protection provisions in their statutes.[5] The ICC in recognition of the importance of witness protection has set up the Victims and Witnesses Unit within its Registry. The unit, among other things, provides protective measures and security arrangements to victims who appear before the court and others who are at risk on account of testimony given by such witnesses. [6] In accordance with Rule 16 of the Rules of Procedure and Evidence the Registrar may negotiate confidential agreements on relocation and provision of support services on the territory of a State on behalf of the Court. The Victims

---

3 See Fred Montanino, *Unintended victims of organized crime witness protection,* (1987) 2/4 Criminal Justice Policy Review, 392-408. See also UNODC, *Good Practices for the Protection of Witnesses Witness Protection in Criminal Proceedings Involving Organised Crime,* (2008, UN, New York) available at <http://www.unodc.org/documents/organized-crime/Witness-protection-manual-Feb08.pdf> (last accessed 21 April 2012).

4 *Ibid*, UNODC, *Good Practices for the Protection of Witnesses in Criminal Proceedings Involving Organised Crime.*

5 For the ICTR see Article 21 of the Statute of the International Tribunal for Rwanda; for ICTY Article 22 of the Statute of the International Tribunal for former Yugoslavia; for ICC Article 68 of the Rome Statute of the International Criminal Court.

6 Article 43(6) of the Statute of the International Criminal Court.

and Witnesses Unit actively pursues a policy of concluding relocation and other cooperation agreements with States Parties and other parties in order to establish an effective national and international protection regime for witnesses and victims who appear before the Court, and others who are at risk on account of testimony.[7]

These advancements towards having witness protection regimes have been based on the acknowledgment that witnesses are susceptible to threats and intimidation aimed at preventing them from testifying in courts and tribunals[8]. A failure to ensure the attendance of witnesses is no doubt a failure to ensure that justice is served. It goes without saying that without evidence being offered, a suspect who would otherwise be convicted will have to be released despite his guilt. This would certainly be contrary to public policy and the interests of society at large.

15.3 Need for Witness Protection

The purpose of witness protection law is to ensure that the due administration of justice in criminal and related proceedings is not prejudiced by witnesses not being prepared to give evidence for fear of reprisal from the accused person/s. Consequently provision of witness protection is a fundamental legal obligation on the part of law enforcement officers for purposes of safeguarding the interests of justice.

The principal objective of any witness protection programme is to safeguard evidence which is under threat of being lost. The successful investigation and prosecution of offences, grave or not, depends primarily on the information and testimony of witnesses. Prosecutors can only rely on witnesses who are willing and able to appear in court and provide evidence. The adage goes that "dead men tell no tales" and in this light, the availability of witnesses underpin successful national and international criminal justice jurisdictions. It

---

7 See the webpage of the Victims and Witness Unit of the ICC, available at http://www.icc-cpi.int/Menus/ICC/Structure+of+the+Court/Protection/Victims+and+Witness+Unit.htm (last accessed 18 April 2012).

8 For an elaborate discussion, see generally, C Mahony, *The Justice Sector Afterthought: Witness Protection in Africa* (2010, Institute for Security Studies).

is therefore good practice for criminal justice systems to afford assistance and support measures to victims and other witnesses which then facilitates their ability to participate in criminal trials and allows them to be more willing to give evidence.

15.4 Forms of Witness Protection

Witness protection can come in various forms. These include the concealment of witness identity during investigation and trial, the assignment of security detail, the grant of restraining orders, the provision of safe houses, the provision of new identity, the allotment of monthly allowances, and other covert plans for protection. Witness protection measures can be assorted into Short-term Measures and Long-term Measures. Both measures factor in legislative and regulatory requirements in determining who and when to protect; strategies on how to protect; and the type of procedural and formal witness protection. Short-term measures are those that cover temporary protection while the case is still under investigation or trial.

Long-term measures are those that cover the after-trial period. They may involve the total relocation and change of identity of not only the witness, but also that of his family or close associates. This is because the risk of retaliation by the accused may remain alive even after the trial process. It is a scenario that is common in cases involving organised crime as the gang may want to send a message for purposes of enforcing a code of silence.[9]It may thus be necessary to give the witness and his close associates a new identity and new residence, sometimes in a different country, to safeguard their safety.[10]

---

[9] *Ibid.*

[10] L Toomey(2007). *Witness Protection in Countries Emerging from Conflict. Consolidated Response* (2007). International Network to Promote the Rule of Law, U.S.A.

15.5 Development of Witness Protection in Kenya

The manifest need to guarantee the protection of witnesses culminated in the enactment of the Witness Protection Act of 2006.[11] With the enactment of this statute, Kenya became only the second country in Africa after South Africa, to launch such a programme.[12] This 2006 statute was amended in 2010, and the 2010 statute, The Witnesss Protection Act, Chapter 79, Laws of Kenya, constitutes the current witness protection regime in Kenya. It is now prudent to look at the initial statute before analyzing the current law embodied in the 2010 enactment.

15.5.1 The 2006 Witness Protection Act

The Witness Protection Act, 2006 (WPA, 2006), was the first ever legislative instrument directly aimed at the protection of witnesses in Kenya. It was assented to on the 30th December 2006 and commenced on the 1st September 2008.[13] The Act was necessitated by the need to ensure successful investigation and prosecution of economic crimes, organized criminal gangs, and cases arising out of ethnic clashes which were on the rise.[14]

The WPA (2006) under Section 4 established the Witness Protection Programme.[15] The establishment and maintenance of the Witness Protection Programme was under the control of the Attorney General who was empowered to take measures he deemed necessary to guarantee protection of the safety

---

11 The Kenya Witness Protection Act, No. 16 Of 2006

12 The South Africa Witness Protection Act, No. 112 of 1998, assented to 19 November 1998.

13 WPA (2006), Section 1.

14 *"Attorney-general launches the Witness Protection Programme"* Office of Public Communications <http://www.communication.go.ke/news.asp?id=135> (last accessed 12 January 2012).

15 WPA (2006), Section 4 (2)

and welfare of witnesses.[16] The control that the Attorney General had under the Act was emphasised in Section 5, as a witness could only be included in the Programme if the Attorney General allowed the witness to be so included and the witness agreed to be so included. In addition a Memorandum of Understanding (MOU) was to be signed by the witness or his parent/guardian where such witness was a child or lacked legal capacity.[17] A request to be included in the Witness Protection Programme had to be made in writing to the Attorney General. Such request could be made by the witness himself, or any law enforcement agency[18] and the Attorney General had to respond to such request within Seven (7) Days.[19] It can therefore be discerned that inclusion into the Witness Protection Programme was at the complete discretion of the Attorney General.

Termination of protection was also to be effected by the Attorney General if the participant requested for termination;[20] or if, anything done or intended to be done by a protected witness was likely to threaten the security or otherwise compromise the integrity of the programme; or the witness had breached the memorandum of understanding entered on admission to the Witness Protection Programme (WPP); or where the circumstances that gave rise to the need for protection had ceased to exist.[21]

The terms under which the particular witness would be under the WPP were to be set out in a Memorandum of Understanding (MOU). The MOU was designed to contain the details of protection and assistance accorded including the obligations of the participant under the WPP; and the terms, surrender and

---

16 *Ibid.* Such measures could included: Making arrangements necessary to allow the witness to establish a new identity or otherwise to protect the witness; relocating the witness; providing accommodation for the witness; providing transport for the property of the witness; providing reasonable financial assistance to the witness; providing to the witness services in the nature of counselling and vocational training services; and doing any other things which the Attorney-General considers necessary to ensure the safety and welfare of the witness.

17 *Ibid*, Section 5(2).

18 *Ibid*, Section 5(3).

19 *Ibid*, Section 5(4).

20 *Ibid*, Section 10(1)

21 *Ibid,* Section 10(2).

issue of passports, the taking and retention of photographs by the participant, the provision of new identity to the participant, activities prohibited, social and domestic obligations, consequences of failure to abide to the MOU and termination of the programme for breach of the provisions of the MOU.[22]

Section 9 of the WPA (2006) provided that, the Attorney General could include a person into a WPP on a temporary basis if the person was in urgent need of protection. An interim MOU could then be signed pending the formal inclusion of the person into the WPP. The Attorney General was also empowered to suspend the assistance provided under the WPP if he was satisfied that the participant had done or intended to do something which would limit the capacity of the Attorney General to provide assistance.[23]

Under the WPP, the Attorney General was granted wide powers for the protection of the identity of the participant witnesses. He could apply for any documents necessary to allow the witness establish a new identity or to restore such person to his former identity or to seek such other documentation for the protection of the witness.[24] The Attorney General was further empowered to seek various orders from the High Court towards the protection of a witness including making an application for authorisation of new entries to be made into the register of births, marriages and death.[25] Any such court proceedings were to be conducted in camera.[26] The new identity could be nullified and the witness restored to his old identity if protection was terminated and the Attorney General was of opinion that it was appropriate for the witness to be restored to his former identity.[27] There were however some limitations to the wide powers granted to the Attorney General. For example the Attorney General was precluded from providing the witness with qualifications that he never had or represent that he is entitled to a benefit that he was not otherwise entitled to.[28]

---

22 *Ibid*, Section 7.

23 *Ibid*, Section 11.

24 *Ibid*, Section 13.

25 *Ibid*, Section 14.

26 *Ibid*, Section 15.

27 *Ibid*, Section 20.

28 *Ibid*, Section 25.

The Act further provided that, the identity of the participant (witness) was not to be disclosed in any proceedings relating to the participant, unless the court considered that it would be contrary to justice.[29] There was also to be suppression of the publication of the evidence given in court. In such proceedings the court was also empowered to direct that no questions be asked which would lead to the disclosure of the identity of the protected person, or his place of abode. The court was also empowered to direct that no statement be made by a person involved in the proceedings that would disclose the protected identity of a participant to a WPP or a former participant to the WPP. This was an important enactment since the essence of witness protection is to protect the witness and such protection could come to naught if the witness had to reveal his identity when giving evidence. His cover would certainly be blown if proceedings were conducted in the traditional way. In recognition of this important aspect, the Act empowered the Chief Justice to make rules for purposes of giving effect to the statute.[30]

The Act provided for Regulations to be made by the Minister for purposes of outlining the operations of the Act.[31] The Regulations were made in 2008 and came into effect in 2009.[32] They provided for various important matters including the establishment of a Witness Protection Unit (WPU) which was to be in the Office of the Attorney General. The Unit was to be headed by an officer appointed by the Attorney General. The Head of Unit was to be in charge of the day to day affairs of the Unit. He was also to designate an officer to take care of a protected witness, take measures for the continuous safety of witnesses, and determine where a person was to be placed for protection.[33] The Unit would also be comprised of other persons who would be appointed by the Attorney General.[34] The functions of the Unit were *inter alia* to ensure

---

29 *Ibid,* Section 24

30 *Ibid,* Section 36 (1) *'The Chief Justice may make such rules of court as may be required or permitted by this Act to be made or as may be necessary or expedient to be made for carrying out or giving effect to this Act.'*

31 *Ibid,* Section 36 (2). *'The Minister may make regulations for or with respect to any matter which by this Act is required or permitted to be prescribed or which is necessary or expedient to be prescribed for carrying out or giving effect to this Act.'*

32 Legal Notice No.10 of 2009.

33 Regulation 12, the Witness Protection Regulations, 2008.

34 *Ibid,* Regulation 3.

that proper protective measures are put in place for the protection of witnesses, recommend to the Attorney General the adoption of protection measures and assist witnesses when called to testify as witnesses.[35] It was the duty of the Unit to ensure confidentiality at all times and act impartially. The regulations provided that the witness be put under an allowance if he was not going to receive an income by virtue of being under the WPP. If he lost income as a result of being in the WPP the allowance would be at least equal to the amount of income forfeited. The standard forms required to be filled when making an application for protection were also provided in the Regulations.

Protection of course came at a cost to the witness. For example under Section 19 a witness who had been given a new identity could not marry unless he provided the Attorney General with a declaration that the marriage would not be contrary to law. If the witness was relocated or granted a new identity, this would of course mean breaking relationships and ties with long term friends. Nevertheless, the benefits of protection would overall outweigh the inconveniences that would be caused to the witness.

The 2006 statute was argued to have too much state control, gave too much discretion to the Attorney General, and of lacking institutional integrity. This necessitated amendments which were effected in the year 2010, culminating in the present Witness Protection Act, Chapter 79, Laws of Kenya.

15.5.2 The 2009 Witness Protection Act

The new statute established a Witness Protection Agency (WPA) as an independent corporate body.[36]The core purpose of establishing the WPA was to remove the witness protection programme away from the office of the Attorney General and place it upon an independent body.[37] The Witness Protection Unit, existing under the 2006 Act, was dissolved and all existing obligations taken up by the WPA.[38]The WPA is tasked with establishing and maintaining a witness

---

[35] *Ibid*, Regulation 4.

[36] Witness Protection Act, (2009), Section 3A.

[37] *Ibid*, Section 3C.

[38] *Ibid*, Section 3O.

protection programme; determining the criteria for admission to and removal from the witness protection programme; determining the type of protection measures to be applied. It also has mandate to advise any Government Ministry, department, agency or any other person on the adoption of strategies and measures on witness protection.[39] For purposes of accountability, the Agency is to report to the Minister in charge of matters of witness protection.[40]

Apart from the WPA, the 2010 statute also establishes The Witness Protection Advisory Board (WPAB).[41] The Board is an unincorporated body with a membership comprising of, the Minister as the chairman, the Minister responsible for matters relating to Justice, the Minister responsible for matters relating to Finance, the Director-General National Security Intelligence Service, the Commissioner of Police, the Commissioner of Prisons, the Director of Public Prosecutions and the Chairperson of the Kenya National Commission on Human Rights. The Board is responsible for advising the Agency on the exercise of its powers and performance of its functions. It is further mandated to advise the Agency on the formulation of witness protection policies, approve the budgetary estimates of the Agency and have general oversight on the administration of the Agency.[42]

The Act stipulates that the Agency shall be led by a Director whose appointment shall be on the recommendation of the Board on terms and conditions as the Minister may, in consultation with the Board approve.[43] It is requisite for the Agency to report to the relevant Minister on the overall realization of its objectives, purpose and the performance of its functions under the Act.[44] This ensures that the Agency is held responsible and accountable. Furthermore the Act demands that the expenditure of the Agency be in compliance with its approved annual estimates or pursuant to an authorization of the advisory Board given with prior written approval of the Minister.[45] The Act obligates

39 *Ibid.*

40 *Ibid*, Section 3G (2).

41 *Ibid*, Section 3P

42 *Ibid*, Section 3Q

43 *Ibid*, Section 3E.

44 *Ibid*, Section 3G (2).

45 *Ibid*, Section 3J (5).

the Agency to make a report to the Board on the activities and operations of the Agency during the financial year. [46]

As regards "protective measures", the Act sanctions the Agency to take measures it deems necessary and reasonable to make certain the safety and welfare of protected witnesses. Such measures could include relocation, physical and armed protection and change of identity. The Agency could also demand other protective measures be taken such as holding proceedings *in camera* or closed sessions, the use of pseudonyms, reduction of identifying information, the use of video link, and employing measures to obscure or distort the identity of the witness.[47]

The Agency is tasked to establish the criteria for inclusion and removal of witnesses in the programme a mandate which has now been removed from the office of the Attorney General.[48] Funding is key for a witness protection programme to be successful. The 2010 Act envisages a state of affairs where the Agency will draw its funding from the Consolidated Fund.[49] The Agency may also accept other funding in the nature of gifts, donations, or bequests but subject to the approval of the Minister.[50] The 2010 statute further provides for a Victims' Compensation Fund from which funds for restitution and compensation of victims of crime may be appropriated from.[51]

Apart from the WPA and The Board, the Act establishes a third institution known as The Witness Protection Appeals Tribunal.[52] The Appeals Tribunal comprises of a Chairman and two other members. The Chairman is appointed by the President on recommendation of the Attorney General and must be qualified to hold the position of a Judge of the High Court of Kenya.[53] The two members are appointed by the Minister and must possess expert knowledge of

---

46 *Ibid*, Section 3L.

47 *Ibid*, Section 4.

48 *Ibid*, Section 3C (1) (b).

49 *Ibid*, Section 3H

50 *Ibid*.

51 *Ibid*, Section 3I.

52 *Ibid*, Section 3U.

53 *Ibid*, Section 3U (2) (a).

the matters likely to come before the Tribunal.[54]The function of the Tribunal is to review and determine grievances by persons not satisfied with the decisions or orders of the Agency in relating to admissions or terminations of placement into the Witness Protection Programme.[55] It will therefore be discerned that the statute establishes an appellate structure in which the decisions of the Agency may be subject to review.

The abovementioned legal framework for the protection of witnesses under the 2010 Act illustrates a progression from the situation under the Witness Protection Act of 2006. The main improvement is on the establishment of the Agency which is independent thus diverging from the position prevailing under the previous Act which established the witness protection programme under the Attorney General's office. The 2010 Act is also credited for the provision of an appeals mechanism on matters of non-inclusion and removal from the witness protection programme as opposed to its antecedent which gave the Attorney General unfettered discretion in deciding matters of inclusion and exclusion. The Agency has not been in operation for long, and its effectiveness will be judged by time. However, the presence of a witness protection program is a big step towards ensuring the integrity of the criminal justice system.

* * *

54 *Ibid,* Section 3U (2) (b).

55 *Ibid,* Section 3U.

INDEX

D

E

F

G

H

I

J

K

L

M

N

O

P

R

S

T

U

V

W

17222867R00218

Printed in Great Britain
by Amazon